CEDAR

Raven and the First Men, *a carving in yellow cedar by Bill Reid,*
Museum of Anthropology, University of British Columbia

CEDAR

TREE OF LIFE TO THE NORTHWEST COAST INDIANS

HILARY STEWART
with drawings by the author

Douglas & McIntyre

University of Washington Press

First paperback printing 1995

14 15 16 17 18 15 14 13 12 11

Douglas and McIntyre (2013) Ltd.
P.O. Box 219
Madeira Park BC Canada V0N 2H0
www.douglas-mcintyre.com

Library and Archives Canada Cataloguing in Publication
Stewart, Hilary, 1924–2014
Cedar
Bibliography: p.

ISBN: 978-1-55054-406-0 (pbk.) · ISBN: 978-1-926706-47-4 (ebook)

1. Cedar—Northwest Coast of North America. 2. Indians of North America—Northwest Coast of North America. I. Title.
E78.N78S74 1984 634.9′7568 C84-091223-4

15 16 17 18 19 14 13 12 11 10

Published simultaneously in the United States by
University of Washington Press
www.washington.edu/uwpress

Library of Congress Cataloging-in-Publication Data
Stewart, Hilary.
Cedar: tree of life to the Northwest Indians.
Bibliography: p.
Includes index.
1. Indians of North America—Northwest coast of North America—Industries. 2. Cedar. I. Reid, William, 1920– II. Title.
E78.N78S762 1984 674′.089970795 84-15156

ISBN: 978-0-295-97448-4 (pbk.)

Editing by Saeko Usukawa
Design by Barbara Hodgson
Typeset by Ronalds Printing
Cover photograph by Derik Murray, artifacts courtesy of University of British Columbia Museum of Anthropology and private collections
Printed and bound in Canada by Friesens
Printed on acid-free paper
Published with assistance from the British Columbia Heritage Trust

We gratefully acknowledge the financial support of the Canada Council for the Arts, the British Columbia Arts Council, the Province of British Columbia through the Book Publishing Tax Credit, and the Government of Canada through the Canada Book Fund for our publishing activities.

To those who know and respect
the spirit of the cedar

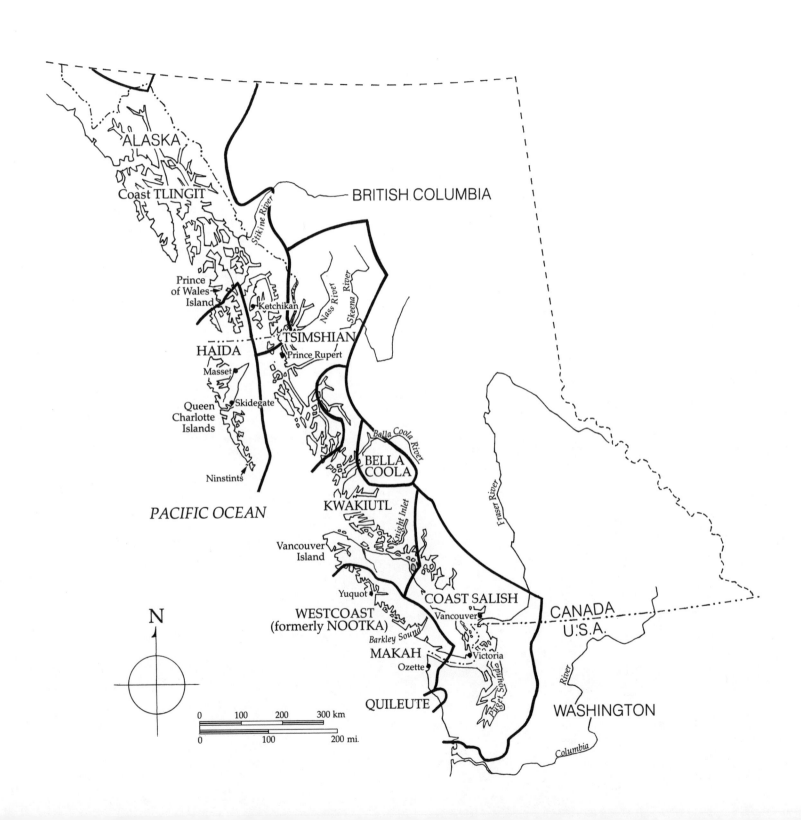

ALASKA

Coast TLINGIT

BRITISH COLUMBIA

Stikine River

Prince
of Wales
Island

Ketchikan

Nass River

Skeena River

TSIMSHIAN

HAIDA

Prince Rupert

Masset

Queen
Charlotte
Islands

Skidegate

Balla Coola River

BELLA
COOLA

Ninstints

PACIFIC OCEAN

KWAKIUTL

Knight Inlet

Fraser River

Vancouver
Island

Yuquot

COAST SALISH

CANADA
U.S.A.

WESTCOAST
(formerly NOOTKA)

Vancouver

Barkley Sound

MAKAH

Ozette

Victoria

Puget Sound

QUILEUTE

WASHINGTON

N

River

0   100   200   300 km

0   100   200 mi.

Columbia

CONTENTS

FOREWORD

Almost twenty years ago, when I was somewhat younger, and could perhaps be forgiven, I wrote about the west coast cedar in prose so purple tinged it might have been considered poetry if it had had a hint of the discipline and control so necessary to that most structured of all the arts.

Today, in response to Hilary Stewart's wonderful book on the subject, I looked again at that unseemly, extravagant outpouring, but, having spent many of the intervening years in the gentle, aromatic presence of those cedars, I find that I can't bring myself to change a word, except perhaps to add a few hyperbolic adverbs and adjectives in which the English language abounds.

I refrained from that excess, but ask you to bear with me in recalling my inadequate but sincere tribute to the cedar, inspired by the dignified generosity with which it has sacrificed its beauty to make my little creations, a few of which may in a small way compensate for that sacrifice.

Oh, the cedar tree!

If mankind in his infancy had prayed for the perfect substance for all material and aesthetic needs, an indulgent god could have provided nothing better.

Beautiful in itself, with a magnificent flared base tapering suddenly to a tall straight trunk wrapped in reddish brown bark, like a great coat of gentle fur, gracefully sweeping boughs, soft feathery fronds of grey-green needles.

Huge, some of these cedars, five hundred years of slow growth, towering from their massive bases. The wood is soft, but of a wonderful firmness and, in a good tree, so straight-grained it will split true and clean into forty-foot planks, four inches thick and three feet wide, with scarcely a knot.

Across the grain it cuts clean and precise. It is light in weight and beautiful in color, reddish brown when new, silvery grey when old. It is permeated with natural oils that make it one of the longest lasting of all woods, even in the damp of the Northwest Coast climate.

When steamed it will bend without breaking. It will make houses and boats and boxes and cooking pots. Its bark will make mats, even clothing. With a few bits of sharpened stone and antler, with some beaver teeth and a lot of time, with later on a bit of iron, you can build from the cedar tree the exterior trappings of one of the world's great cultures.

That is what I said about the cedar, giving a few of its possible uses and so showing its importance to the peoples who, until a few short years ago, ruled the Northwest Coast.

Now Hilary Stewart has performed the much more difficult feat of telling of the wonder of the cedar tree with the same loving awe experienced by us for whom it forms a constant part of our lives, and at the same time explores extensively every aspect of this marvellous arboreal giant and gives us a true account of how well it served our precursors on the coast. If we will only treat it with the respect in which they held it, the great west coast cedar will always be with us, to serve with the same regal philanthropy it always has, as a powerfully beautiful asset to our coastal vistas when alive, and as a source of some of the finest materials for making objects of use and beauty.

Bill Reid

ACKNOWLEDGEMENTS

During the three years and more that it has taken to put this book together, a good number of people have given generously of their time, knowledge and expertise in a broad range of subjects. Their warm support and enthusiasm for my work have been really encouraging.

My warmest thanks to the people unnamed here who added directly or indirectly to the enrichment of these pages, including those, wishing to remain anonymous, who loaned me items from their private collections. My thanks also to John Hauberg, Bill and Marty Holm, Neil Smith and Shyamali Tan for kindly allowing me to use choice pieces from their collections. Some items drawn from auction catalogues are in collections that I have not been able to trace, but I wish to extend my thanks to their owners through this page.

For their input on the archaeological aspects of this book, my appreciation goes to archaeologists Val Patenaude and Kathryn Bernick. For dragging me through the underbrush in search of culturally modified trees on distant islands, and for his interest and collaboration, I am grateful to James Haggarty, archaeologist at the British Columbia Provincial Museum in Victoria. My thanks to Marcus Bell, Head of Environmental Studies at the University of Victoria, for checking the botanical data

and answering my queries, and to paleobotanist Richard Hebda for important insights into the antiquity of the cedar tree. I am indebted to Laurence C. Brown, professor of metallurgical engineering at the University of British Columbia, for his special interest and expertise in testing the strengths of a selection of cedar withe and bark samples and ropes.

To Bill Reid, my thanks for giving from the storehouse of his knowledge to help fill the gaps in mine. Particular thanks and appreciation to Bill Holm for his thorough and meticulous checking of the manuscript, drawings and photographs, as well as for correcting my errors, answering my questions and adding valuable information.

I am indebted to Ulli Steltzer for her generosity in providing several expressive photographs of Indian artists at work. To my friend and fellow writer Paula Gustafson, who proffered research and photographs, my very grateful thanks. Special thanks also to my good friend, colleague and kindred spirit Joy Inglis, anthropologist, for her warm support and shared discoveries.

Canadian, American and overseas museums played a major role in providing me with access to information about the many cedar products illustrated here and gave permission to use their material. For those courtesies I would like to acknowledge the following: British Columbia Provincial Museum, Victoria, with special thanks to Collections Technician Marilyn Chechik for her many hours of valuable help; British Museum, London, with thanks to Assistant Keeper Jonathan King for his courtesies; Campbell River and District Museum, Campbell River; Denver Art Museum, Denver; Field Museum of Natural History, Chicago, with much gratitude to Education Officer Carolyn Blackman and guest curator Ronald Weber for extensive help in many aspects of my research there; Glenbow Museum, Calgary; 'Ksan Treasure House, 'Ksan; Kwakiutl Museum, Cape Mudge; Milwaukee Public Museum, Milwaukee; Museum of Anthropology, University of British Columbia, Vancouver, with appreciation for the help and support of Curator of Education/Ethnology Madeline Brondson-Rowan and Conservator Miriam Clavir; Museum of the American Indian, New York; Museum of Archaeology and Ethnology, Simon Fraser University, Burnaby; Museum of Northern British Columbia, Prince Rupert; National Museum of Ireland, Dublin; National Museum of Man, Ottawa; National Museum of Natural History, Washington, D.C.; Oakland Public Museum, Oakland; Portland Art Museum, Portland; Royal Ontario Museum, Toronto; Taylor Museum, Colorado Springs; Thomas Burke Memorial Washington State Museum, Seattle; Tongass Historical Society Museum, Ketchikan; Vancouver Museum, Vancouver, and Washington State Historical Society, Tacoma.

For special and long-suffering research assistance, I must give particular thanks to Norah McLaren, librarian at the Vancouver Museum. In many weeks of cheerfully foraging through shelves, she uncovered a wide assortment of helpful publications, and I am most appreciative.

Several people have provided me with the kind of information not generally found in either libraries or museums: these were the knowledgeable elders of various cultural groups who often took me into their homes and patiently discussed and demonstrated traditional skills they had learned in childhood. In special appreciation, I would like to thank Florence Davidson, Mary Jackson, Ed Leon, Vic Mowatt, the late Hannah Parnell, Alice Paul and Mabel Taylor for sharing their expertise in working with cedar bark, roots and withes; also, though not an elder, Wally Henry, Coast Salish expert in working with cedar bark.

Canoe builders and carvers of all ages gave of their specialized knowledge, and I extend my warm thanks to Joe David, Andy Dick, David Frank, Sr., the late Chief Dan George, (Ron Hamilton) Hupquatchew, Roy Hanuse, Jim Hart, Norman Tait and (Richard Wilson) Wanagun. The wealth of their personal experience has added a richness to the pages of this book, and for this I am greatly indebted.

INTRODUCTION

With my lifelong interest in wild flowers, trees and all things growing outside the garden wall, it was only natural that I should be drawn to the early Northwest Coast Indians' use of the plants of their environment — both for food and in technology. Because I always cared less about cooking than creating things with my hands, the early technologies have always held my interest, and they still do. Having lived on the Northwest Coast for some twenty-eight years and travelled much of its length and breadth, I feel on close and comfortable terms with a lot of its natural history, botany especially. It intrigues me that people lived so well and for so long using almost exclusively the materials of their environment, and I am endlessly curious about the "hows" and "whys" of those materials, their technologies and their uses. Having the same trees, shrubs, barks, grasses and other raw materials at my feet is the incentive for trying out and discovering for myself how things worked. It is a learning process that continues to broaden with each year's travel, experience or field trip.

While lecturing on plant uses of the Northwest Coast peoples, I found that half the time was taken up outlining the basic technologies and products of the cedar tree, both the red and the yellow, though mainly the former. Gradually, I began to realize what a vital part this tree played in the lives of coast peoples — literally from cradle to grave. In making some of the tools for and experiencing the process of working with the wood, bark, roots and withes, I became so fascinated by the cedar that I knew it must be the subject for my next book.

In search of the broadest range of items made from the cedar tree, I browsed through exhibitions, museum display and storage shelves, private collections, auction and exhibition catalogues, and archival photos. Further research on technologies and uses took me through popular and academic books, many of them buried in special collections of libraries, as well as field reports, newsletters, student papers, MA theses and PhD dissertations. I read biographies and prowled through diaries and journals of early explorers, traders, botanists, miners and missionaries. For answers to my questions I communicated in person and by mail with archaeologists, ethnologists, ethnobotanists, paleobotanists, curators and other academics. I talked to botanists, foresters and loggers; I hiked islands and scrambled through underbrush to find old cedars that bore evidence of aboriginal use in the past.

I talked to young native carvers about their experiences, their tools and their feelings towards the cedar, but best of all were the native elders with whom I talked:

gentle, thoughtful people, with gnarled hands and bright minds and memories, who demonstrated or told me about the old skills, sharing so much of their knowledge stored in the pages of rich memory. In early times the memories of elders were the "books" of the young, and phrases such as "That's how my mother-in-law taught me" or "My grandfather, he always did it that way" took the technology back one or two generations. I began to realize how many different ways there were of achieving the same result, some the outgrowth of regional differences, some personal innovation. If occasionally I enquired why a person did something in that particular way, the answer often was: "Because that is how it is done," meaning that the method was old, time-tested and, therefore, there was no need to question it.

The majority of the drawings illustrate specific items, made from cedar materials, that are now in existence, though some are not; others depict the technologies used. Here I have often drawn from early or recent photos, but at times I had only written and verbal descriptions to guide my interpretations.

The time frame I have used for the book is from the earliest times up to and including early contact of the indigenous peoples with those from other lands. Because this book looks at the broad range of Northwest Coast cultures through the peoples' use of the cedar tree, I have chosen to divide the contents into categories pertaining to the four main parts of the cedar: wood, bark, withes and roots. Within each of these categories I have created subheadings that cover significant subjects, or grouped objects that share a common factor. But I could not complete the book without including other aspects of importance to the people: the prayers, beliefs and taboos associated with the cedar, as well as its uses in medicinal rites and healing.

So thoroughly did the cedar permeate the cultures of Northwest Coast peoples that it is hard to envision their life without it. Indeed, perhaps the cedar's fourfold supply of the essential materials of their culture — wood, bark, withes and roots — contributed to their special mystical regard for the number four.

REFERENCE KEYS

Each specimen illustrated is accompanied by a measurement, except where none is available, together with a letter-number combination. The measurement, given in both metric and Imperial, represents the maximum length or height of an item. The letters refer to the linguistic or cultural group who used that item, and the numbers represent the source and/or location.

By referring to the keys, the reader may determine that a specimen notated HA 2 was used by or collected from the Haida people and is to be found in the British Columbia Provincial Museum, Victoria. The cultural designation refers to that particular specimen and does not necessarily imply that no other group used that type of item.

Drawings that reconstruct a technique, such as splitting bark, or show the use of a specimen, such as tree-climbing equipment, carry a number that refers to the source of that information.

Cultural Key

TL Tlingit
HA Haida
TS Tsimshian
KW Kwakiutl
BC Bella Coola
WC Westcoast (formerly Nootka)
CS Coast Salish
NWC Northwest Coast, specific area not known.
QL Quileute
MK Makah

Location/Source Key

* Drawn from written or verbal description

1 National Museum of Man, Ottawa
2 British Columbia Provincial Museum, Victoria
3 Museum of Anthropology, University of British Columbia, Vancouver
4 Vancouver Museum, Vancouver
5 Museum of Archaeology and Ethnology, Simon Fraser University, Burnaby
6 Royal Ontario Museum, Toronto
7 Kwakiutl Museum, Cape Mudge
8 Museum of the North, Prince Rupert
9 Glenbow Museum, Calgary
10 Campbell River and District Museum and Archives, Campbell River
11 'Ksan Treasure House, 'Ksan
12 Field Museum of Natural History, Chicago
13 National Museum of Natural History, Washington, D.C.

14 Museum of the American Indian, New York
15 Denver Art Museum, Denver
16 Portland Art Museum, Portland
17 Oakland Public Museum, Oakland
18 University Museum, University of Pennsylvania
19 Taylor Museum, Colorado Springs
20 American Museum of Natural History, New York
21 Thomas Burke Memorial Washington State Museum, Seattle
22 Tongass Historical Society Museum, Ketchikan
23 Milwaukee Public Museum, Milwaukee
24 Washington State Historical Society, Tacoma
25 Saxman Totem Park, Ketchikan
26 British Museum, London
27 Museum of Anthropology and Ethnography of the Academy of the Sciences, Leningrad
28 Museum of the Lomonosav State University, Moscow
29 Museum für Volkerkunde, Berlin
30 National Museum of Ireland, Dublin
31 Private collection
32 The Coast Indians of Southern Alaska and Northern British Columbia, Albert Niblack
33 In the Wake of the War Canoe, William Henry Collison
34 Ethnology of the Kwakiutl, Franz Boas
35 The Social Organisation and Secret Societies of the Kwakiutl Indians, Franz Boas
36 Kwakiutl Ethnography, Franz Boas
37 Adventures in Vancouver Island, R.H. Pidcock
38 The Quinault Indians, Ronald Olsen
39 Adze, Canoe and House Types of the Northwest Coast, Ronald Olsen
40 Indians of the Northwest Coast, Pliny E. Goddard
41 6th Report on the North-Western Tribes of Canada, British Association for the Advancement of Science
42 The Tlingit Indians, Aurel Krause
43 Contributions to Clayoquot Ethnology, Vincent A. Koppert
44 Indian Canoes of the Northwest Coast, Bill Durham
45 Fine American Indian Art, Sotheby Parke Bernet, April 1981
46 Fine American Indian Art, Sotheby Parke Bernet, October 1981
47 Indian Primitive, Ralph Warren Andrews

48 Arts of the Raven, Wilson Duff
49 Art of the Northwest Coast Indians, Robert Bruce Inverarity
50 Quileute: An Introduction to the Indians of La Push, Jay Powell and Vickie Jensen
51 Indian Artists at Work, Ulli Steltzer
52 Kwakiutl Art, Audrey Hawthorn
53 Notes on the Ethnology of the Indians of Puget Sound, T.T. Waterman
54 Art in the Life of the Northwest Coast Indians, Erna Gunther
55 The Nootkan Indian, John Sendy.
56 The Coast Salish of British Columbia, Homer Barnett
57 The Chilkat Dancing Blanket, Cheryl Samuel
58 Salish Weaving, Paula Gustafson
59 The Northern and Central Nootkan Tribes, Philip Drucker
60 The Lummi Indians of Northwest Washington, Bernhard J. Stern
61 Plants in British Columbia Technology, Nancy Turner
62 Crow's Shells, Nile Thompson and Carolyn Marr
63 Traditional Salish Textiles, Native Research Project
64 Shed Roof Houses of the Ozette Archaeological Site, Jeffrey E. Mauger
65 The Excavation of Water-Saturated Archaeological Sites (Wet Sites) on the Northwest Coast of North America, Dale Croes
66 The West Coast (Nootka) People, E.Y. Arima
67 Haida Monumental Art, George F. MacDonald
68 Mabel Taylor
69 Wally Henry
70 Ed Leon
71 Alphonse Peters
72 Alice Paul
73 Photograph by the author
74 Provincial Archives of British Columbia, Victoria
75 Archival photograph
76 Nootka Sound: a 4,000 Year Perspective, John Dewhirst
77 From History's Locker, Anthony Carter
78 Indian Fishing: Early Methods on the Northwest Coast, Hilary Stewart
79 The Kwakiutl of Vancouver Island, Franz Boas

PART 1

PEOPLE OF THE CEDAR

In a small clearing in the forest, a young woman is in labour. Two women companions urge her to pull hard on the cedar bark rope tied to a nearby tree. The baby, born onto a newly made cedar bark mat, cries its arrival into the Northwest Coast world. Its cradle of firmly woven cedar root, with a mattress and covering of soft-shredded cedar bark, is ready. But first, the baby must remain on the cedar mat until its umbilical cord withers.

The young woman's husband and his uncle are on the sea in a canoe carved from a single red cedar log and are using paddles made from lengths of knot-free yellow cedar. When they reach the fishing ground that belongs to their family, the men set out a net of cedar bark twine weighted along one edge by stones lashed to it with strong, flexible cedar withes. Cedar wood floats support the net's upper edge.

Kwakiutl canoeists, circa 1910 to 1914. Photograph by E. Lazare, courtesy Edmonton Art Gallery, No. 78-12-90

The light green foliage of yellow cedar, Chamaecyparis nootkatensis, *stands out from other conifers. 73*

Wearing a cedar bark hat, cape and skirt to protect her from the rain and the cold, the baby's grandmother digs into the pebbly sand of the beach at low tide to collect clams. She loads them into a basket of cedar withe and root, adjusts the broad cedar bark tumpline across her forehead and returns home along the beach.

The embers in the centre of the big cedar plank house leap into flame as the clam gatherer's niece adds more wood. Smoke billows past the cedar rack above, where small split fish are hung to cure. It curls its way past the great cedar beams and rises out through the opening between the long cedar roof planks. The young girl takes red-hot rocks from the fire with long tongs, dips them into a small cedar box of water to rinse off the ashes, then places the rocks into a cedar wood cooking box to boil water for the clams her aunt has gathered.

Outside the house stands a tall, carved cedar memorial pole, bearing the prestigious crests of her family lineage. It had been raised with long, strong cedar withe ropes and validated with great ceremony. The house chief and noblemen had taken out their ceremonial regalia from large storage chests of cedar wood, dancers had worn cedar wood masks adorned with cascades of soft-shredded cedar bark and performed in front of screens made of cedar planks. Guests had been served quantities of food from huge cedar wood bowls and dishes, wiping their hands clean on soft-shredded cedar bark.

A young slave woman coils two fresh diapers from soft-shredded cedar bark and goes to tend a crying baby, while the child's father prepares long, slender cedar withes to lash a stone hammer head to its shaft. When the hammer is finished, he uses it to pound wedges into a cedar log to split off a plank for a tackle box to fit in the bow of his canoe. He will use the other withes he prepared to sew the corner of the box once he bends the plank into shape. In a year or more he will make a cedar wood cradle in a similar fashion for his sister's new baby, when it grows too big for the woven cedar root cradle. He smiles at the reassuring cries of the newborn infant resounding through the forest.

Throughout her life the newborn baby girl, born before the coming of sailing ships from far-off lands, would rely on the magnificent cedar as an integral part of her life on the Northwest Coast. The child would grow up to respect the cedar tree above all others, believing in its spirit and power. She would refer to the cedar's supernatural spirit as ''Long Life Maker'' and ''Rich Woman Maker,'' because it provided the necessities for a comfortable and full life.

Her people would travel by canoe on long trading journeys to bring back foods, raw materials and various goods not otherwise available. A large canoe would carry her entire family out to their summer village on the outer coast to fish for salmon and gather other resources that would see them through the winter. Without the nets, traps, weirs and harpoons, all made of cedar, to harvest the salmon, and the large cedar wood boxes or root baskets in which to store foods for the long winter, her family would have found it difficult to survive. Practical clothing on the raincoast also came from the cedar, as did large structures to house and shelter extended families from the storms of winter and rains of spring. When people died, their remains were wrapped in cedar bark mats, put in cedar burial boxes and sometimes lashed to the branches of a cedar tree. From birth to death, the wood, bark, roots, withes and leaves of the mystical, powerful cedar tree provided generously for the needs of the peoples of the Northwest Coast — materially, ceremonially and medicinally.

*   *   *

Growing along the rainforest coast of the Pacific Northwest, the cedar, together with other conifers, flourishes in a climate kept temperate by the Japanese Current. The warmed air is trapped by the high peaks of the Coast Mountains, a barrier that also prevents cold, continental air from dominating the climate. Mild winters and moist summers nurture a lush abundance of vegetation to provide edible berries, roots, bulbs, young green shoots and other potherbs that were gathered, preserved, cooked and eaten by the early coastal inhabitants.

In addition, they hunted waterfowl and land and sea mammals, both for food and the raw materials they provided. Low tides laid bare a varied assortment of foods from the intertidal zone: shellfish, chitons, sea urchins, crabs and seaweeds, to name a few. As well as the incomparable salmon — five species annually returning to the various rivers of their birth — the ocean supported halibut, cod, flounder, dogfish and more, with rivers providing sturgeon and trout. Spring brought teeming millions of herring, eulachon and smelt to spawn in the bays or rivers. Food was plentiful, though hunger lurked behind salmon runs that failed or were late, preserved foods that spoiled and enemy raiders who plundered a village for its food and other trophies of war.

When food was abundant, the people enriched their spiritual lives with ceremony, ritual, dancing, drumming, singing and myth telling. They enhanced their material lives with sumptuous feasts, drama, gambling, games and lavish gift giving. They embellished all areas of their lives with a marvellous creativity that included intricately woven and ornamented baskets, hats and dance blankets; finely carved and painted masks made in the images of birds, animals and supernatural, mythical creatures; large storage chests, carved or painted (sometimes both) with complex and sophisticated designs; rattles and drums painted with animal figures, and wide plank dance screens elaborately designed with crests and mythical creatures. Canoe-sized wooden bowls and enormous ladles were used to serve quantities of food to great numbers of visiting guests accommodated in huge houses, and the feasting often lasted for days or weeks. A high-ranking chief arrayed his prized possessions in a conspicuous display of wealth calculated to impress his rivals as well as maintain and enhance his status.

Underlying the power of property — be it possessions, privileges or the ownership of special masks, songs and dances — was the peoples' oneness with all creatures. They recognized that all beings of land, sea and air, as well as the vegetation, were part of the same world; all were to be revered, for each possessed its own spirit. Bears, whales, thunderbirds, wolves or salmon — and supernatural beings — had their own villages, their own chiefs and their own structured societies; all were important to the overall scheme of things. Those that presented themselves as food did so willingly, because the hunter held them in respect and observed the appropriate taboos and rituals. He often spoke to their spirits, thanking them for coming or for giving so generously of their products.

The marine-oriented peoples of the Northwest Coast dwelt on the fringes of the great evergreen forests and were encompassed by a mystic world of spirit beings. They held the supernatural cedar in high esteem, for, like the bountiful salmon of the sea, the ubiquitous tree of the forest gave of itself to sustain and enrich their lives.

*   *   *

For some 9000 years — and probably longer, as archaeology on the Pacific Northwest Coast is still in its infancy — peoples have migrated, settled and moved on, or been displaced by succeeding waves of other peoples. The history is a long one, recorded only in part by myth and legend until quite recently. It has been only a little over two hundred years since men with paper, pens and ink arrived on the coast in sailing ships to write down where they went, what they saw and whom they met. The men brought with them items of trade: iron, beads, mirrors, buttons, copper, cloth, iron pots and muskets. Unwittingly, they also brought diseases that had never been known in the land, and to which the people had no immunity. The worst was smallpox, which raged along the coast, wiping out whole families and sometimes entire villages, until populations dwindled to a pitiful few.

The early explorers and traders were followed by missionaries and settlers, who were followed by Indian agents and the paternal hand of government, which saw fit to ban the potlatch — an institution that lay at the very heart of the native culture. The swift destruction of a thriving people is well documented by historians and anthropologists, and by some of the people themselves. Time passed, but the quiet strength and pride of the peoples did not. With a new awareness of their place on the coast — and of their rights and privileges to the land, the sea and the rivers — they began to emerge with a stronger voice and a rejuvenated sense of identity.

The Northwest Coast peoples are again a positive force in the land, facing up to governments, industry and the business world — and to themselves. Many are grasping the tools of education to enable them to compete in a complex twentieth-century society, and many are focussing on the re-emergence of the old art forms. The cedar tree is often central to that art, providing, as in the past, the raw materials they need: wood, bark, roots and withes. Women have not only revived the weaving skills they learned in their youth, exhibiting and selling their exquisite basketry, but are teaching it to the young people. Men and, occasionally, women, often with apprentices at their side, carve crest poles and canoes, make baskets and steambent boxes, and create masks, drums and rattles. Large plank houses are again being built and used for feasts and ceremonies — and the return of the potlatch.

Great cedar trees, with clear, true grain, are becoming difficult to find as more of them succumb to the logger's saw, yet there is no other tree that can provide so generously, so totally and so beautifully.

PART 2

CEDAR: THE TREE

BOTANICAL DESCRIPTION All conifers are now divided into four distinct families, but at one time botanists grouped them together in the pine family. Thus, when early explorers and various other visitors to the coast recorded that native houses, canoes and clothing were made from the pine tree, they were simply using the generic name. In Britain, where deciduous trees dominate, people still refer to conifers collectively as pines. On the Pacific Northwest Coast, the tree is commonly referred to as cedar, though that name is a general term for two different trees that share common characteristics. Popular use defines one as the red cedar and the other as yellow cedar.

The Red Cedar *Thuja plicata* Tall and straight like its companion conifers, the red cedar is conspicuous by being a lighter green. Towards the top, its branches spread hori-

Photograph by Hilary Stewart

This red cedar in an open area has branches growing to the base of its trunk. 73

zontally, tips upturned; then, below, they take a down curve. Cascading from the branches are the withes, long, slender, curved twigs that bear a bright lacework of flat, fernlike sprays of foliage. On islands and coastlines rimmed with cedars, the boughs gracefully sweep down over the water, the tide drawing a straight basal line along the leafy growth, as though neatly clipped by some unseen gardener.

The finest cedars, however, are not found at the water's edge, for they prefer to be rooted in the deep, moist, porous soils of cool slopes, lakesides, river estuaries and rich bottom lands. Growing in the shade of a dense forest, the cedar reaches up for light, producing a tall straight trunk uninterrupted by branches for much of its height.

In some areas where cedars thrive, they often form groves of large trees with a luxuriant undergrowth of ferns, salal, devil's club and perhaps skunk cabbage, if the land is swampy. Some real giants of the forest have so far managed to escape the power saw's bite and still stand, leviathan-like, among the spruce and hemlock of the Queen

A giant red cedar, probably eight or nine hundred years old, towers over the author standing at the base. Windy Bay, Queen Charlotte Islands. 73

Charlotte Islands. There, at Windy Bay, cedars estimated to be nearly one thousand years old occasionally tower to an awesome 70 m (230'), diminishing the beholder to insignificance. Their trunks, some convoluted and deformed with great age, carry grey-brown bark, ridged and fissured into long fibrous strips. The moss-covered base of one tree, flared by its buttressed roots, measures 4.3 m (14') in diameter. With increasing age, many cedars develop multiple crowns with two, three or more erect divisions that eventually die, leaving the tree with a spiked tip commonly called a "cake-fork" because of its shape.

Red cedars range from sea level to 1370 m (4500'), growing from Baranof Island, Alaska, southward down the coast of British Columbia, Washington, Oregon and northern California. They venture eastward and into higher elevations, but lacking moisture their growth there is considerably diminished.

The long, slender branches and withes of the coastal cedars are both strong and flexible, bending under the weight of snow so as not to break. The cedar's inner bark, composed of many fibrous layers, also has strength and flexibility. Its roots, mostly shallow and widespread, find support mainly by interlacing with the roots of other trees and in a soil without stones run straight and even. But it is the wood, above all else, that gives the cedar such distinction. Beneath its near-white sapwood runs the straight-grained heartwood in shades of reddish brown — aromatic with the characteristic cedar scent. The loose, cellular structure creates air spaces, giving the red cedar better insulating properties than hardwoods; and though cedar is not as strong, it is considerably lighter — an important factor for Northwest Coast native builders. The easily opened cleavage planes allow it to be readily split, and the wood even has its own preservative, a toxic oil called thujaplicin that acts as a fungicide to resist rot in mature trees. Consequently, the wood of a fallen tree often remains sound for a hundred years after it has fallen. A sapling, however, does not have this protection, and may grow into an adult tree with a decayed or hollow centre to its trunk.

The tree is known by many names: red cedar, Western red cedar, Pacific red cedar, giant cedar, British Columbia cedar, giant arborvitae and canoe cedar. In spite of all that, it is not, in fact, a true cedar, nor does it belong to

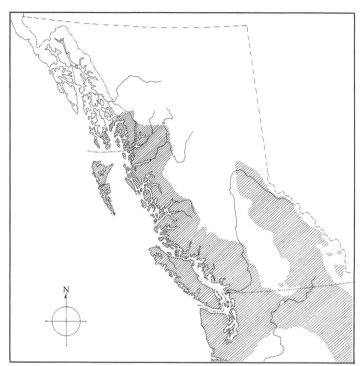

Distribution of Red Cedar on the Northwest Coast

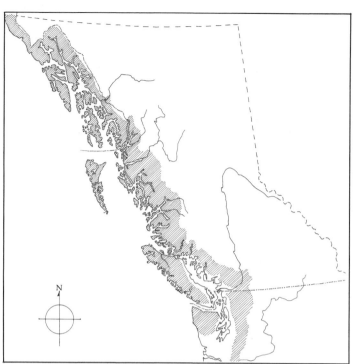

Distribution of Yellow Cedar on the Northwest Coast

Cedar boughs frame a carver working on a cedar canoe. 73

RED CEDAR TREE GROWING IN THE OPEN — CROWN REACHES NEARLY TO THE GROUND — SAME APPLIES TO YELLOW CEDAR.

CEDAR TREE [RED OR YELLOW] GROWING IN DENSE FOREST HAS CROWN AT TOP OF TRUNK WITH MOST BRANCHES ON SIDE FACING THE LIGHT.

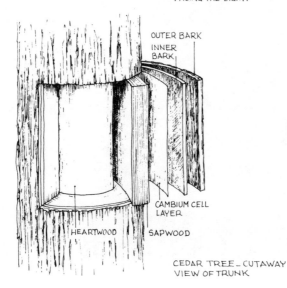

OUTER BARK
INNER BARK
CAMBIUM CELL LAYER
HEARTWOOD
SAPWOOD

CEDAR TREE — CUTAWAY VIEW OF TRUNK

A giant red cedar at Windy Bay, Queen Charlotte Islands. 73

the cedar family, *Cedrus*, of which none is native to North America. Only one of the above names is actually correct, since the tree is a species of arbor-vitae, of which there are only two native to North America. One, *Thuja occidentalis*, (American Arbor-vitae) is the eastern or northern white cedar; the other, *Thuja plicata*, (Giant Arbor-vitae), is the red cedar, the name it is best known by in British Columbia. The name *plicata* is derived from a Greek word meaning "folded in plaits," and refers to the braidlike arrangement of the small, scaly leaves. The most appropriate of the cedar's names must surely be arbor-vitae, Latin words meaning "tree of life" — an apt description for a tree that contributed so much to the life of the Northwest Coast peoples, who addressed the supernatural spirit of the cedar as "Long Life Maker."

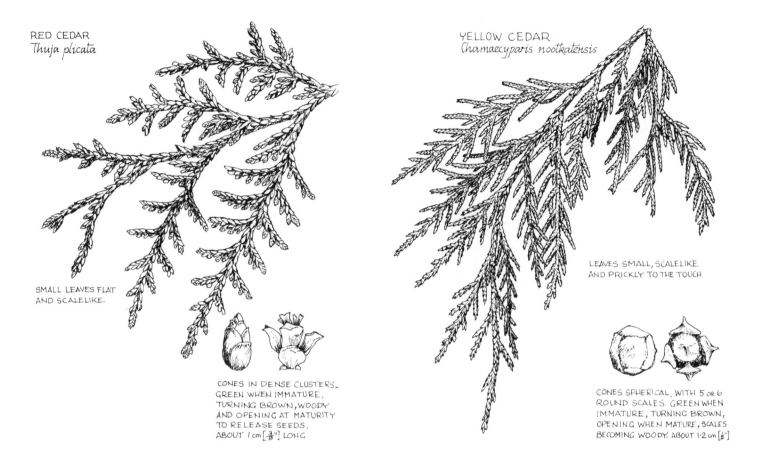

RED CEDAR
Thuja plicata

SMALL LEAVES FLAT
AND SCALELIKE.

CONES IN DENSE CLUSTERS,
GREEN WHEN IMMATURE,
TURNING BROWN, WOODY
AND OPENING AT MATURITY
TO RELEASE SEEDS.
ABOUT 1 cm [⅜"] LONG

YELLOW CEDAR
Chamaecyparis nootkatensis

LEAVES SMALL, SCALELIKE,
AND PRICKLY TO THE TOUCH

CONES SPHERICAL, WITH 5 OR 6
ROUND SCALES. GREEN WHEN
IMMATURE, TURNING BROWN,
OPENING WHEN MATURE, SCALES
BECOMING WOODY. ABOUT 1·2 cm [½"]

The Yellow Cedar *Chamaecyparis nootkatensis* The yellow cedar is similar in many respects to the red cedar, and both belong to the *Cupressaceae* or cypress family. Most Canadians refer to the tree as a cedar, but some Americans call it a cypress, which is why its popular names include these variations: yellow cedar, yellow cypress, Sitka cedar, Sitka cypress, Alaska cedar, Alaska cypress, Nootka cedar, Nootka cypress. Its botanical name is *Chamaecyparis nootkatensis*. The first part of the name is derived from the Greek word for an Old World shrub, the ground cypress; the second refers to Nootka Sound on the west coast of Vancouver Island, where the tree was first documented botanically.

The yellow cedar presents a weeping silhouette, the long withes pendant, the foliage drooping vertically, its soft yellow-green making the tree conspicuous among the other conifers. The outer bark, greyish brown and scaly on young trees, is furrowed in light grey, loose ribbonous strips on mature trees; the whole trunk appears shaggy and almost white against the dark of the forest or in sunlight. The yellow-gold inner bark is exceptionally strong, like satin to the touch, and has a fine fibrous content. Yellow cedar derives its common name from the colour of its wood, which is a light creamy yellow throughout. The softness of the fine-grained, evenly textured wood, wonderfully pungent to smell, makes it highly suitable for carving, since it does not split as readily as red cedar and is also durable.

Growing to a height of 44 m (145') and more, with a trunk diameter of 0.9 m (3') or greater, the yellow cedar may live as long as the red, but never comes near its huge size. It thrives in a cold, wet maritime climate, along streams, in valleys and on mountain slopes, preferring deep, slightly acidic soil, though it can grow on a

Branches of a yellow cedar. 73

thin layer of soil over bedrock. It is found on western coastal mountains and islands northward from Oregon through British Columbia to Alaska, but chooses sub-alpine elevations of 610 m to 2130 m (2000' to 7000') in the south, descending to sea level only from about Knight Inlet northward.

EARLY EVIDENCE   Just how long the cedar has flourished along the entire Northwest Coast is difficult to say with certainty, but pollen analysis studies are significant. Botanist Richard Hebda and palynologist Rolf Mathewes examined plant pollen preserved in the sediments of Marion Lake, in the Lower Fraser Valley, and determined their age through carbon-14 dating. They then charted a diagram showing that the cedar (probably red cedar) first made an appearance in the Lower Fraser Valley around 6600 years ago. It slowly flourished and by about 500 years ago accounted for nearly fifty per cent of the vegetation of the area, diminishing to about twenty per cent from then to the present.

Archaeological excavations in the southern regions of the Northwest Coast have unearthed ample evidence of the indigenous peoples' use of the cedar tree over a lengthy span of time. The now-famous wet-site of Ozette, Washington, yielded great quantities of items made from wood, bark, roots and withes, including complete (though destroyed) houses and their contents, all dating from between 300 and 500 years ago. At another wet-site, the Little Qualicum River site (DiSc 1) on the east coast of Vancouver Island, finds included light and heavy-duty rope of withes, bark matting and rope, as well as a canoe bailer, dating from around 1000 years ago. Great quantities of wooden items and bark baskets from the water-logged Lachane site (GbTo 33) in Prince Rupert harbour are evidence of the use of the cedar tree 2000 years ago.

A waterlogged section of the Pitt River site (DhRq 21), near Vancouver, produced two carved items, possibly adze hafts, made of heartwood, as well as evidence of wood chopping, carving and incising. Also present were baskets of split withes and bark, showing three different weaving techniques, all around 2900 years old. Finds dating from a century earlier showed that the people of the Musqueam site (DhRt 4), near Vancouver, produced bark basketry in five distinct weaves (both coarse and fine), matting and heavy ropes suitable for use with sealing harpoons. In addition, large amounts of cedar chips, as well as split and drilled wood fragments, are evidence of considerable use of the cedar tree 3000 years ago. A whalebone bark beater from Yuquot (DjSp 1), on the west coast of Vancouver Island, also dated from 3000 years ago, and woodworking tools from another strata dated from between 3000 and 4000 years ago.

In the final days of the Pitt River excavation, archaeological work located an adzed plank in the floor of a deep trench. The plank, about 30 cm (12″) wide and probably cedar, had to remain embedded in its muddy matrix when the trench was backfilled but was well enough below dated strata for dig director Val Patenaude to believe it could possibly be as much as 5000 years old.

At the Glenrose site (DgRr 6), near Vancouver, archaeologists unearthed woodworking tools from the deep levels of midden dating from between 5000 and 8000 years ago. It is impossible to know whether or not an early woodworker made the antler wedges for the purpose of splitting cedar boards some 6000 years ago — but he might have.

In future years, excavations will no doubt bring to the surface positive evidence of enormous antiquity for the use of the cedar tree.

LEGENDS   To all things there was a beginning. The need for Northwest Coast peoples to rationalize, understand and record these origins was manifest in the many creation legends found along the entire coast. Legends made order out of the world, defined certain behaviour and rituals and confirmed the existence of a supernatural power.

The Origin of   "There was a real good man who was
the Red Cedar   always helping others. Whenever they needed, he gave; when they wanted, he gave them food and clothing. When the great Spirit saw this, he said, 'That man has done his work; when he dies and where he is buried, a cedar tree will grow and be useful to the people — the roots for baskets, the bark for clothing, the wood for shelter.' "

Told by Bertha Peters to Wally Henry and reproduced by their kind permission. Coast Salish.

The Origin of   Long ago, when the world was not as it
the Yellow Cedar   is now, Raven, the great creator and trickster, came across three young women drying salmon on the beach. Ever hungry, the wily bird approached the women and asked: "Are you not afraid to be here alone?"

"No," they said.

"Are you not afraid of bears?"

And again they replied, "No."

Persistent, Raven asked if they were not afraid of wolves, marten and various other creatures. Each time they answered no, until he mentioned owls, at which the three women confessed to their terrible fear of owls.

Raven went off but quickly hid himself in some nearby bushes, where he began making owl calls. Terrified, the women fled, running and running until they were halfway up the mountain. They stopped, finally, out of breath. Standing together on the mountainside, the three of them turned into yellow cedar trees. That is why yellow cedars are always found on high slopes of the west coast of Vancouver Island and why they are so beautiful; their long graceful branches and silky inner bark resemble the women's hair, and their young trunks are smooth to the touch.

Adapted by the author from the original told by Alice Paul in *Ethnobotany of the Hesquiat Indians of Vancouver Island* by Nancy J. Turner and Barbara S. Efrat. Westcoast.

PART 3

CEDAR: THE WOOD

THE WOODWORKER AND HIS TOOLS   In a culture where so much of daily life depended on products made of wood, all men — for woodworking was solely the task of men — acquired a well-rounded knowledge of the art. By constructing plain boxes for general family use, making fishing and hunting gear, tools and other implements, as well as small dugout canoes, a man provided many of the necessary requirements of his family.

Major objects in wood and items of particular artistic merit were made by a craftsman specializing in one type of work. The master carver, who was highly regarded and enjoyed a prestigious place in society, received payment in food, clothing and other items for his work. When a specialist was commissioned by someone in another village to make a canoe, carve a pole or complete a lengthy task, he and his family went to live in the household of his employer, usually a chief, who provided all their food.

A young boy who showed an interest in and a natural talent for woodworking was encouraged by a specialist to watch and copy his work — the typical method of Northwest Coast schooling. In addition, the young carver would seek a spirit helper through magical practices, since no one could succeed in anything important without the guidance of a specific power. An especially talented carver was considered to be supernaturally endowed with his gift or to have inherited it from an ancestor. Apprenticed under a good carver, the novice learned to make and handle quality tools. He was instructed in their use and practised until he became advanced enough to work on a major project such as a pole, with the master carving one side and the pupil copying the design on the other side.

In modern times, as the revival of woodworking continues to flourish along the Northwest Coast, several top

Photograph by Richard Renshaw-Beauchamp. Courtesy British Columbia Provincial Museum, PN 16035-24A
Kheykhanius, a carver, seated on a cedar bark mat; he is holding a finished cedar bentwood bowl and demonstrating the method of using a curved knife. In the foreground are a stone palette and paintbrushes. Kwakiutl, no date. Courtesy Field Museum of Natural History, Chicago, 13572

29

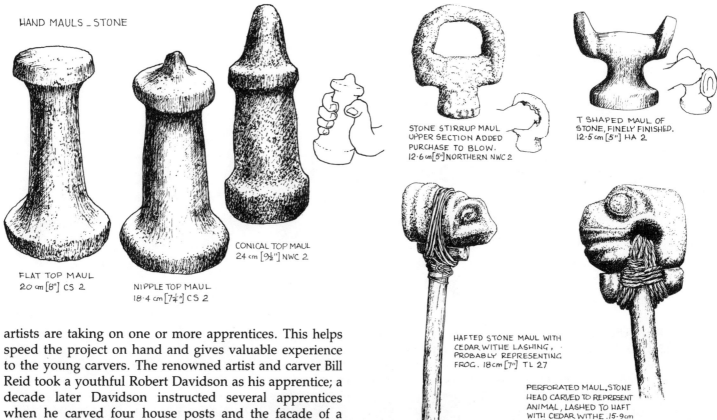

HAND MAULS – STONE

FLAT TOP MAUL
20 cm [8"] CS 2

NIPPLE TOP MAUL
18·4 cm [7¼"] CS 2

CONICAL TOP MAUL
24 cm [9½"] NWC 2

STONE STIRRUP MAUL
UPPER SECTION ADDED
PURCHASE TO BLOW.
12·6 cm [5"] NORTHERN NWC 2

T SHAPED MAUL OF
STONE, FINELY FINISHED.
12·5 cm [5"] HA 2

HAFTED STONE MAUL WITH
CEDAR WITHE LASHING,
PROBABLY REPRESENTING
FROG. 18 cm [7"] TL 27

PERFORATED MAUL. STONE
HEAD CARVED TO REPRESENT
ANIMAL, LASHED TO HAFT
WITH CEDAR WITHE .15·9 cm
[6¼"] HA 1

artists are taking on one or more apprentices. This helps speed the project on hand and gives valuable experience to the young carvers. The renowned artist and carver Bill Reid took a youthful Robert Davidson as his apprentice; a decade later Davidson instructed several apprentices when he carved four house posts and the facade of a Haida plank house built in Masset, Queen Charlotte Islands, as a memorial to the great Haida master artist Charles Edenshaw. (Unfortunately, this work was destroyed by fire in 1981.) Following a new concept of the apprentice system, experienced carvers teach students at the Gitenmax School of Northwest Coast Indian Art in 'Ksan, a replica Gitksan village at Hazelton in British Columbia.

* * *

For scores of generations of Northwest Coast woodworkers, the marvel of the cedar tree was that it could be worked in so many ways with a minimum of tools. Uncomplicated though most of these tools were, their very simplicity speaks of knowledge and experience refined over a long time span.

A man's tools, especially those used for carving, were very personal items. He made each to fit his own hands and his own way of working, sometimes devising a special tool for a particular need and, with the pride that stems from creativity, he often sculptured the handles with intricate crest figures.

Three basic tools — the hammer, the wedge and the adze — and a number of other special tools — contributed to the development of a major woodworking industry that became established along the entire Northwest Coast, wherever the cedar grew.

Hammers A simple, early form of maul was the hammer stone, a waterworn cobble chosen for its shape, hardness and resistance to cracking or chipping. Unmodified, the oval stone was grasped in the hand, and either end could be used for pounding. Later, two types of stone hammers characterized the north and the south. While the southern peoples used the hand maul (held directly in the hand), the northern nations, Tsimshian,

SPLITTING WEDGE
OF ALDER WOOD,
GROMMET OF CEDAR
WITHE. 49·5cm [19¼"]
NWC 4

LARGE WOODEN
WEDGE WITH CEDAR
WITHE GROMMET.
57·8 cm [22¾"] WC 12

WEDGE WITH WITHE
GROMMET. 35cm [13¾"]
NWC 9

WEDGE OF ELK
ANTLER BEAM.
36·8cm [14½"] CS 12

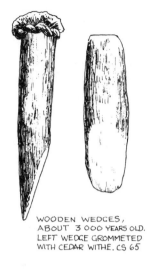

WOODEN WEDGES,
ABOUT 3 000 YEARS OLD.
LEFT WEDGE GROMMETED
WITH CEDAR WITHE. CS 65

Haida and Tlingit, devised a heavy-duty implement —
the hafted maul, which was a heavy stone head lashed
onto a long haft. Using a hafted maul, a man could
deliver a blow with great force, much like a sledge
hammer. Many of these stone mauls were sculpted with
bird or animal figures, which may have represented the
woodworker's spirit helper.

Wedges   Wedges, which were hammered into cedar
logs to split them into planks, had to withstand heavy
abuse. Tough, fine-grained yew wood provided the best
material for their manufacture, though other woods such
as spruce, maple and crabapple were often used. The
wedgemaker scorched the wood to increase its hardness,
rubbed tallow into the heated wood to stop it from warping, and twisted a grommet of cedar withe around the
top end to prevent hammer blows from splitting it. The
opposite end he bevelled, to allow it to be driven into the
wood.

As an alternative to wood, a section of the thick beam
of an antler, usually elk (wapiti), bevelled at one end,
also made a tough, serviceable wedge. These are often
found archaeologically, providing evidence of woodworking at sites where wooden wedges have long since rotted
away.

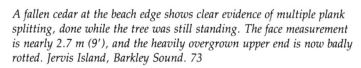

*A fallen cedar at the beach edge shows clear evidence of multiple plank
splitting, done while the tree was still standing. The face measurement
is nearly 2.7 m (9'), and the heavily overgrown upper end is now badly
rotted. Jervis Island, Barkley Sound. 73*

This cedar tree may have had its base chopped by adzing to obtain kindling. Jervis Island, Barkley Sound. 73

Adzes and Chisels Woodworkers along the coast wielded several different types and sizes of adzes to cut and shape wood. Most universal was the elbow adze, so called because of its shape. The most southern peoples used an elbow adze with a stone head on a short haft, while Coast Salish, Westcoast and Kwakiutl peoples used a long-handled implement. The northern woodworkers had a heavy-duty version, with a wedge-shaped stone head lashed to a haft longer and thicker than the southern elbow adzes; this hefty tool could be wielded with both hands. Since the blade edges of museum specimens never appear to be at all sharp, this tool may have served the purpose of splitting cedar rather than cutting and shaping it; one early account, in fact, refers to it as a "splitting adze."

Since metal-bladed adzes have been used on the coast for several hundred years, very little is known of the use of adzes with stone blades, and to date no examples of wood worked with stone-bladed adzes are available for study. An adzed plank was discovered at an archaeological excavation at the Pitt River site (DhRq 21), but it could not be removed for lack of time. Since the plank might have been a few thousand years old, it is possible that the adzing had been done with a stone-bladed tool.

A woodworker used the large-sized elbow adze for rough shaping and chopping, such as removing branches from a log, carving out the basic shape of a canoe or the initial stages of roughing out the figures on a pole. This adze was also used on other materials: a piece of elk skull found at an old village site had the adzed stub of the antler beam still attached — the rest likely made into a wedge.

Contemporary carvers use a wide range of elbow adzes, particularly for large works, and almost always make their own tools. Kwakiutl carver Roy Hanuse prefers alder wood for the haft because it is soft to carve while still green and when dried retains the spring necessary for proper use. He uses an elbow adze with a wide blade for general use and roughing out; for finer work, he switches to an adze with a narrow blade which, he says, "can be bounced along down the surface of the wood." This rebounding helps to set up the steady rhythm that creates a uniform texture as the adze moves down the grain in parallel, overlapping rows. Handling the adze with such apparent ease takes a great deal of practice.

Used only by the woodworkers from Vancouver Island southward, the D adze, so named for the shape of its haft, generally had a blade narrower than that of the elbow adze. Many of the old D adze hafts were carved to represent creatures, either minimally or quite elaborately. The protuberance on the blade end of the haft was functional; when wielding the tool, the ball of the user's hand pressed down onto the projection to add to the force of the strike.

The carpenter used the D adze for finer work and for finishing. Worked with precise, repeated strokes in a continuous line, the adze created a textured groove. Several of these grooves, side by side, were sometimes used to create simple designs. Sometimes an object was fine-

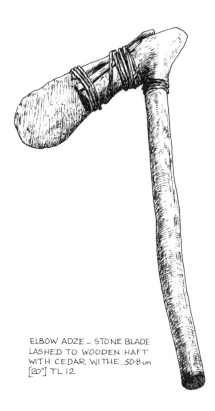

ELBOW ADZE — STONE BLADE
LASHED TO WOODEN HAFT
WITH CEDAR WITHE. 50·8 cm
[20"] TL 12

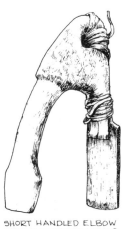

SHORT HANDLED ELBOW
ADZE WITH METAL BLADE,
LASHING OF RAWHIDE. FROM
PUGET SOUND. CS 53

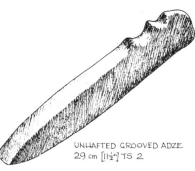

UNHAFTED GROOVED ADZE
29 cm [$11\frac{1}{2}$"] TS 2

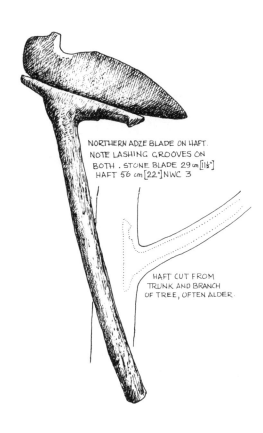

NORTHERN ADZE BLADE ON HAFT.
NOTE LASHING GROOVES ON
BOTH. STONE BLADE 29 cm [$11\frac{1}{2}$"]
HAFT 56 cm [22"] NWC 3

HAFT CUT FROM
TRUNK AND BRANCH
OF TREE, OFTEN ALDER.

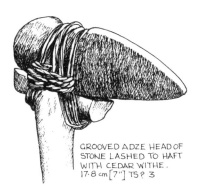

GROOVED ADZE HEAD OF
STONE LASHED TO HAFT
WITH CEDAR WITHE.
17·8 cm [7"] TS? 3

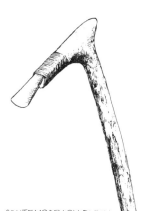

CONTEMPORARY ELBOW
ADZE WITH STEEL BLADE
BOLTED TO ALDER HAFT,
LASHED WITH NYLON
CORD. 40 cm [$15\frac{3}{4}$"] OWNED
BY NISHGA CARVER
NORMAN TAIT.

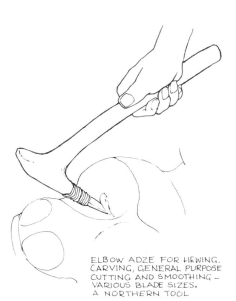

ELBOW ADZE FOR HEWING,
CARVING, GENERAL PURPOSE
CUTTING AND SMOOTHING —
VARIOUS BLADE SIZES.
A NORTHERN TOOL

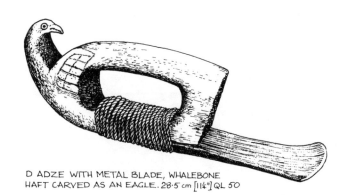

D ADZE WITH METAL BLADE, WHALEBONE
HAFT CARVED AS AN EAGLE. 28·5 cm [11¼"] QL 50

D ADZE – FOR CUTTING, SHAPING
AND FINE FINISHING WOOD. A TOOL
OF SOUTHERN AREAS.

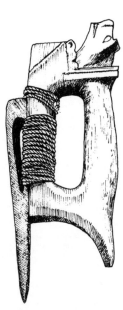

D ADZE – WOODEN HAFT
CARVED TO REPRESENT
BEAR COMING OUT OF BOX.
METAL AXE HEAD FOR
BLADE 15·2 [6"] LONG. MK 12

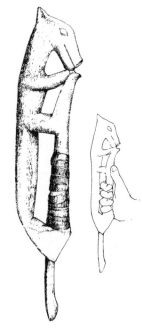

STRAIGHT ADZE WITH ANTLER
HAFT. UNLIKE D ADZE, CARVER'S
GRIP WAS ALIGNED WITH BLADE.
PROBABLY FROM LOWER COLUMBIA
RIVER AREA. 21·5 cm [8½"] COURTESY
UNIVERSITY OF OREGON MUSEUM OF
ANTHROPOLOGY.

CHISEL WITH STONE
BLADE, WOODEN
SHAFT, CEDAR
WITHE LASHINGS.
33·6 cm [13¼"] NWC 32

CHISEL WITH METAL
BLADE, SET IN ELK
ANTLER SLEEVE –
LASHED WITH TWINE –
CEDAR WITHE GROMMET.
45·6 [18"] CS 2

CHISEL WITH
BONE BLADE.
40·6 [16"] WC 2

CHISEL WITH
IRON BLADE,
LASHED WITH
CHERRY BARK.
33 cm [13"] WC 2

CHISEL DRIVEN DOWN INTO WOOD
[LEFT], THEN ANGLED BACK AND
HAMMERED ALONG TO REMOVE CHIP.

CHISEL – USED WITH HAND
MAUL, FOR CUTTING, HOLLOW-
ING AND REACHING INTO
RECESSED PLACES – VARIOUS
BLADE SIZES AND HAFT LENGTHS.

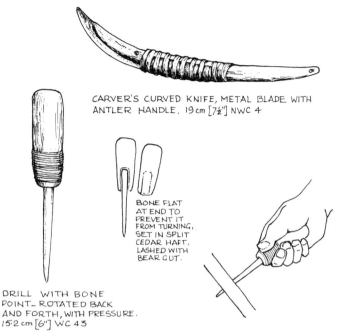

CARVER'S CURVED KNIFE, METAL BLADE WITH ANTLER HANDLE. 19 cm [7½"] NWC 4

BONE FLAT AT END TO PREVENT IT FROM TURNING, SET IN SPLIT CEDAR HAFT, LASHED WITH BEAR GUT.

DRILL WITH BONE POINT- ROTATED BACK AND FORTH, WITH PRESSURE. 15·2 cm [6"] WC 43

finished by adzing to achieve the characteristic ripple effect so often seen on poles and house beams; indeed, in early times most cultural groups considered a pole was not finished unless it was textured all over in this manner. Northern woodworkers, who did not have the D adze, used the metal-bladed elbow adze for fine finishing.

A third type of adze, the straight adze, was similar to the D adze except that the blade was aligned with the knuckles instead of being set off and had a knuckle guard of leather or wood.

Another important cutting tool for the woodworker was his chisel, which generally had a long shaft topped by a grommet or crown of cedar withe to prevent it from being split. While adzes bit into the wood with a swinging motion of the carpenter's hand, the chisel had a different action. Holding the chisel in place against the wood, the woodworker drove it in a short way with a hammer, angled it back, then drove it along to remove a thin chip of wood. He could also drive the chisel more deeply into the wood to create a groove or to split off wood in recessed areas of carvings, where the adze could not reach.

Chisels used in felling large trees had a haft up to 1.2 m (4') in length to reach deep into the trunk. Before the

introduction of iron, cutting tools had blades of a fine-grained stone (in the south, generally nephrite) or bone. The nephrite could hold a reasonably sharp edge and be resharpened on a grindstone when dulled. The bone of elk is extremely tough and can be honed to quite a sharp edge.

When I tried roughly hollowing out a cedar bowl using a maul and a bone-tipped chisel I had made, I was surprised by the blade's strength and cutting ability. Early ethnographies also mention chisels with blades of mussel shell (*Mytilus californianus*), but in experiments with such a tool I found the blade to be not nearly strong enough: after several blows, the thick shell cracked and broke. The hafted shell blade does, however, make a sharp tool for scraping and shaving wood, a method I found practical in shaping and smoothing various types of wood. Sharp-edged tools of flaked stone would have served the same purpose.

Other Tools   For decorative woodworking, the carver probably employed a curved, split beaver-tooth knife. The introduction of metal gave rise to knives that had a similar blade, but with varying widths and curves. Clenching the wooden handle in his fist almost horizontally, the carver drew the knife towards him with long, sure strokes. Among other things, he used this tool for making spoons, ladles and bowls, for hollowing out the back of a mask and for making the sharp or gentle curves of three-dimensional carving. This specialized tool made it possible to create the beautiful, subtle curves characteristic of Northwest Coast carving and sculpture.

Fine carving required small, sharp scrapers, either hafted or hand held, for shaving and shaping cedar. Easily controlled, scrapers allowed precise shaping for such items as yellow cedar pegs, arrow or spindle shafts and paddles. Originally the blades of scrapers were quartz, obsidian, sharpened bone, mussel shell, beaver teeth and probably other materials. With the coming of iron, carvers and woodworkers discovered the advantages that metal had over stone and adapted the metal to their carving needs.

Fine-pointed quartz tools, called gravers, allowed the carver to incise fine lines into wood or to score marked lines.

To make holes in wood, the woodworker used a sharp,

pointed bone awl or stone drill bits. He pierced the soft wood with the awl and rotated it back and forth while applying pressure. By directing the awl diagonally through the grain, the wood did not split. This work was surprisingly fast, taking about fifteen seconds to drill through 10 mm (⅜") of cedar. To drill larger and deeper holes, he rotated a shaft, tipped with a serrated stone drill bit, between his hands, though he mainly used this tool on woods harder than cedar.

To keep his bone and stone chisel and adze blades sharp, the woodworker used abraders of sandstone.

Although the native woodworker's tool chest held no measuring tape or yardstick, he had, nevertheless, a system of measurement that worked quite adequately. Instead of centimetres and metres, or inches and feet, he used finger, hand and arm widths and lengths. More important than standard measurements was accuracy in making, for instance, a bentwood box. The carpenter achieved that with sticks cut to the length and width that he required for the sides of the box and perhaps a gauge for the kerfs to ensure the necessary precision. An artist often used cedar bark templates for perfect symmetry in a flat design, but when it came to matching the two sides of a canoe, the craftsman relied on many years experience and a deep, innate sense of the nature and spirit of the remarkable cedar.

* * *

It is popularly thought that early explorers of the late eighteenth century were the first to introduce iron to the coast, but it is clear that iron was known and used long before that. An archaelogical excavation at Ozette, in Washington, unearthed rusted iron tools that dated from about 500 years ago, but from where the metal came has not been ascertained. One speculation is that it may have originated with some iron-age source in Siberia and slowly worked its way down the coast through a series of trade exchanges. This could possibly account for the woodworking tradition in the north being more highly developed and extensive than that in the south. Another speculation is that iron may have drifted ashore on wood from the wrecks of ocean-going Asian ships.

When Capt. James Cook arrived on the Northwest Coast in 1778, the native peoples seemed to have few

tools that were not tipped with iron. He recorded: "Their great dexterity in works of wood, may, in some measure, be ascribed to the assistance they received from iron tools. For as far as I know, they use no other; at least, we saw only one chisel of bone." Some reports say that the iron blades were the width and thickness of a barrel hoop, which suggests shipboard origin — Spanish or Russian explorers, perhaps, who sailed the coast some years before Cook.

For quite some time after European tools became accessible to native woodworkers, they continued to prefer their own style of implements and the familiar ways of working with them. For instance, an iron axe head was used as the blade of a D adze, files were made into curved knife blades and trees were felled in the old ways in spite of the availability of the axe. Alexander Walker, an ensign on the fur-trading ship *Captain Cook*, visited Yuquot (Friendly Cove) in 1786 and in his journal noted: "They are much dissatisfied with the shape of our tools, that they generally altered it after buying them." He also wrote: "A chisel, five inches long, and very broad towards the end, they preferred over all our tools, even to a Saw, Hatchet or Sabre, although we had instructed them in the use of these Instruments."

It is not surprising that the native carpenter felt more at ease using the tools he knew so well than those of European origin, for his culture had a long history of expertise in woodworking, and there were elders to advise and guide him when he needed it.

TECHNOLOGIES   As a result of working with the versatile cedar for thousands of years, generations of woodworkers devised and perfected various technologies for felling and transporting trees, splitting and cutting planks, joining pieces of wood together, steaming and bending wood and sanding finished products, as well as patching and repairing damaged wooden objects.

Felling Trees   In early times, when a drift log of good cedar landed on a beach fronting an Indian village, it was a welcome gift — but drift logs could not supply all the needs of a village, so it was necessary to fell trees. Large cedar trees were valuable, particularly to people who required them for huge canoes and big plank houses, and wealthy families laid claim to good stands of cedar near

FELLING A TREE
BY BURNING AND ADZING KW 34

RED-HOT STONES, SET IN
CAVITY CHISELLED INTO
CEDAR TREE, BURNED WOOD.
TREE FALLER CHOPPED
AWAY CHARCOAL, RENEWING
HOT STONES AS NEEDED.

UPPER END OF FELLED
TREE REMOVED BY
CONTROLLED BURNING
WITH HOT ROCKS

ROCKS HEATED IN FIRE, REMOVED
WITH WOODEN TONGS.

HEMLOCK BRANCHES, DIPPED
INTO BOX OF WATER AND
APPLIED TO TREE, CONTROLLED
BURNING.

A cedar with a "test hole" about 45.5 cm (18") wide. Note the strip of bark removed prior to chiselling. Queen Charlotte Islands. 73

water. A family without such rights had to pay the owner of a stand for the privilege of cutting and using his trees.

As there were specialists in every major field of endeavour, so there were men particularly skilled at felling trees. The time preferred was late summer to early spring, as felling a tree when the sap was up hastened the rotting of the wood. Also, it was important to find the right cedar tree for the purpose required: house construction, canoe, mortuary pole and so on. Straight, clear-grained wood was generally preferred, and a trunk with a minimum number of limbs would provide wood largely free of knots. A Westcoast canoemaker ritually fasted and prayed for success in choosing the right tree. For the best trees, he looked in the darker parts of the forest, hoping to find one not too far from a river or the sea, though evidence shows that on occasion trees were cut several kilometres inland.

Many large, old cedar trees on the coast bear a deep rectangular or square hole chiselled well above the flare of the trunk's base. Today these are referred to as "test holes," and several ethnographic accounts explain that if such a hole proved that the wood inside was rotten, the tree was not felled. Because of the renewed interest in early woodworking technologies, the function of these holes is now being questioned. A Haida from Skidegate,

FELLING A TREE
BY BURNING WC 66

FIRE BURNED THROUGH BASE OF
TREE, WET CLAY ON TRUNK ABOVE
CONTROLLED FIRE.

FELLING A TREE
WITH CHISEL, WEDGE AND MAUL CS 38

TREE RINGED WITH TWO CHISEL CUTS, WOOD
BETWEEN SPLIT OUT WITH WEDGE AND MAUL.
PROCESS REPEATED UNTIL TREE FELL.

MOVING A LOG TO WATER'S EDGE. WC 43

SIXTY OR MORE MEN PULLED ON
A HEAVY-DUTY ROPE, HAULING
LOG DOWN INCLINE TO SEA.

SEVERAL MEN
PUSHED AT ONE
END...

...OTHERS USED POLES TO LIFT
AND MOVE THE LOG FORWARD...

SHORT POLES BENEATH
LOG LESSENED DRAG

An unusual adzed cavity appears in three equidistant places around the base of a large, old cedar; it may have been the start of felling this tree. The width of the cavity at top is about 61 cm (24"). Queen Charlotte Islands. 73

(Richard Wilson) Wanagun, who is studying early woodworking sites on the Queen Charlotte Islands, thinks that there are too many trees in good condition for all the cavities to be test holes. The two trees I examined had only a small core of rot, which could have developed since the hole was made (possibly even because of it), supporting his doubt. Although the literal translation of the Haida word for the hole is "feeling the heart" — appropriate for the test hole — Richard has other theories. One is that the cut might identify the owner of the tree to ensure that no one else felled it. Since the holes do vary in shape and size, though some are extremely wide, this is a possibility. Another theory is that the cavity marked the tree for

the faller, since the man who chose the tree was not necessarily the man who felled it.

There are also some other ways to test a tree for rot. Jeoff White of Old Masset, a man in his seventies and grandfather of present-day carver Jim Hart, said that he judges the condition of the wood by studying the crown of the tree: dead wood at the top indicates rot in the heartwood. Veteran canoemaker eighty-four-year-old David Frank of Ahousat, on the west coast of Vancouver Island, also told me about his method of testing a cedar for soundness. "I walk all around that tree, hit it with a piece of wood, and I listen to the sound it makes. If it's got some rot in it, then it's gonna be hollow inside, and it's gonna make a different sound. I listen to the tree — it tells me." When questioned about the holes cut in cedars, he said they were "to see if the tree was rotten. The hole was chiselled on the side opposite the sun . . . with some people making up to three holes to test how far the rot went up."

Another theory is that the test hole could have served to check on the quality of the cedar's grain, a particularly important factor in canoe making. Perhaps further study and research will fully answer the enigma of the test hole.

Before starting the task of felling a cedar, the faller respectfully addressed the spirit of the tree with a prayer, asking for the trunk to topple in the direction he wished. David Frank said that he would calculate the direction so that the cedar's fall was cushioned by hitting other trees on its way down, to prevent the trunk from landing too heavily and cracking. Care also had to be taken to ensure that the tree would not become hung up in another.

One method of felling the tree was by burning. The faller set red-hot rocks inside a chiselled-out cavity — the test hole? — to burn the wood. Under his direction, workers, often slaves, then chiselled and adzed out the charred wood. With a back cut chiselled out, the great cedar let go, falling to the ground where the faller had asked it to. A similar burning technique involved setting fire to the base of the tree and using wet clay to prevent the rest of it from catching fire.

Another method of cutting down a tree entailed building a scaffold and platform around the trunk, just above the flaring base. The woodworkers removed sufficient bark to enable them to chisel two parallel grooves, about

30 cm (12″) or more apart, around the trunk. The men then used wedges and stone mauls to split out the wood from between the grooves. They repeated the chiselling and wedging process to cut away the trunk, making sure the lower chisel cut remained horizontal, while the upper one was chiselled downward at a forty-five degree angle. When these cuts became too deep for the chisel to reach into, the men switched to one with a longer haft; then one man held the chisel while another wielded the stone maul.

Among the Makah, only a chief who owned many slaves would attempt to fell very large cedars. The method there was to encircle the tree with as many slaves as possible, each with an adze. No doubt supervised by an expert tree faller, relays of workers chopped away at the trunk, beaver style, until the tree fell. In the early nineteenth century, during his two years as a captive of the Yuquot, John Jewitt wrote: "The felling of trees, as practiced by them, is a slow and most tedious process, three of them being generally from two to three days in cutting down a large one."

Once a tree was felled, the next step entailed removing the upper portion by setting red-hot stones on the trunk at the place where the top was to be cut off by controlled burning and chopping. The workers then removed any limbs on the trunk and adzed off the bark and sapwood. If the log was exceptionally large and intended for a canoe, it was hollowed out before being taken out of the forest.

Skidding out the log, especially a large one, was another major undertaking. Men drove a series of long poles under the log to act as a skid in hauling it out. About sixty men pulled on cedar bark ropes tied around the log, while others pushed from the opposite side. Still others used poles to lift and propel the log forward on its downward journey to the water. The time involved in this procedure depended on the size of the log, the nature of the terrain and the distance to the water; on average, it took two hundred men a total of twenty-four hours.

Once the log was in the water, several canoes, each with two paddlers, lined up in single file to tow the massive cedar back to the village; the men paddled in unison for greater power. They beached the log at high tide and put rocks beneath to prevent it from rolling back; there it

was trimmed and shaped. If the log was for house construction, two to three hundred men and women used a system of ropes and sloping planks to haul it up the incline to where the house was being constructed.

As I walked among the remains of the twenty-four houses in the old village of Tanu, on the Queen Charlotte Islands, I thought about the process of felling, bucking, skidding, towing and hauling the massive beams and posts. When I stood beside one of these giants, now thickly moss covered and sprouting spruce seedlings, the immensity of its size was a far greater reality than the actual measurements: close to 13.7 m (45′) long, with a diameter of about 91 cm (3′). I could not even guess at the weight, but the thought of the amount of physical labour and teamwork involved in acquiring and raising this single beam stirred my imagination. Near the Yakoun River, in the northern Charlottes, there are several areas with evidence of a great deal of early woodworking activity, including canoe blanks. The stumps of huge cedar trees and their discarded tops, now draped with yellow-green moss, ferns and sprouting vegetation, remain in the silent forest — monuments to the skilled, audacious tree fallers of another era.

Splitting Planks   The single most useful woodworking technique took advantage of the cedar's special characteristic — its ability to be split easily and in one continuous plane for great lengths, thus giving maximum return for minimum effort.

Splitting planks was skilled work, and some men specialized in it. After a tree was felled and the top portion removed, the plankmaker trimmed the upper end to an even, vertical surface. From his wedge bag, he took up a "marker" wedge and repeatedly hammered it in a short way, moving it along each time to make a horizontal groove across the face of the top end, four finger-widths above the centre of the log. He always split the log from the top towards the base to ensure an even thickness all the way.

Next, the woodworker drove in a series of wedges along the grooved line, placing them quite close together and hitting each in succession, so that they penetrated the end of the log, splitting it open. When the crack widened sufficiently, the woodworker inserted a round "spreading stick" (wider than the diameter of the log)

SPLITTING OFF PLANKS. KW ✳ 34

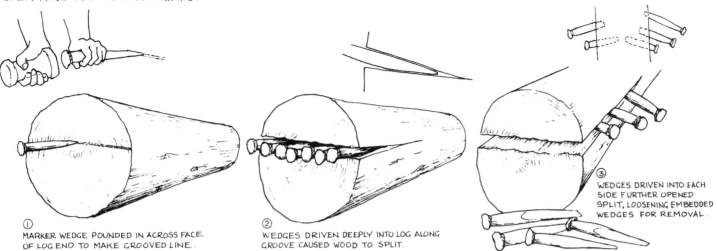

① MARKER WEDGE POUNDED IN ACROSS FACE OF LOG END TO MAKE GROOVED LINE.

② WEDGES DRIVEN DEEPLY INTO LOG ALONG GROOVE CAUSED WOOD TO SPLIT.

③ WEDGES DRIVEN INTO EACH SIDE FURTHER OPENED SPLIT, LOOSENING EMBEDDED WEDGES FOR REMOVAL.

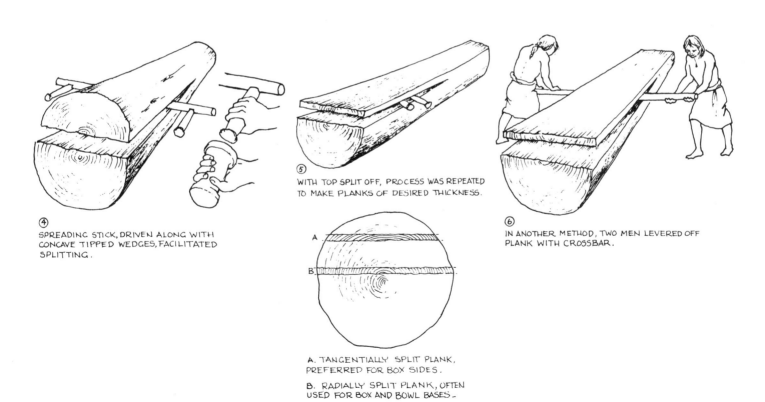

④ SPREADING STICK, DRIVEN ALONG WITH CONCAVE TIPPED WEDGES, FACILITATED SPLITTING.

⑤ WITH TOP SPLIT OFF, PROCESS WAS REPEATED TO MAKE PLANKS OF DESIRED THICKNESS.

⑥ IN ANOTHER METHOD, TWO MEN LEVERED OFF PLANK WITH CROSSBAR.

A. TANGENTIALLY SPLIT PLANK, PREFERRED FOR BOX SIDES.

B. RADIALLY SPLIT PLANK, OFTEN USED FOR BOX AND BOWL BASES.

SPLITTING PLANKS FROM A STANDING TREE.

CHISELLED CAVITIES IN TREE TRUNK ALLOWED FOR WEDGES TO BE DRIVEN IN AT TOP, PLANK TO COME AWAY AT BASE. KW*34

PULLING ON ROPE HELPED TO SPLIT PLANK AWAY FROM TRUNK. WC* PERS.COMM. RON HAMILTON.

SLOW, BUT ENERGY-SAVING, METHOD OF SPLITTING PLANK: AFTER INITIAL WEDGING, CROSSPIECE WAS INSERTED AND LEFT. WIND AND WEATHER COMPLETED WORK OF SPLITTING OFF PLANK. WC*59

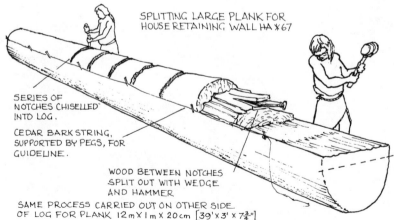

SPLITTING LARGE PLANK FOR HOUSE RETAINING WALL HA*67

SERIES OF NOTCHES CHISELLED INTO LOG.

CEDAR BARK STRING, SUPPORTED BY PEGS, FOR GUIDELINE.

WOOD BETWEEN NOTCHES SPLIT OUT WITH WEDGE AND HAMMER

SAME PROCESS CARRIED OUT ON OTHER SIDE OF LOG FOR PLANK 12m X 1m X 20cm [39' X 3' X 7¾"]

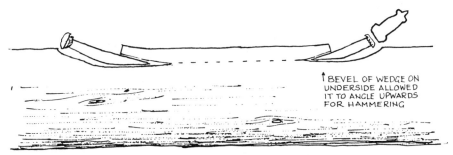

BEVEL OF WEDGE ON UNDERSIDE ALLOWED IT TO ANGLE UPWARDS FOR HAMMERING

TO SPLIT A SHORT PLANK FROM FALLEN LOG: CAVITIES CUT AT DISTANCE PLANK REQUIRED, ROW OF WEDGES DRIVEN IN AT EACH END. KW

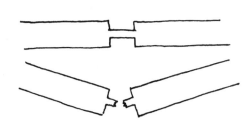

TO CUT A CEDAR PLANK: GROOVE CHISELLED ON EACH FACE, ACROSS THE WIDTH, THEN PLANK BENT UNTIL IT BROKE. WC *43

STRAIGHTENING WARPED PLANKS. KW *34

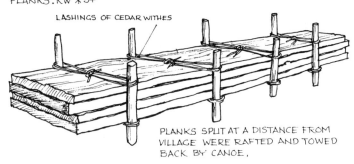

LASHINGS OF CEDAR WITHES

PLANKS SPLIT AT A DISTANCE FROM VILLAGE WERE RAFTED AND TOWED BACK BY CANOE.

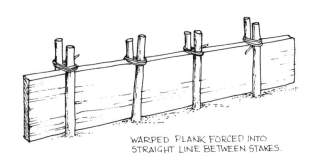

WARPED PLANK FORCED INTO STRAIGHT LINE BETWEEN STAKES.

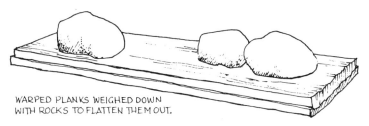

WARPED PLANKS WEIGHED DOWN WITH ROCKS TO FLATTEN THEM OUT.

across the horizontal opening. One man on each side then drove the stick along by means of a maul and wedge that was concave at one end so as to fit the stick's shape. This extended the split the full length of the log.

After removing and turning over the upper section of the log, the woodworker split a plank from it by repeating the process, inserting wedges at whatever thickness he required for the plank. This gave him a radially split plank, with the grain crossing the thickness of the board, suitable for the base and lid of a bentwood box. A plank taken farther away from the log's centre — tangentially split — was generally used for the sides of the box because it would bend more easily.

Ensign Walker admired the results of this technique and wrote: "The Trees are cut down and formed into Planks by means of Wedges. They are split into Boards of a great breadth and length. Considering the rudeness of the method, they are wonderfully straight and even."

Not all planks were wonderfully straight and even, but the woodworker knew how to straighten warped or twisted planks. In one method he laid the uneven plank on a flat surface and placed heavy rocks on it in strategic places; in another, he stood the plank on edge and forced it between pairs of stakes driven into the ground in a

The author splitting planks from a beached log of red cedar, using yew wood wedges and a stone maul. Photograph by Vickie Jensen, courtesy of the photographer.

The result of a few hours work. Photograph by Vickie Jensen, courtesy of the photographer.

straight line. In both methods he left the wood thus under pressure until it dried to its corrected shape.

The nineteenth-century missionary Myron Eells was impressed by the size of the planks he saw in the Puget Sound area: "One was two and a half feet wide, and forty feet long, and another three and a half wide and twenty long. Such boards were split by wedges and trimmed by hewing."

I wanted to experience splitting planks, so I took five yew wood wedges I had made and a stone hand maul (found in a friend's garden) down to the beach. From among the host of drift logs, I chose a red cedar 4.9 m (16′) long, with a 61 cm (2′) diameter and no visible knots. At the end of the log I drove four wedges all the way in, hitting each in succession. This opened up a cleavage plane but also left the wedges deeply embedded in the wood. However, pounding a fifth wedge in at the side opened the cleavage enough to release the other four.

From then on the splitting progressed by driving a wedge deeply into each side of the cleavage, and following this with another ahead of it. Each time, the forward wedge widened the crack, releasing the other from the grip of the wood. Each pounding was followed by several seconds of cracking sounds as the fibres of the wood let go and split apart a few more centimetres, releasing the cedar's pungent scent. After considerable work I had the top slab of the log split off. The next day I returned with a friend, and we split off two planks, using wedges for the first, and a combination of wedges and the spreading stick for the second. Our hand mauls had seemed inefficient for driving the spreading stick along the cleavage plane, and I could see that for a thick plank, a northern hafted maul would have been an advantage. I also observed the damage to these wooden wedges and understood why ones of elk antler would have worked well. Thoughts on such ancient tools were interrupted, and the twentieth century quickly brought back into focus, as a tall young man with a large chainsaw slung over his shoulder came up and offered his help.

Joining Wood   The ability to drill fine holes allowed for two techniques of joining wood. In one method, the carpenter drove yellow cedar pegs through drilled holes and cut off the surplus length flush with the wood before sanding it smooth. Although mainly used for joining the

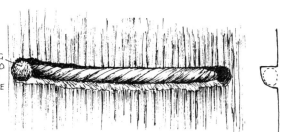

WOODEN PEG DRIVEN INTO HOLD AND TIGHTEN THE WITHE.

WIDE BOARDS OF PAINTED SCREEN ORIGINALLY HELD IN PLACE BY TYING WITH CEDAR WITHE TO BACK SUPPORTS. FACE OF TIE. 7·5cm [3"] TS 3

CROSS SECTION OF GROOVE FOR COUNTERSUNK WITHE.

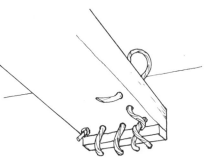

COUNTERSUNK GROOVES ON TWO PLANKS OF SCREEN SHOW WHERE PAIR OF CEDAR WITHE TIES HELD THEM TOGETHER. TWO WOODEN PEGS REMAIN IN GROOVES. TS 3

METHOD OF SECURING THWARTS TO HULL OF CANOE USING CEDAR WITHES LASHED THROUGH DRILL HOLES. KW 34

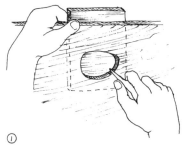

① DAMAGED OR ROTTEN SPOT ON PLANK OR CANOE HULL CAREFULLY TRIMMED. CEDAR BOARD HELD IN PLACE, AND LINE TRACED AROUND WITH POINTED BONE.

② PLUG CUT TO SHAPE AND FITTED WITH PRECISION, THEN PEGGED IN PLACE. WC 43

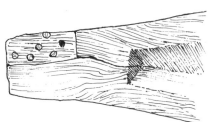

DAMAGED CORNER OF CANOE PROW HAS BEEN REPLACED AND PEGGED IN. HA 8

CRACK IN CANOE HULL CLOSED BY SEWING WITH CEDAR WITHES. KW ✳ 34

SHREDDED YELLOW CEDAR BARK DRIVEN INTO CRACK IN CANOE FOR CAULKING. CRACK THEN SEWN WITH WITHES, THE WHOLE COVERED WITH PITCH. KW ✳ 35

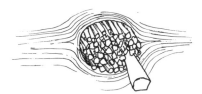

TEMPORARY REPAIR. KNOTHOLE IN CANOE FILLED WITH CEDAR TWIGS, AND COMPRESSED BY PEGS DRIVEN IN. KW ✳ 34

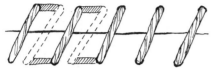

TWO TECHNIQUES FOR SEWING CRACKS
IN PLANK OR CANOE. KW 34

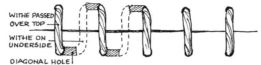

WITHE PASSED OVER TOP
WITHE ON UNDERSIDE
DIAGONAL HOLE

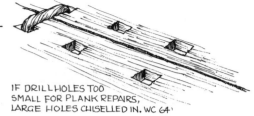

IF DRILL HOLES TOO
SMALL FOR PLANK REPAIRS,
LARGE HOLES CHISELLED IN. WC 64

FOUR METHODS OF TYING CEDAR WITHE TO CLOSE CRACK IN PLANK MK 64
AFTER MAUGER

DOUBLE LOOP,
HELD BY
FRICTION

SINGLE LOOP,
HELD BY
WHIPPING

DOUBLE LOOP,
HELD BY
PEGGING

SINGLE LOOP,
HELD BY
WHIPPING WITH
ANOTHER WITHE

TYING SEQUENCE

BEFORE SEWING, LARGE CRACKS
IN WOOD WERE CLOSED BY TYING
TOGETHER WITH CEDAR WITHE. SPLINT
DRIVEN UNDER TIE PULLED SIDES
CLOSER TOGETHER. KW 34

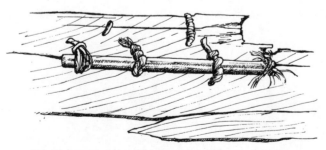

PLANK FRAGMENT FROM OZETTE SITE SHOWS TWO
CRACKS REPAIRED WITH CEDAR WITHE TIES. SPLINT
PUSHED BENEATH TIES FORCED SIDES OF CRACK TOGETHER
BY TIGHTENING TIES. WC 64

DETAIL OF MORTUARY POLE AT
NINSTINTS, QUEEN CHARLOTTE
ISLANDS. CARVED WING
ORIGINALLY HAD TWO PATCHES
TO REPLACE DAMAGED WOOD.
TOTAL LENGTH OF PATCHES
ABOUT 1m [36"] HA 73

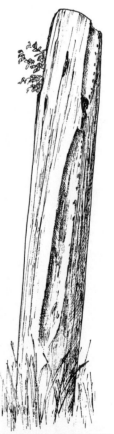

BACK OF MORTUARY POLE
ORIGINALLY HAD ROTTED
WOOD REPLACED WITH TWO
PATCHES. HOLES SHOW
WHERE PEGS ONCE HELD
PATCHES IN PLACE. POLE
3.6m [12'] HA [NINSTINTS] 73

ONE METHOD OF MAKING DRUM FRAME – STRIP OF YELLOW CEDAR STEAMED AND BENT AROUND ROUND ROCK. WC ✕ 34

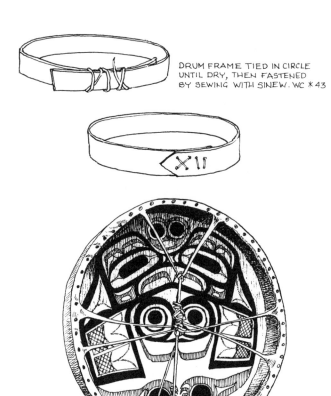

DRUM FRAME TIED IN CIRCLE UNTIL DRY, THEN FASTENED BY SEWING WITH SINEW. WC ✕ 43

TAMBOURINE DRUM – HIDE STRETCHED OVER FRAME OF YELLOW CEDAR WOOD. EAGLE DESIGN PAINTED ON INSIDE 40·6 cm [16"] HA 12

open corner of a bentwood container and attaching its base, pegging also served to patch damaged wood and to add appendages to an elaborate feast dish or pole.

The second method of joining wood, sewing, had a wider variety of uses. In this method, the woodworker passed a thin, flexible cedar withe in and out through a series of drilled holes and pulled it tightly to secure the join. With this technique he could join two pieces of wood at different angles or several planks to make a dance screen. He could also repair a crack in a canoe or bentwood box; a cooking box found at the Ozette archaeological site had the bottom burned out and a wooden patch sewn in place. In some cases, the woodworker tightened the cedar withe stitch by driving a wooden peg into the drillhole, up against the stitch. Usually the stitch itself was countersunk in a narrow groove to make it flush with the surface of the wood; this helped both to conceal it and protect it from abrasion.

Steaming and Bending   The nature of cedar allowed it to be steambent without difficulty. Other woods could also be bent through steaming, but cedar was the one most often used. The process of steambending, described later in the section on steambent wood, involved cutting kerfs at places where a plank was to be bent. This method was also suitable for shaping a child's wooden cradle and a multisided drum. The woodworker could make a circular tambourine drum by steaming a long thin strip of yellow cedar and bending it into a complete circle, sewing the two ends where they overlapped.

Finishing   Many cedar items, especially those that were carved or were to be painted, required a smooth surface. To smooth a plank, the woodworker rotated a flat, heavy block of sandstone on the surface, applying pressure to grind down the ridges of adze marks. The addition of a sprinkling of sand helped the process. Small areas of carving were smoothed with small sandstone abraders. To further smooth the wood, the carver rubbed it with dried dogfish skin, using it like modern sandpaper, with a new piece for coarse, through to a well-used piece for extra fine. Alternatively, he took fresh horsetail or scouring rush (*Equisetum* spp.), which contained natural silica, and used it in the same way.

*　　*　　*

The basic tools and technologies outlined here enabled men in the woodworking industry to create and to build anything that their culture required. Their knowledge and skills, particularly those of the specialists, enriched the daily and ceremonial lives of the coast peoples and elevated their standard of living to an impressive degree.

CANOES   Made of a single log that was hollowed and shaped with simple tools by skilled hands and a spirit helper, the dugout canoe of the Northwest Coast was central to the way of life of the marine-oriented peoples of the area. Nowhere else in the world was a dugout developed to such a degree of sophistication; no other people had a dugout that could match the speed, capacity and seaworthiness — or the elegant grace — of the sleek canoes of the Northwest Coast Indian.

The earliest Europeans to visit the coast — explorers and seamen who knew good boats — marvelled at the construction and capability of the fragile-looking canoes that flocked around their ships; early missionaries who had a chance to watch canoes being made by master craftsmen were impressed by their skills. Describing this process in his diary while at Hesquiat early in this century, the Rev. Charles Moser summed it up by saying: "All the work is done without instruments to go by or measure; yet most of these Indian canoes are so true and so well shaped and proportioned that not even an expert could detect the least flaw or imperfection."

If the superb lines and craftsmanship stirred the imagination of the white men, so did the quantity of canoes that plied the waterways of coast and river; many people commented on this in their journals. When Capt. George Vancouver was anchored near Yaculta, on Quadra Island, he recorded that 18 canoes came out to meet his ship, leaving 70 still on shore. At a village on the west coast of Vancouver Island, Capt. James Cook estimated that 500 people occupied the 80 canoes that swarmed around his vessel for trading, while Jewitt described a raiding party that consisted of 40 vessels carrying 10 to 20 warriors each. The factor at Fort Langley, on the Fraser River, recorded the daily passing of canoes going home from the fishing grounds after the salmon run, and entries such as "150 Cowichans families stopped at the wharf" and "200 canoes of Whooms stopped alongside" or "100 more canoes passed" are frequent. In the Queen Char-

Norman Tait's canoe Little Beaver resting on a bed of cedar boughs prior to its launching and naming ceremony. 73

lotte Islands, in 1791, Captain Barnet recorded that the staggering number of 600 Haida canoes surrounded his trading ship in Cloak Bay.

Without the canoe as a means of travel and transport, few villages could have prospered. The intricate contours of the coastline, the high and steep slope of mountains, rugged and densely tangled with undergrowth, made coastal travel on foot forbidding and nearly impossible. Where calm waters laced together myriad islands with channels, passages and straits, and where long fingers of sea pointed their way through steep, narrow valleys to link with river mouths, there the sea-going peoples established well-defined routes for their journeys. And journey they did, sometimes canoeing long distances to trade

River canoes with updated equipment, still used by fisherman at the Quileute village of La Push, Washington. 73

"Return of the Whale Hunters" is the caption of this 1911 postcard. Note the canoe is being beached stern first. Probably Makah. 75 Author's collection

or to raid other villages, as well as to visit villages for feasts, potlatches and betrothals. Seasonal travel included moving from winter to summer villages and back again. From early spring to late fall they went by canoe to hunt and harvest whatever food sources were in season: fish, shellfish, waterfowl, seal, sea otters, fruits, potherbs and more, returning with laden craft. The Kaigani Haida paddled 40 km (25 miles) or more to the outer islands of the Prince of Wales archipelago to gather gull eggs, and whaling could take Westcoast hunters considerable distances from shore. Gathering raw materials for manufacturing household goods and implements — roots, grasses, logs, bark and minerals, for example — often

necessitated lengthy voyages, and they also used their canoes to tow logs and planks back to their home villages.

The Haida, who dwelt on a group of islands well separated from the mainland, were, of necessity, an ocean-going people. They took trading fleets of their great canoes, some 18.3 m (60') long, and navigated them down the coast to Victoria, paddling a round trip of over 1600 km (1000 miles). Ensign Walker observed that the people from Yuquot "navigate a great way both North and South, and on such voyages have been often absent several months."

Esteemed for their superb craftsmanship, the northern canoes were a valuable trade item. Indeed, the canoe was the most important item of trade for the Haida, who towed newly made craft over to the mainland to trade for eulachon grease and other commodities not available in their homeland. The Tlingit, too, found a ready market for their canoes, which even in 1888 were reported to be their chief source of revenue. Among the Quinault Coast Salish, in Washington, a sealing canoe was worth ten to fifteen blankets, while an ocean-going canoe had the value of one slave.

The high value placed on canoes made them an important symbol of wealth. Playing for high stakes in a lengthy gambling game, a man might add his canoe to the already massive jackpot, heightening the players' excitement. At a large gathering, a chief often demonstrated his wealth and generosity by giving his canoe as overpayment for a deed, as a prize in a game or simply as a lavish gift to an honoured guest. A large canoe was sometimes paid to people chosen to be bitten during Hamatsa initiation ceremonies, in which the initiate was required to bite human flesh as part of a dramatic enactment of being possessed by the mythical Cannibal Spirit. On other occasions, when a person was abused in some way during the ceremony, payment of a canoe might also be made. To northerners, especially, the canoe became a symbol of such wealth that its deliberate destruction enhanced the owner's prestige. At a potlatch given to celebrate and pay helpers for the construction of a house, a Haida chief once had a large canoe brought in and smashed up for kindling. But to damage or destroy the canoe of a personal enemy was to bring the satisfaction of revenge.

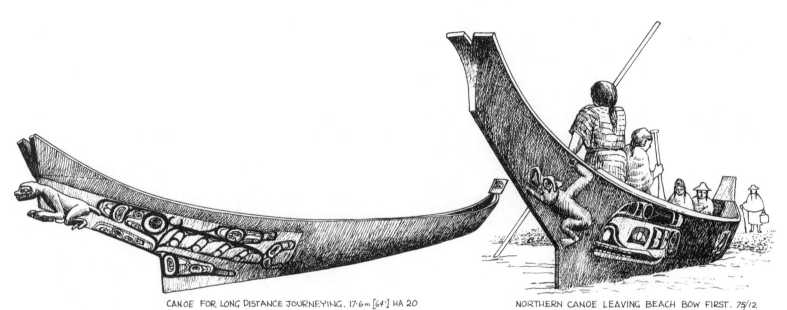

CANOE FOR LONG DISTANCE JOURNEYING. 17·6 m [64'] HA 20

NORTHERN CANOE LEAVING BEACH BOW FIRST. 75/12

When a northerner died, his canoe often rested beside the burial place; the body of a high-ranking southerner might be interred in his canoe, often with a smaller one serving as a cover. A hole was cut in the hull of the burial canoe to prevent it from being stolen. The Salish of Washington put the deceased, along with his most precious possessions, into a dugout and placed it on stilts or lashed it to a tree.

Styles and Sizes The variation in styles and sizes of canoes used by coastal Indian peoples was a reflection of both use and maritime conditions. Nineteenth-century canoes developed from earlier styles now known mainly from small models in museums, early paintings and drawings, and the observations of eighteenth-century explorers. With increased travel, trading and potlatching, canoe designs merged and hybridized until three basic styles came to represent most canoes travelling coastal waters, with the addition of river canoes.

Northerners, especially the Haida, who made long journeys and often crossed open stretches of water, required a large craft with a high prow and vertical cutwater for throwing off high waves. This northern style of canoe also had flaring sides and a rounded bottom for buoyancy and speed. To give extra height to the sides of

a Haida canoe, perhaps to prevent waves from breaking over the side, wash strakes in the form of long planks were occasionally added to the gunwales, from stem to stern. Captain Grey, who sailed the Queen Charlotte Islands in 1792, noted: "Their canoes are dug out of one log, with a narrow piece of board sewed around the upper edge." One impressive canoe measured 17.1 m (56') long, with a beam 2.4 m (8') wide and stood 2.2 m (7'3") at the bow. Even larger is the astounding 19.5 m (64') Haida canoe now housed at the American Museum of Natural History, New York. A beamy, high-sided freight canoe of good size had a carrying capacity of 4.5 t (5 tons). Cook reported that the size of the average canoe was 12.2 m (40'), with a 2.1 m (7') beam and 91 cm (3') deep.

General family or transportation canoes of the coast ranged from 5.5 m to 10.7 m (18' to 35') long, with a beam 0.9 m to 1.8 m (3' to 6'), carrying fifteen people and about 2.7 t (3 tons). Lighter, portable, hunting and fishing canoes averaged around 6.7 m (22') in length, while a two-man dugout, used for gathering purposes and inshore fishing, measured 6.1 m (20') or less.

Used mostly in relatively sheltered waters, the canoe of the Coast Salish had a more gently sloping bow than its northern counterpart, and a rounded bottom. The

50

NORTHERN
SEALING CANOE

RIVER CANOE BEING POLED UP STREAM

COAST SALISH CANOE FOR GENERAL TRAVEL

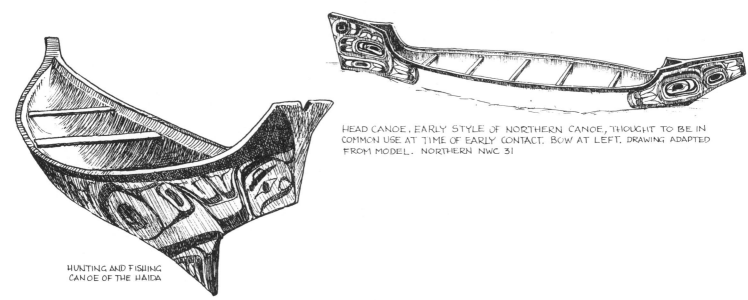

HEAD CANOE, EARLY STYLE OF NORTHERN CANOE, THOUGHT TO BE IN
COMMON USE AT TIME OF EARLY CONTACT. BOW AT LEFT. DRAWING ADAPTED
FROM MODEL. NORTHERN NWC 31

HUNTING AND FISHING
CANOE OF THE HAIDA

gunwales terminated in a characteristic concave flare, with the wood only one finger-width thick at the edge; the sides of the hull measured two finger-widths in thickness, with the bottom a little thicker. The Salish also fashioned a makeshift or emergency canoe from a large piece of cedar bark, as described later under unprocessed bark uses. These were used to cross a river or lake and had the advantage of being lightweight for portage.

The Westcoast people, together with the Makah and Quileute, spent much of their summer travelling on open water heaving from ocean swells or whipped by westerly winds. They also ventured out to sea in pursuit of the whale. Needing a stable and roomy craft, they fashioned their canoes with a relatively flat bottom and a vertical stern. The flat gunwales swept up at the bow, terminating in an elegantly carved bow piece, which resembled a stylized wolf head. A groove between the "ears" supported harpoon shafts. Whaling canoes measured between 9.1 m and 10.7 m (30' and 35'), with a beam of about 1.5 m (5'), and carried an eight-man crew and all the whaling gear. Although the body was made from one red cedar log, the entire bow and stern sections were added as separate pieces, being fitted with perfect precision to ensure that the canoe was watertight.

The Quileute also used slender, simply built canoes for going upriver to set their fishing nets, as did others living on rivers. These practical craft are still in use, and one may see, at the Quileute village of La Push, tied up at a wharf alongside modern power boats, two or three traditional dugouts with an outboard motor on the vertical stern.

Making a Canoe   Although some people made small dugouts for themselves, most canoes were made by a specialist working with one or more assistants. It took two men, working a few hours a day, about two months (less, if it was urgently needed) to complete a canoe of about 7.6 m (25'). To be successful in his work, the master canoemaker required a spirit helper, as did those undertaking any major task. He was also subject to a variety of restraints, such as not combing his hair lest the ends of the canoe split, and remaining continent so the wood would not rot.

The canoemaker carefully chose a cedar for its size and straight, even growth, as well as its proximity to the

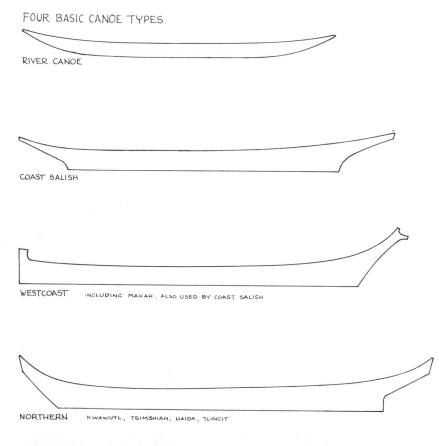

FOUR BASIC CANOE TYPES.

RIVER CANOE

COAST SALISH

WESTCOAST   INCLUDING MAKAH, ALSO USED BY COAST SALISH

NORTHERN   KWAKIUTL, TSIMSHIAN, HAIDA, TLINGIT

A Coast Salish canoemaker using an adze to rough out the hull of a small dugout; unfinished and finished canoes are in the background. Courtesy Provincial Archives of British Columbia, F-7440

52

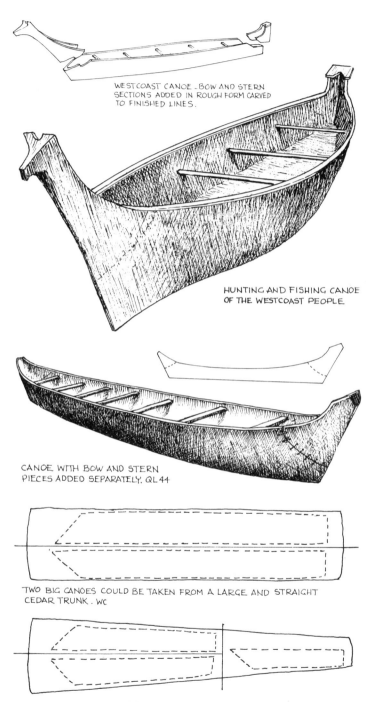

WESTCOAST CANOE . BOW AND STERN
SECTIONS ADDED IN ROUGH FORM CARVED
TO FINISHED LINES.

HUNTING AND FISHING CANOE
OF THE WESTCOAST PEOPLE.

CANOE WITH BOW AND STERN
PIECES ADDED SEPARATELY. QL 44

TWO BIG CANOES COULD BE TAKEN FROM A LARGE AND STRAIGHT
CEDAR TRUNK . WC

TWO MEDIUM AND ONE SMALL CANOE COULD BE TAKEN FROM A
TAPERED CEDAR TRUNK. WC

water. For a large canoe he required a tree with a butt of about 1.8 m (6') or more; if the butt was not too tapered, he could split two canoes from the same log, depending on the style of dugout. He might even get three smaller canoes from one log: two from the butt and one from the top. Since the wood could be lighter on the south side of the trunk, it was important to split it in the east-west direction of its growth to avoid a list to the finished craft.

After the tree was felled, the canoemaker cut off the top section with the branches and removed the bark and sapwood. Next he made a wide V cut towards each end, split out the wood between and adzed both ends to a point, keeping the butt end for the bow. He then turned the log over and completely shaped the outside, ensuring that it was symmetrical from end to end. The unfinished canoe was left in the forest for the winter to allow the wood to mature.

The following spring, the master craftsman and his assistant turned the unfinished craft over and roughly hollowed out the inside, using one of two techniques, depending on regional tradition. In one, he split out the wood with chisel and hammer, either in sections or all in one piece. In the other, controlled burning of the wood with hot rocks did most of the work for him. Coast Salish canoemaker Andy Dick said that his grandfather would sail 80.5 km (50 miles) up the coast of Vancouver Island to Qualicum Beach in order to obtain a particular kind of rock that was resistant to cracking when heated. He never used the rocks a second time but made another journey to collect fresh ones. The burning seared the wood, sealing and hardening it, he told his grandson.

When the hollowing out had considerably lightened the weight, the hull was skidded down to the water and towed back to the village for finishing. The master canoe-maker adzed out the final shape with extraordinary precision, eyeing it for perfect symmetry and for the graceful lift of the gunwales at bow and stern. Next, he carefully adzed out the interior, until the hull of the craft reached an even thickness — two finger-widths for the sides and three finger-widths for the bottom of a large canoe. Often an experienced man knew when the sides were the right thickness simply by feel. Many years ago I watched the elderly Michael Peters, of the Chehalis band in the Fraser Valley, doing this. The gnarled knuckles of his workworn hands flexed and straightened as his sensitive palms and finger tips responded to the feel of the canoe sides. I realized that his hands carried the kind of knowledge that could never be explained in words.

The canoemaker had another method of finding the right thickness by using drilled holes and measured wooden pegs to indicate when he reached the correct thickness.

Canoes of the Westcoast people, the Makah and Quileute, among others, had separate stern and bow sections fitted on. This technique made it possible to use a log with a rotted centre for a dugout; indeed, much of the hollowing out had already been done by the rot.

The final stage of shaping most canoes involved steaming in order to spread the sides; this gave the craft a wider beam for better stability and greater carrying capacity. When Norman Tait, a Nishga of the Coast Tsimshian group, finished carving a 5.8 m (19') canoe, I watched the steaming process with deep interest. Reading about and hearing lecturers talk of this was academic, but seeing the rocks become red hot in the fire pit and watching them being dropped into the canoe partly filled with water was to understand. Tait, his apprentice carvers and other helpers used paddles to slop the water up the sides of the fresh yellow-gold wood of the hull. Billowing clouds of steam engulfed the scene, filling the air with the pungent scent of wet cedar. Gradually, the sides of the canoe began to soften and spread outward. Tait kept measuring the spread, slopping water and calling for more hot rocks, until he was satisfied the gunwales had spread wide enough. Then he drove pairs of posts into the ground up against each side of the hull to prevent the upper edges from spreading any farther. Finally, he put in the thwarts. The whole process took most of the day. In another method of steam spreading, sticks were eased into the steamed hull to gently force the sides outward.

Some small canoes were carved the full width and not steamed, but all were singed on the outside with burning cedar sticks and pitch to remove any slivers and to harden the wood. Finally, the canoemaker rubbed the hull smooth with either dogfish skin or hemlock boughs, depending on local custom.

David Frank Sr., a canoemaker in Ahousat, on the west coast of Vancouver Island, made his first canoe when he was twelve years old; he learned from his uncle. His alert

CARVING A CANOE KW ✗ 34

① CANOEMAKER REMOVED BARK FROM CEDAR LOG AND CHISELLED OUT SECTION FROM EACH END.

② HE SPLIT OUT WOOD FROM BETWEEN CUTS, USING WEDGES AND HAND MAUL.

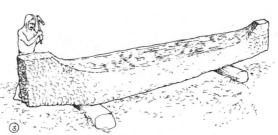

③ USING LARGE-BLADED ADZE, CANOE MAKER ROUGHLY SHAPED CRAFT, NARROWING BOTH ENDS.

④ WITH LEVERS AND MANPOWER, CANOE WAS TURNED OVER, SAPWOOD ADZED OFF, THEN HULL, BOW AND STERN ADZED TO SHAPE.

⑤ TO ROUGHLY HOLLOW CENTRE, CANOEMAKER CHISELLED DEEP HOLES, SPLIT OUT WOOD BETWEEN WITH WEDGES AND MAUL.

⑥ USING SMALLER BLADED ADZE HE CONTOURED INSIDE OF CANOE, THINNING HULL SIDES.

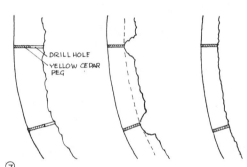

DRILL HOLE
YELLOW CEDAR PEG

⑦ TO ENSURE EVEN THICKNESS OF CANOE HULL, CANOEMAKER:

a] DRILLED HOLES THROUGH ROUGHLY HOLLOWED HULL, AND INSERTED MEASURED PEGS OF YELLOW CEDAR.

b] HE CARVED AWAY INNER SIDE OF HULL AT HOLES, UNTIL HE REACHED PEGS, THEN CUT VERTICAL GROOVES BETWEEN THEM.

c] FINALLY HE SPLIT OUT WOOD BETWEEN GROOVES, LEAVING SLENDER SIDED HULL OF EVEN THICKNESS.

⑧ WHEN FINAL SHAPING COMPLETED, MEN PARTIALLY FILLED CANOE WITH FRESH WATER, ADDED HOT ROCKS FROM FIRE, THEN SPLASHED BOILING WATER OVER HULL INTERIOR.

⑨ MAN SCORCHED BOTTOM OF CANOE WITH LIGHTED TORCH, ADDING HEAT AND HARDENING WOOD. CEDAR SIDES EVENTUALLY SOFTENED, ENABLING CANOEMAKER TO SPREAD SIDES OF HULL BY FORCING SPLIT CEDAR STICKS BETWEEN GUNWALES.

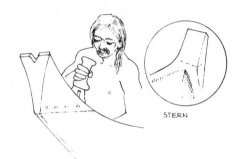

STERN

⑩ ADDITION OF BOW AND STERN PIECES, SECURED BY PEGGING, ADDED HEIGHT AND GAVE GRACEFUL LINES TO DUGOUT.

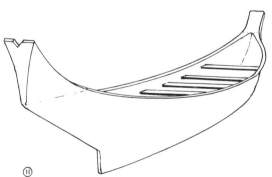

⑪ FINISHED CANOE – SANDED SMOOTH WITH DOGFISH SKIN, RUBBED WELL WITH DOGFISH OIL FOR PRE-SERVATION. FINAL STEP WAS DESIGN PAINTED ON EXTERIOR. LARGE CANOE MIGHT ALSO HAVE CARVED FIGURE EACH SIDE OF BOW.

"Indians of British Columbia pitching a 'dugout' canoe" is the caption of this illustration from the New York magazine Harper's Weekly, 1865.
75 Author's collection

mind and good memory belied his eighty-four years of age as he talked to me about canoes he had made — forty-seven of them: fishing, sealing, packing and whaling, the largest 10.4 m (34') long. He gestured with large, strong hands as he described the final process of canoe-making — the oiling: "I take that dogfish oil, make it real hot. And I wrap a rag on a stick; dip it in, rub it all over, around the canoe. That oil, it goes into the wood, stops it splitting. Then I turn it over, and I heat the oil again. Do the same thing on the inside. That canoe last maybe thirty years — if you treat it good." Records seem to indicate that the average lifespan for a much used canoe would have been closer to ten years.

The skill of the canoemaker, or his faults, show up in the initial testing, and David Frank also described this: "I test the canoe in a place where the water is quiet, no wind, no current. I put a big rock in the stern and I push it way out. If it keeps going straight, you know you got a good canoe. Some fellows, they make a canoe in too much of a hurry . . . then it will twist, not go straight." I witnessed the naming ceremony and launching of Norman Tait's canoe Little Beaver on a bright golden day one fall. Gentle waves lapped at the beach as he pushed the craft out on the end of a rope. The traditional lines of the bow, painted with a red and black design, curved gracefully upwards, matching the sweep of the mountains beyond. Looking like a floating autumn leaf, the fragile wood sculpture made a heartwarming contrast to the

56

Men hollowing out a canoe with adzes, on the beach in front of Metlakatla in northern British Columbia, no date. Courtesy National Museums of Canada, 72-18064

enormous grey steel freighter in the distance. Little Beaver was a good canoe.

Many early canoes bore elaborate ornamentation, at the bow only or on both bow and stern with a black section between or along the full length of the hull. Some had a carved and painted totemic figure attached to the bow with cedar withes or cord; this figure was removed when using the canoe for freighting. Some canoes had their interior painted in red ochre or white, or occasionally a complex traditional design in the standard red and black. Westcoast whaling canoes almost always had two parallel rows of opercula just below the gunwales, fore and aft, and the Chinook often decorated their canoes handsomely with wolf and sea otter teeth.

Paddles and Seamanship Paddles bore elegant designs created to fit the blade's tapering shape. The style of paddle that was used varied according to tribe, but those used for steering generally had a broad blade. Craftsmen usually made the paddles out of yew wood, which was strong and durable, but they also often made them out of yellow cedar.

A man who spent considerable time paddling canoes developed powerful arms and shoulders, and often calloused knees from paddling small canoes in the kneeling position. In medium- or large-sized canoes, however, paddlers sat on the thwarts. For general travel, the owner of the canoe or the most experienced person took the position of steersman. Among the Tlingit, this was considered an honour that usually fell to an older person of rank, often a woman. Women also assisted the men with paddling and excelled at the task. One explorer declared: "In the management of these canoes, the women are equally as expert as the men, for in the smaller boats, which contain four oarsmen, the helm is generally given to a female."

In family travel, children also helped to paddle — a perfect example of learning by doing. With all the members of a family or household in one canoe, the seating arrangement reflected the living arrangement in their house, and they were seated according to rank.

Paddle songs kept the rhythm of a steady stroke and helped to pass time on a long or tedious journey, such as towing a dead whale back to the village. On various occasions, the paddlers struck the butt end of their paddles in unison against the side of the canoe for a drumming effect, beating time as they sang.

In the spring of 1847, Paul Kane, painter of many native Indian scenes, made a storm-tossed crossing of Juan de Fuca Strait in a native canoe. His words paint a vivid image of the scene and pay tribute to the skill of the crew: "The Indians on board now commenced with their wild chants, which increased to a perfect yell whenever a wave larger than the rest approached. . . . It was altogether a scene of the most wild and intense excitement: The mountainous waves roaming round our little canoe as if to engulf us every moment, the wind howling over our heads, and the yelling of the Indians made it actually terrific. I was surprised at the dexterity with which they managed the canoe, all putting out their paddles on the windward side whenever a wave broke, thus breaking its force and guiding the spray over our heads to the other side of the boat."

In open water, a heavy, quartering sea pounding the hull presented the most danger to a canoe as it could crack the hull or even split the vessel asunder. To maintain buoyancy of a whaling canoe that was shipping water in heavy seas, the crew tied inflated sealskin floats along the sides and bailed as much as possible. Landing at a beach, they brought the canoe in stern first, allowing the incoming waves to be deflected by the bow. The paddlers waited for a large wave to lift the canoe high onto the beach or up the canoe runway; with the vessel facing

CANOE PADDLES

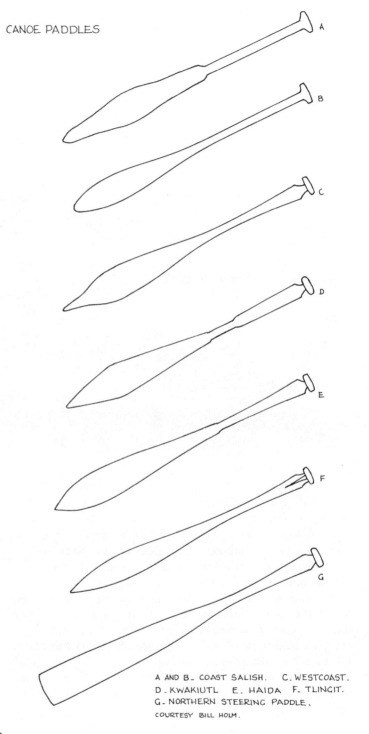

A AND B - COAST SALISH.   C. WESTCOAST.
D - KWAKIUTL   E. HAIDA   F. TLINGIT.
G - NORTHERN STEERING PADDLE,
COURTESY BILL HOLM.

LARGE NORTHERN CANOES RIGGED WITH MASTS AND CLOTH SAILS. KW 75/2

out to sea, they could later make a quick launching without waves breaking over the stern. If they needed to anchor offshore, they dropped over the side a large stone that had a long rope secured to it through a perforation. Several stones served as ballast for a single paddler in a small canoe without freight.

It is generally believed that the Northwest Coast Indians did not use sails on their craft until European sailing ships introduced the principle. Some canoe owners then stepped a mast, sometimes two or three, and rigged sails; at first they used coarse matting or thin boards joined together and later cotton sheeting. Not having a keel or rudder, the craft could not quarter or sail into the wind, but a stiff following breeze or sailing on a beam reach propelled canoe, passengers and possessions with welcome speed as the loaded vessel headed home on a long voyage.

The native mariners of the coast felt completely at home on the water and became as one with their canoes. Veteran canoemaker Andy Dick said: "A canoe is like a person, you talk to it by name, you tell it where you want to go." All canoes, of course, had names. These could be clan crest names or some reflection of the craft's character, such as Dancing Canoe, Steelhead Canoe, Crooked Canoe, Red Cod Canoe or Lazy Canoe, to mention a few.

Maintenance　　Care and maintenance of canoes were of utmost importance, since not only the life of the crew depended on them but the very life of the family or household. A chief or wealthy person would retain a top canoemaker to keep his craft in good repair. Damaged or rotten sections of a canoe could often be cut out and replaced with new wood that was sewn on by means of tough cedar withes or spruce root. Cracks or splits in a canoe could be sewn closed, then coated with fresh pitch gum of spruce or fir to make them waterproof. Regular polishing of the hull minimized friction and was important for speed. When a canoe was beached in hot weather, old matting, boards or branches covered the craft to prevent the wood from cracking; a canoe that was not going to be in use for a while was hauled up on the beach and turned upside-down, preferably in the shade.

Because whaling was a cult rather than merely the hunting of a resource, the whaling canoe was treated with a special reverence. Always kept in immaculate condition, the craft was used for no other purpose, and no

The framework of a large house with fluted beams in the Kwakiutl village of Mimkwumlis, 1915. Courtesy Milwaukee Public Museum, 2492

woman was ever allowed to enter one lest she bring misfortune to the canoe and its crew. Often a whaler stored his craft indoors when not using it or at the end of the season turned it upside down and braced it to prevent the hull from spreading.

*　*　*

The ancient tradition of canoeing has never died out. Contemporary Indians may drive late-model cars and run diesel-powered fishboats, but in many Coast Salish areas the intertribal canoe races draw together contestants from many villages, and the competition is keen. The canoes are now elongated racing shells — the largest is 15.2 m

(50′) and carries an eleven-man crew — but are still carved from a single log and are named, polished and cared for. The sound of the paddlers' chant in unison with the flash of their paddles, as the fragile craft speeds across the water, hints at an ancient heritage when the canoe was an essential part of the culture.

HOUSES AND OTHER STRUCTURES The greatest achievement of early Northwest Coast peoples must surely be their building technique. Newcomers to their land were always impressed by the massive size and construction of the cedar dwellings they came upon. Their journals and diaries made frequent mention of the structures, giving measurements and descriptions that often cap-

This keyhole corner post of a Haida house still supports one end of a barge board. Note the adzing on the post. Tanu, Queen Charlotte Islands. 73

tured the sense of wonder experienced by the writers. A visit to a house of the Westcoast people staggered the imagination of Capt. John Meares, who sailed the coast in 1788, and his journal entry well expressed his feelings: "The trees that supported the roof were of a size which would render the mast of a first-rate man of war diminutive, on a comparison with them; indeed our curiosity as well as our astonishment was on its utmost stretch, when we considered the strength that must be necessary to raise these enormous beams to their present elevation; and how such strength could be found by a people wholly unacquainted with mechanical powers."

Along the entire Pacific Northwest Coast, villages of sturdily built cedar houses hugged the water's edge wherever there was a beach, fresh water and an economic reason to be there. On the banks of major rivers that flowed to the sea, on islands, in bays and coves, at the heads of inlets, on peninsulas, along channels, narrows and even atop defensive sites, the peoples of the coast built their houses and villages and claimed ownership to specific resources within range of their area.

All the houses of these marine-oriented peoples faced the water. Generally built close to each other, the houses were strung out in a single row; occasionally, there was a second row if the population was large and the terrain did not allow for linear expansion. Most peoples had both a summer and a winter village, with some even having a third village for the salmon and sealing seasons. Families moved out in the spring to places where resources were readily available in order to collect basketry materials, dig roots, gather and dry berries and seaweeds, trap salmon, set hooks for halibut, harpoon seals and sea otter, and hunt bear and mountain goats; some people even ventured out to sea to hunt the whale. Before fair weather gave way to the cold and storms of winter, before wind-whipped seas made canoe travel dangerous, families returned to their winter villages, laden with provisions for the long, dark months ahead. They returned to the security of sheltered places, where their villages were protected from the full force of ocean storms by deep river valleys, offshore islands or steep mountains.

House-building was the work of a specialist. He chose the cedars to be used and directed the felling (often done by slaves) and the work of hauling the logs out of the forest to the building site. He supervised a variety of skilled craftsmen, whom he assigned to make the posts, beams, roof and wall planks and do other work as required, and with another specialist co-ordinated the task of raising the posts and beams. The owner paid each person for his work, and when trade blankets became a form of currency, the price was usually a set number of blankets. Prices ranged from one to four blankets for each man digging post holes, four blankets for each man working on the roof beams, and eight blankets for each man making roof planks. Occasionally the house front was painted, but that was an additional and great expense. Only a wealthy family could afford to build a house, and the size depended on the ability to not only reimburse all the workers but to provide for the ceremony and feasting that was required at its completion. Often a Haida family had a house built over a period of several years, paying and giving a potlatch for each stage as it was completed.

In all Northwest Coast villages, the chief had the largest house since he did much of the entertaining and feast giving. Public gatherings and ceremonies also took place in his house because it could accommodate a large crowd. The Rev. Charles Moser described an Ahousat chief's house in the late nineteenth century: "The house of the chief was over one hundred feet in length by sixty in

HAULING HOUSE POST UP FROM BEACH WC 43

SCAFFOLDING SUPPORTED PLANK RAMP.
ROPES, ATTACHED TO STAKES BESIDE AND
BENEATH RAMP, PASSED BETWEEN PLANKS, UP
OVER BEAM TO TOP OF INCLINE.
PEOPLE PULLED ON ROPES, HAULING BEAM TO
TOP. ROCKS PLACED BEHIND BEAM ACTED AS
BACKSTOP — TWO TO THREE HUNDRED MEN
AND WOMEN TOOK PART.

RAISING A HOUSE POST. WC 43

MEN PUSHED UP ON FIVE HARDWOOD POLES
WHILE OTHERS PULLED ON ROPE.
SINGLE STOUT POLE HELD BEAM'S WEIGHT
WHEN MEN TOOK FRESH GRIP, ADJUSTED
SMALL POLES — TOTAL OF EIGHTY' MEN
INVOLVED.

RAISING A HOUSE BEAM. KW 40

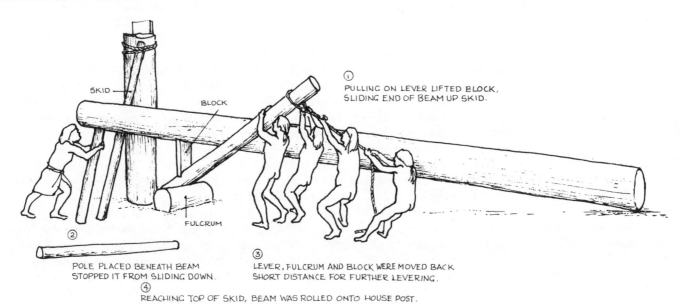

SKID

BLOCK

FULCRUM

① PULLING ON LEVER LIFTED BLOCK,
SLIDING END OF BEAM UP SKID.

② POLE PLACED BENEATH BEAM
STOPPED IT FROM SLIDING DOWN.

③ LEVER, FULCRUM AND BLOCK WERE MOVED BACK
SHORT DISTANCE FOR FURTHER LEVERING.

④ REACHING TOP OF SKID, BEAM WAS ROLLED ONTO HOUSE POST.
PLANK LASHED TO POST PREVENTED IT FROM ROLLING TOO FAR.

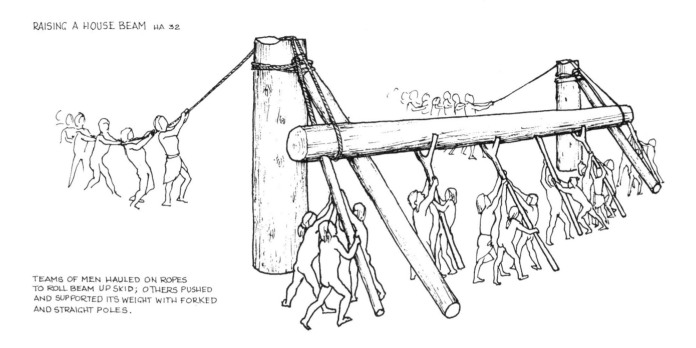

TEAMS OF MEN HAULED ON ROPES
TO ROLL BEAM UP SKID; OTHERS PUSHED
AND SUPPORTED ITS WEIGHT WITH FORKED
AND STRAIGHT POLES.

The Coast Salish village of Comox on Vancouver Island, with shed roof houses and a Wakashan house; the latter may have belonged to a wealthy person. Note the great width of the wall planks, though vertical use of them on this type of house was not typical. Courtesy Provincial Archives of British Columbia, F-8547

width. The corner posts were immense pieces of cedar twenty feet high; they were met at top by long sticks three feet through. One monster beam was laid across the centre and served as a crosspiece to support the roof planks . . . cedar roof planks are chiselled out to leave a groove for the rain.''

Large extended families lived together under the same roof, and to them the house was not only a home but a symbol. It was the container of their lineage and held their identity as a family and as a people in warm security. Both inside and out, the house carried crest figures in proud recognition of those who lived within. The house was also the spiritual centre of family life and social organization.

All houses had a framework of posts and beams, but styles fell into two main categories. Along the northern half of the Northwest Coast, the house walls were an integral part of the building, with the wall planks set vertically into sills. On the southern half of the coast, the walls formed a separate shell around the framework, with the planks placed horizontally. To this latter style belonged two house types, the shed roof and the Wakashan.

SHED ROOF HOUSE _ COAST SALISH. 64

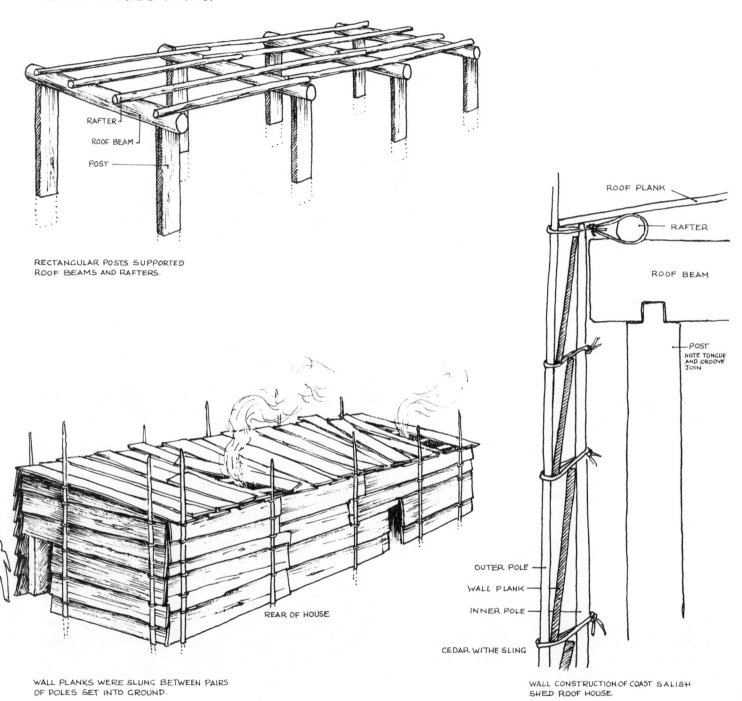

RAFTER

ROOF BEAM

POST

RECTANGULAR POSTS SUPPORTED
ROOF BEAMS AND RAFTERS.

ROOF PLANK

RAFTER

ROOF BEAM

POST
NOTE TONGUE
AND GROOVE
JOIN

OUTER POLE

WALL PLANK

INNER POLE

CEDAR WITHE SLING

REAR OF HOUSE

WALL PLANKS WERE SLUNG BETWEEN PAIRS
OF POLES SET INTO GROUND.

WALL CONSTRUCTION OF COAST SALISH
SHED ROOF HOUSE

A roof of split cedar planks on a house in the Bella Coola Valley, no date. Courtesy National Museums of Canada, 56938

In the midst of a jungle of vegetation, the posts and beams of a Wakashan house still stand in the long-abandoned village of Keeshan on the west coast of Vancouver Island. 73

The Shed Roof House   The shed roof house, built in southern areas of the coast throughout the Coast Salish region, was about 11.6 m (38') wide and about 24.4 m (80') long, with a roof height averaging 3 m (10'). The framework consisted of rectangular posts 61 cm to 91 cm (2' to 3') wide, and from 12.7 cm to 20.3 cm (5" to 8") thick. Placed in two rows, the posts on the seaward side stood a little taller than those on the forest side, giving the roof a slight pitch or shed. Inside, the flat-faced posts often had carved figures that stood out in high relief, and corner posts sometimes depicted three-dimensional figures. Large roof beams connected each pair of posts; rounded rafter poles were placed over these to support the roof planks, which overlapped each other. The wall planks ran horizontally, and a doorway faced the beach or opened at the side, with another at the rear.

Shed roof houses were sometimes built onto another, end to end, creating a single building of extraordinary length. This practice gave rise to the term "longhouse," a name often applied, incorrectly, to the big plank houses of northern areas. In 1808, the explorer Simon Fraser described a longhouse in a village near Langley (near Vancouver, B.C.), once a trading post on the Fraser River: "The houses are built of cedar planks . . . the whole range, which is six hundred and fifty feet long by sixty broad, is under one roof; the front is eighteen feet high and the covering is slanting: all the appartements, which are separated by partitions, are square, except the chief's, which is ninety feet long. In this room the posts or pillars are nearly three feet in diameter at the base and diminish gradually to the top. In one of these posts is an oval opening answering the purpose of a door through which one man may crawl in or out. Above, on the outside, are carved a human figure as large as life, with other figures in imitation of beasts and birds."

The interior of the shed roof house had a wooden platform along the walls and housed many families. Each family had its own hearth and generally occupied the entire space between two pairs of upright posts, about 4.6 m (15'), by the width of the house.

The Wakashan House   This style of house, also built in southern areas, had a sturdy framework of nine upright posts, in three rows of three, which supported the eave beams on the outside rows and the ridge beam on the centre row. Because the ridge beam was of greater diameter than the two eave beams, the extra height at the centre created a gently sloping gable roof.

In general, Wakashan houses measured from 11 m (36') to 12.2 m (40') in width, with a length ranging from 12.2 m

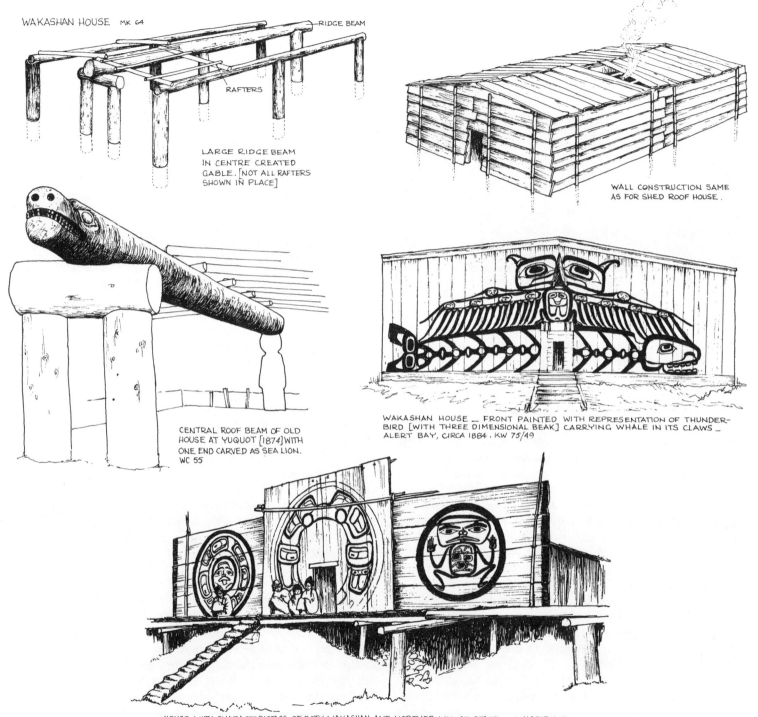

WAKASHAN HOUSE   MK 64

RIDGE BEAM

RAFTERS

LARGE RIDGE BEAM
IN CENTRE CREATED
GABLE. [NOT ALL RAFTERS
SHOWN IN PLACE]

WALL CONSTRUCTION SAME
AS FOR SHED ROOF HOUSE.

CENTRAL ROOF BEAM OF OLD
HOUSE AT YUQUOT [1874] WITH
ONE END CARVED AS SEA LION.
WC 55

WAKASHAN HOUSE — FRONT PAINTED WITH REPRESENTATION OF THUNDER-
BIRD [WITH THREE DIMENSIONAL BEAK] CARRYING WHALE IN ITS CLAWS —
ALERT BAY, CIRCA 1884. KW 75/49

HOUSE WITH CHARACTERISTICS OF BOTH WAKASHAN AND NORTHERN HOUSE STYLE — i.e. HORIZONTAL,
SUSPENDED WALL PLANKS, WITH VERTICAL PLANKING AND HOUSE FRONT PAINTING. BC 75/2

The interior of an abandoned Kwakiutl house, about 1912 to 1915. All the rafters and beams show decorative fluting done with an adze: horizontally, verticaly and diagonally. Compare the size of these pieces and the platform planks with that of the seated man. Mimkwumlis, on Village Island. Courtesy Vancouver City Archives, N.53 P.105

(40') to 45.7 m (150'). The average roof height was 3 m (10'), but a chief's house was larger and taller; that of Chief Maquinna, at Yuquot, had a lofty height of 4.3 m (14'). The ridge beam measured from 0.6 m (2') to a hefty 1.2 m (4') in diameter and was occasionally fluted with an adze or painted with rings of black and red (according to Jewitt); in a notable chief's house, the ends of the ridge beam protruded beyond the walls and were carved with an animal head, such as a seal. Inside, the house posts of a chief's house bore designs carved with family crest figures; Captain Cook's artist, John Webber, depicted a pair of these posts in his well known and often published illustration, "The Inside of a House in Nootka Sound."

The walls of the house were structurally separate from the framework. Wide cedar planks hung horizontally between pairs of tall vertical poles placed at intervals along the outside of the house frame. The planks rested on cedar withes that lashed together the pairs of poles, which in turn were tied to the beams. The bottom wall plank was positioned first; subsequent planks overlapped to prevent rain from entering the house. Wall planks

ranged to an astounding width of 1.5 m (5'), with a length of about 1.8 m (6').

Roof planks, about 5.5 m (18') long and of varying widths, sloped down from the ridge beam to the eave beams on each side and often had a chiselled groove at each edge to allow them to fit snugly together to keep out the rain. The roof planks were not permanantly fixed and could be shifted aside to let light come in or smoke go out. Jewitt wrote: "they are wholly with out a chimney, nor is there any opening left in the roof, but whenever a fire is made, the plank immediately over it is thrust aside, by means of a pole, to give vent to the smoke." Loose, overlapping roof planks were convenient until a windstorm blew up, and Jewitt's first-hand experience of this situation provides a graphic description of the necessary action that had to be taken: "in a high storm I have often known all the men obliged to turn out and go upon the roof to prevent them from being blown off, carrying large stones and pieces of rock with them to secure the boards, always stripping themselves naked on these occasions, whatever may be the severity of the weather, to prevent their garments from being wet and muddied, as these storms are almost always accompanied by heavy rains." Another method of holding down the roof planks was to place long poles, weighed down with rocks, across them.

The door of the house was generally at the end, though occasionally it might be on the side. The interior of the house had a platform set on rows of short stakes that ran along the walls; the space underneath was used for storage. Sometimes the opening beneath a platform was covered by a plank. The platform held quantities of boxes and chests that contained various dried foods, fishing gear, raw materials, tools and other household goods, as well as ceremonial and valued possessions. From the beams hung fish racks with segments of salmon or other fish draped over them to dry and smoke; long harpoons and spears were stored over the beams.

The head of the house and his family occupied the rear right corner of the house, and the family next in importance had the rear left; others had specified places along each side, according to their rank. Piled-up boxes, baskets and various equipment divided one family area from the next, though some large houses had plank partitions to create private cubicles for sleeping. By day, the occupants

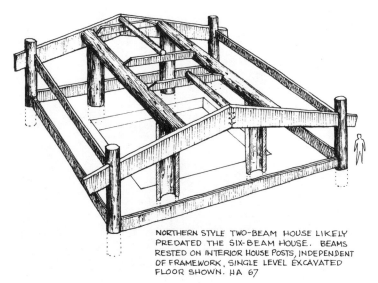

NORTHERN STYLE TWO-BEAM HOUSE LIKELY PREDATED THE SIX-BEAM HOUSE. BEAMS RESTED ON INTERIOR HOUSE POSTS, INDEPENDENT OF FRAMEWORK. SINGLE LEVEL EXCAVATED FLOOR SHOWN. HA 67

A small part of Tanu, the largest and most flourishing Haida village on the Queen Charlotte Islands in the nineteenth century. Six-beam houses rim the beach; in the centre is a house under construction. Courtesy National Museums of Canada, 242

made use of the low platforms fronting the sleeping areas, and each family had its own hearth.

When families moved from summer village to winter village or vice versa, they took down most of the wall and roof planks, loaded them across two canoes lashed together, and set them up again around the bare frameworks at the other village. John Jewitt wrote about this in his narrative: "Immediately on our arrival, we all went to work very diligently in covering the houses with the planks we had brought, the frames being ready erected, these people never pretending to remove the timber. In a very short time the work was completed, and we were established in our new residence."

Variations of the Wakashan House Farther north along the coast, among the Bella Coola and the Kwakiutl (except for the northernmost Kwakiutl, the Haisla), villages often had both shed roof houses and regional variations of the Wakashan house; the latter was considered more prestigious. The basic framework of the Wakashan

NORTHERN STYLE TWO-BEAM HOUSE WITH ENTRANCE THROUGH HOUSE PORTAL POLE. HA 67

68

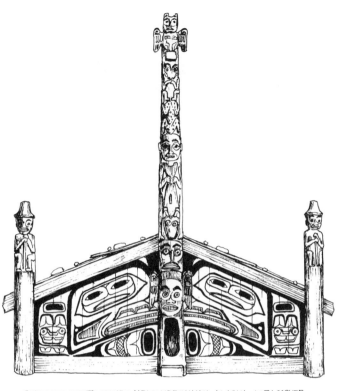

RECONSTRUCTED HOUSE NEAR KETCHIKAN, ALASKA, WITH CARVED
CORNER POSTS [RARE], RAVEN PAINTED ON HOUSE FRONT. TL 73

CHIEF'S HOUSE PAINTED WITH BEAR CREST, WITH ROOF APPENDAGES
FOR EARS — GASH VILLAGE, CAPE FOX. TL 75/12

TSIMSHIAN HOUSE

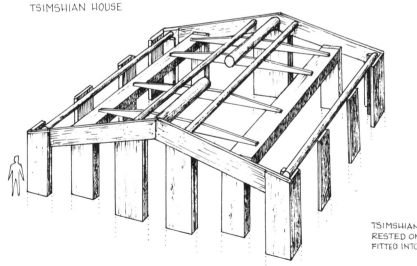

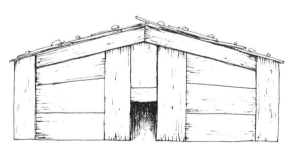

TSIMSHIAN HOUSE OF THE NISHGA PEOPLE. SQUARED TIMBERS
RESTED ON SEPARATE HOUSE POSTS. HORIZONTAL PLANKS
FITTED INTO GROOVED WALL POSTS. TS 41

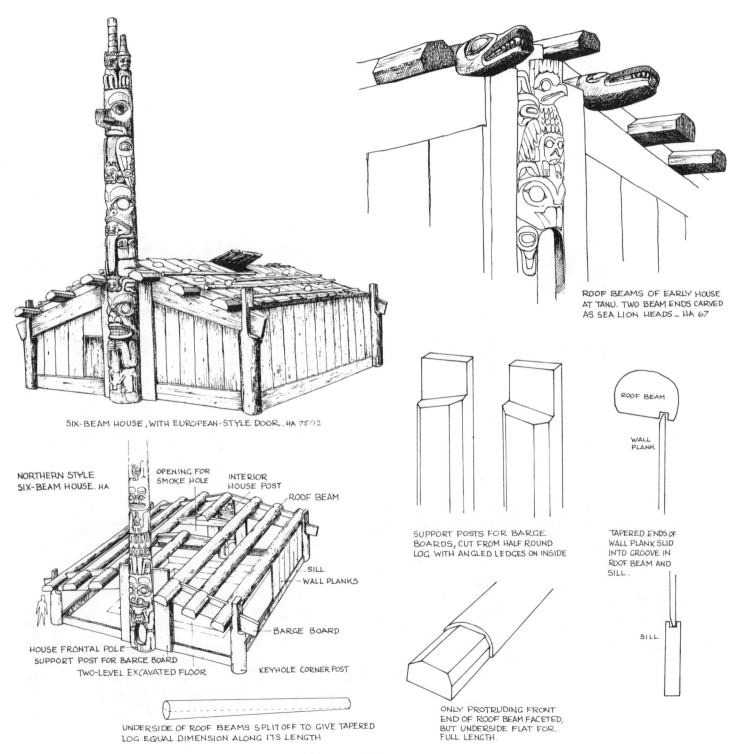

SIX-BEAM HOUSE, WITH EUROPEAN-STYLE DOOR. HA 75/12

ROOF BEAMS OF EARLY HOUSE AT TANU. TWO BEAM ENDS CARVED AS SEA LION HEADS – HA 67

NORTHERN STYLE SIX-BEAM HOUSE. HA

OPENING FOR SMOKE HOLE

INTERIOR HOUSE POST

ROOF BEAM

SILL

WALL PLANKS

BARGE BOARD

HOUSE FRONTAL POLE
SUPPORT POST FOR BARGE BOARD
TWO-LEVEL EXCAVATED FLOOR

KEYHOLE CORNER POST

UNDERSIDE OF ROOF BEAMS SPLIT OFF TO GIVE TAPERED LOG EQUAL DIMENSION ALONG ITS LENGTH

SUPPORT POSTS FOR BARGE BOARDS, CUT FROM HALF ROUND LOG WITH ANGLED LEDGES ON INSIDE

ONLY PROTRUDING FRONT END OF ROOF BEAM FACETED, BUT UNDERSIDE FLAT FOR FULL LENGTH.

ROOF BEAM

WALL PLANK

TAPERED ENDS OF WALL PLANK SLID INTO GROOVE IN ROOF BEAM AND SILL.

SILL

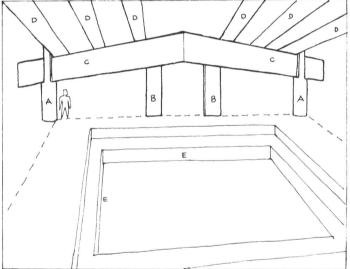

DRAWING RECONSTRUCTS REMAINS OF HOUSE IN PHOTO — HOUSE ORIGINALLY MEASURED 13·2 m X 13·5 m [43'6" X 44'6"] NINSTINTS. HA 73

family crest figures; even the beams were occasionally carved to represent some animal. The rear house posts sometimes depicted two great mythical thunderbirds, their colourful wings spread wide in a regal and powerful manner.

Wooden platforms ran around the inside walls of the house. The chief and his family occupied quarters in the rear, and other related families lived in places to the left and right according to their rank.

The people of some divisions of the Kwakiutl and the Bella Coola, who lived along narrow inlets with barely any level ground for housing, built their homes on pilings. The explorer Alexander Mackenzie, on his epic journey across British Columbia to the coast in 1793, wrote about houses "raised and supported near 30 feet from the ground by perpendicular spars of a very large size," with "access formed by a long tree in an inclined position from a platform to the ground, with notches cut in it by way of steps about a foot and a half asunder." This latter described the typical ladder of the Northwest Coast peoples, often used to gain access to a house roof, a raised food cache and other places.

The Northern House Style Up the Nass and Skeena rivers, on the Queen Charlotte Islands and up into Alaska, the Tsimshian, Haida and Tlingit built impressive, sturdy houses in what is referred to as the northern house style. The Haisla, the northernmost of the Kwakiutl peoples, also built in this style. Very large houses, the property of the wealthy, occasionally measured 15.2 m (50') by 18.3 m (60'), and had gabled roofs and thick plank walls set vertically. Generally, each village had one house with an excavated floor, and that house belonged to the head chief.

The Haida had two structurally different house styles, one of which is thought to have preceded the other. The earlier style had two ridge beams that rested directly on top of two house posts, generally carved, that stood within the house walls, independent of the framework. The bases of the vertical wall planks were set into the ground, lashed together with cedar withes. The more recent style, often seen in archival photos of old Haida villages, had six ridge beams (mostly with only their protruding ends faceted) that rested directly on two barge boards that formed the gable. These barge boards were

style remained the same, but the house floor was nearly square, and the wall planks were vertical instead of horizontal. Houses of high-ranking persons often had a large crest design painted across the entire front.

The main structural change was that there were two ridge beams rather than one. These two great timbers rested on tie beams that lay across pairs of posts at the front and rear of the house. The long ridge beams often had decorative grooves adzed along their length and around their circumference. Frequently the posts at both ends of the house bore elaborately carved and painted

The framework of an old-style two-beam house at Kayang on Masset Inlet, Queen Charlotte Islands. Courtesy Field Museum of Natural History, Chicago, 17459

supported at the outside ends by corner house posts and at the inside ends by a pair of vertical uprights at the centre of the house; all these were part of the frame construction. The vertical wall planks, tapered at both ends, fit into slotted roof beams and sills, allowing for removal of the wall planks during good weather or for other purposes. Long planks, held down with rocks and logs, formed the roof, with a central opening for the smoke hole.

Large houses that belonged to wealthy Haida chiefs generally had an excavated floor, with a platform along the four walls and partitioned cubicles for sleeping areas. The partition planks could be removed for feasts and other crowded events. Long single planks, about 61 cm (2') wide, were placed on edge to serve as retaining walls for the earthen platform, which was covered with planks. The highest ranking chiefs had two or more tiers of platforms in their houses. The head of the house and his family occupied the rear centre section, and other families were placed around the house according to rank.

The remains of an excavated floor house stand amid the new growth of spruce trees in the old village of Tanu, on the Queen Charlotte Islands. The dirt floor is level and clear, save for the ever-present moss, and so is the platform. One retaining wall leans inward under the weight of earth, pushed over, perhaps, by the growing roots of a spruce. One massive, round ridge beam, now fallen, hangs suspended over the floor, each end supported at ground level. The other beam lies with one end atop a corner post that has adzed fluting around the upper portion.

The scene is similar at Ninstints, but the remains are more complete. All the posts, beams and barge boards are there, some standing, some fallen, and the excavated floor is clearly defined. Massive, round ridge beams straddle the low floor level instead of being held aloft; roof planks, now covered with overburden, lie some centimetres from the damp earth. When they were new, some of these houses stood 3.6 m to 5.5 m (12' to 18') high at the gable. Before the introduction of hinged doors, the entrance was an oval opening in the base of the house pole, elaborately carved with the crests or history of the resident family, as were the house posts inside.

All the major posts, beams and supports were named, and, of course, the house itself received a significant name at a special ceremony and potlatch held at its completion. Eventually, some houses acquired a second name. Often the names alluded to some physical aspect of the house or referred to an event during its construction; others were boastful and reflected the owner's wealth and status. For example, Mountain House and House Pole Looks Down were names of houses built on higher ground than the others. The name Cloudy House, of which there were several, was usually associated with fog during the house preparation or construction, while Rainbow House was so called because rainbows rested upon it. Grease House indicated the abundance of food always available within, and People Wish To Be There and House People Never Pass By no doubt also had plenty of food and a hospitable, generous owner. Thunder Rolls Upon It and House Upon Which Clouds Sound implied the houses were so large (they were the largest of the village) that they were brushed by the passing elements. The following are the names of houses that I feel I might have enjoyed living in or visiting: Peaceful House, House In Which It Is Always Summer and Shining House.

On the mainland across the water from the Queen Charlotte Islands, the Tsimshian built their houses using a similar style of construction, but often with squared-off posts and beams. An average house measured 15.2 m by 16.8 m (50' by 55'), not quite square. The sleeping quarters of a chief and his family were built of specially selected planks, often painted with his family crest. Excavated-floor houses often had a secondary step or bench below the main platform.

Farther north, the Tlingit also built their houses in the northern house style, in similar sizes. Entry to a large house was by two or three steps up to the doorway; inside was a raised level around the perimeter and two or three platform levels below. Occupants cooked at a central hearth, above which there was a smoke hole in the roof. Where feasible, they left a wide strip of land between their houses and the beach to serve as a general thoroughfare.

Not far from the coastal town of Ketchikan, Alaska, there is a replica of an early nineteenth-century Tlingit house, complete with painted front and three steps up to the oval doorway. The corner posts, slotted to carry the barge boards, are each topped by a carved figure of a man wearing a spruce root hat and holding a staff; carved corner posts were rare. The tall carved frontal pole, of the type which came into popularity in late years, has been built into the replica. Inside, the house posts are carved and painted with lineage crests, like those of the Haida. Tlingit house names mostly referred to birds, animals and fish, such as Raven Bone House, Eagle Claw House, Beaver Dam House, Halibut House and Giant Rock Oyster House.

As village populations declined through warfare and disease, more and more houses became vacant and suffered neglect. Inevitably, the few remaining people moved away, returning at first for the fishing or the sealing, then eventually not at all. Collectors and museums "acquired" the better carved poles, while missionaries encouraged the cutting down and burning of others to ensure an end to the old, pagan life. Over the years, wind, rain, insects, fungi and seedlings slowly gave back to the forest all but a few scattered remnants of the great cedar dwellings.

Other Structures In addition to houses, Northwest Coast peoples built many types of structures using cedar planks. By taking along several of the removable house planks to a fish camp, clam-digging beach or other resource area, they could quickly set up a temporary shelter; at regularly visited places the framework remained from year to year. The planks also made a good lean-to for overnight stops on a long journey.

Outside many houses along the coast, people built a type of deck, similar to the patio of contemporary homes, for outdoor living in good weather, particularly in spring and fall. Often built on stilts over the beach, the deck had low plank walls sloping outward for people to lean comfortably against, and they gathered there to gamble, to gossip or tell yarns and to generally watch the world go by.

Many Northwest Coast peoples performed ritual cleansing in some form of sweat lodge. The Quinault Coast Salish dug a pit about 1.5 m by 2.1 m (5' by 7') and 1.8 m (6') deep, close to a stream. They covered the floor with sand and roofed over the pit with planks, leaving an opening for entry at the side closest to the river. After pouring water onto hot rocks, they closed the entrance with a mat and steamed themselves before plunging into the cold water.

An important structure at the salmon fishing camp was the smokehouse, especially in the north. Each family or household generally owned its own smokehouse, a structure built of rough planks attached to a strong framework, with many poles running its length for hanging up butchered fish. The unreliable weather during the spring and autumn salmon runs meant that the fish had to be moved into a smokehouse after an initial period on the drying rack. Rows of such houses jostled each other for space along the banks of good salmon rivers, the smoke escaping through cracks between the planks and curling up in white clouds to mingle with the deep green of the forest. A family or household often stored large quantities of smoked fish at the site of the catch; to protect it from predators, they built a cache of cedar boards raised up on stilts.

GRAVE HOUSE WITH BURIAL BOXES. CS 75/2

OUTDOOR GATHERING PLACES,
POPULAR IN SPRING AND FALL,
FOR GAMBLING, TALKING ETC. KW 75/23

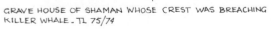

GRAVE HOUSE OF SHAMAN WHOSE CREST WAS BREACHING
KILLER WHALE. TL 75/74

SEPULCHRES OF WIDE PLANKS HELD BOXES
CONTAINING REMAINS OF DECEASED. HA 32

SMOKEHOUSE – AFTER INITIAL DRYING ON OUTDOOR RACK,
FISH WERE MOVED INTO SMOKEHOUSE AND HUNG ON POLES.
SMOULDERING FIRES CURED FLESH FOR PRESERVATION.
ROOF AND WALLS OF CEDAR PLANKS. TS 75/12

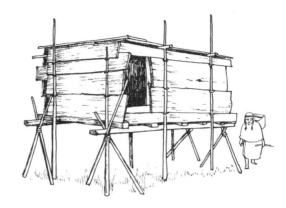

SALMON CACHE – FOR STORING QUANTITIES OF
PRESERVED FISH AWAY FROM DOGS AND OTHER
PREDATORS. CS 75/47

Various cultural groups built different types of mortuary houses in which to deposit their dead. The Coast Salish often used broad planks, horizontally placed, to build a small shed roof shelter with a platform inside to hold the box containing the deceased. The Tsimshian and Tlingit put their dead in small gravehouses raised up on poles, usually situated on a rocky promontory.

The Haida built scaled-down replicas of their own houses, and short keyhole corner posts, a few metres apart, can still be found in some old village sites on the Queen Charlotte Islands. Built next to the family house, the mortuary house was a depository for members of the same house lineage. The burial boxes of commoners were stacked on top each other in several tiers along the walls. Those of high-ranking people generally held a special position in the mortuary house, until the family accumulated sufficient wealth to commission the carving and raising of a mortuary pole (in which to place the burial box) and to pay for the accompanying feast.

CARVED POLES, POSTS AND FIGURES Perhaps the best known and most distinctive feature of Northwest Coast Indian cultures is the tall, carved cedar log commonly referred to as a "totem pole." Massive, mystical and always intriguing, the large-scale carvings readily command attention and admiration.

The antiquity of these poles has not been positively established, since wood cannot long survive the moist climate of the Northwest Coast. One of the earliest recorded sightings of the carved pole is a rough sketch by fur trader John Bartlett of Boston, Massachusetts, who anchored off the Haida winter village of Kiusta, in the Queen Charlotte Islands. The sketch depicts a tall, carved column built into the front centre of a plank house. The year was 1791, and part of his journal reads: "We went ashore where one of their winter houses stood. The entrance was cut out of a large tree and carved all the way up and down. The door was made like a man's head, and the passage into the house was between his teeth. . . ." The sketch is crude, and without any comprehension of the zoomorphic figures that were undoubtedly carved on the pole; indeed, Bartlett may even have made the sketch from memory after leaving the village.

Although Bartlett does establish the existence of tall, carved poles at this time, they must have been few in number since they were seldom mentioned in early journals, even those detailing the people and their habitat. A later illustration of the same village in 1799 shows a row of plank houses and two free-standing poles. One house has a frontal pole more like a massive plank, not much taller than the house. It is quite probable that the monumental pole carvings originated as large blocks of carved wood attached to house fronts and developed into house poles. In the south, at least, carved poles might have been an extension of the interior house posts described and illustrated in Cook's journals of his visit to Yuquot in 1778: "At the upper end of many appartments, were two large images, or statues placed abreast to each other and three or four feet asunder, they bore some resemblance to the human figure, but monstrous large."

Studies indicate that carved poles likely originated with the northern peoples, then spread south along the coast and up the major river valleys. The only coastal people who did not have such poles were the Coast Salish; they did, however, have large carved planks attached to the inside and/or outside of their ceremonial dance houses.

As the numbers of trading ships arriving on the coast to barter for furs and other goods increased, so increased the wealth of many chiefs and high-ranking people. Trade also brought a proliferation of metal-bladed tools. The combination of new wealth and better tools resulted in the commissioning of more and larger poles — a reflection of the rivalry that became widespread, particularly in the north. By the mid- to late nineteenth century, villages positively bristled with complex, sculptured poles — elegant, bold and imaginative — many of great girth or height. Sunbleached or painted, ravens, eagles, bears, beavers, wolves, whales, dogfish, frogs, humans and mythical creatures interlocked or rose one above the other in elaborately carved columns. Even the earliest explorers recognized that the carved poles did not depict gods and were not objects of worship. Rather, the heraldic poles proclaimed the crests of family lineages that had been inherited, gained through marriage or acquired in some other way. They declared certain rights and privileges of the owners and documented legends of tribal origins, as well as recounting the memorable adventures of ancestors and various other family histories. Substituting for written documentation, the poles stood as visible proof of declarations that had been witnessed and validated by all those attending the ceremony of their raising. Honouring both the living and the dead, the monuments of cedar presented an impressive display of wealth and identity, as well as stunning evidence of a sophisticated, powerful art, unequalled in North America at that time.

SINGLE REMAINING POLE AT OLD VILLAGE OF EHATISAT, VANCOUVER ISLAND. WC 77

MEMORIAL POLE BY MUNGO MARTIN. 15·2 m [50'] KW 3

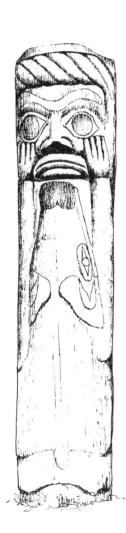

HOUSE PORTAL POLE, WITH
ENTRANCE THROUGH BODY
OF EAGLE, ONCE STOOD AT
HAINA, QUEEN CHARLOTTE
ISLANDS. HA 75/21

HOUSE FRONTAL POLE
REPRESENTING SUPER-
NATURAL MAN AND BEAR
WIFE. OPENING AT BASE
WAS ENTRANCE TO HOUSE.
ABOUT 4·5m [15'] TL 25

HOUSE POST AT CENTRE BACK OF
HOUSE INTERIOR, ORIGINALLY AT
NINSTINTS. 3·9 m [13'] HA 3

HOUSE POST REPRESENTING
ANCESTOR AND WOLF. WC 75/12

HOUSE POST, WITH SLOT TO
CARRY ROOF BEAM. 2·8 m
[9'2"] CS 3

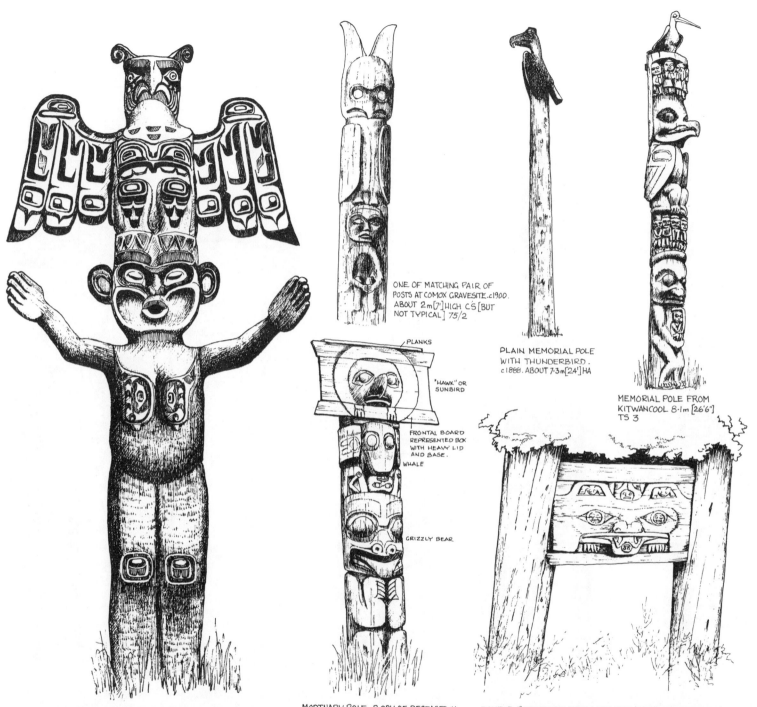

ONE OF MATCHING PAIR OF
POSTS AT COMOX GRAVESITE. c1900.
ABOUT 2 m [7'] HIGH CS [BUT
NOT TYPICAL] 75/2

PLANKS

"HAWK" OR
SUNBIRD

FRONTAL BOARD
REPRESENTED BOX
WITH HEAVY LID
AND BASE.

WHALE

GRIZZLY BEAR

PLAIN MEMORIAL POLE
WITH THUNDERBIRD.
c1888. ABOUT 7·3 m [24'] HA

MEMORIAL POLE FROM
KITWANCOOL 8·1 m [26'6"]
TS 3

MEMORIAL POLE, THUNDERBIRD AND LEGENDARY
WILD WOMAN OF THE WOODS, DZONOQUA, IN
GRAVEYARD AT ALERT BAY. ABOUT 5 m [16½'] KW 2

MORTUARY POLE, BODY OF DECEASED, IN
BOX, PLACED IN HOLLOWED TOP OF POLE,
COVERED WITH FRONTAL BOARD, PLANKS
ON TOP. HA 75/67

DOUBLE-POST MORTUARY WITH CARVED FRONTAL BOARD,
HELD REMAINS OF VERY HIGH-RANKING CHIEF. NOTE WIDE,
BUTT END OF LOGS PLACED UPPERMOST TO PROVIDE
MAXIMUM WIDTH FOR BURIAL BOX. HA 67

78

House, mortuary and memorial poles at Cumshewa, Queen Charlotte Islands, in 1878. Courtesy National Museums of Canada, 243.

Different types of poles had significantly different functions. Perhaps the most striking was the *house portal pole* of early times: this tall pole, standing at the centre of the house front, rose high above it, with the open mouth of the creature at the base forming the entrance. When European-style doors were later built into house facades, no opening was cut in the pole, and it became simply the *house frontal pole*.

About a year after an important chief's death, his successor raised a pole in his memory. On this *memorial pole* were depicted the appropriate crests and symbols that represented outstanding achievements or events in the life of the deceased chief. At the potlatch given at this time, the titles and prerogatives of the dead chief were passed on to his successor, whose family and relatives helped pay for and shared in the festivities. A memorial pole could also be raised for a high-ranking person whose achievements during his life merited this honour.

The *mortuary pole* of the Haida had a cavity at the top, into which was placed the burial box that held the remains of a chief or high-ranking person a year after the death. In order to accommodate the box, the cavity was generally cut into the wide end of the pole, with the tapering end set into the ground. The box was hidden from view by a frontal board, painted and/or carved with a lineage crest, placed across the front. The shape and design of the frontal board gave the appearance of a large chest, with its characteristic heavy lid and base. Planks covered the top of the grave cavity and were held in place with rocks. At Ninstints, in the Queen Charlotte

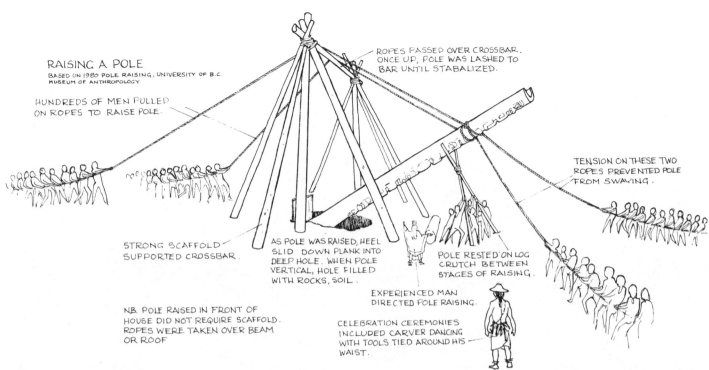

RAISING A POLE
BASED ON 1980 POLE RAISING, UNIVERSITY OF B.C.
MUSEUM OF ANTHROPOLOGY

HUNDREDS OF MEN PULLED ON ROPES TO RAISE POLE.

ROPES PASSED OVER CROSSBAR. ONCE UP, POLE WAS LASHED TO BAR UNTIL STABALIZED.

TENSION ON THESE TWO ROPES PREVENTED POLE FROM SWAYING.

STRONG SCAFFOLD SUPPORTED CROSSBAR.

AS POLE WAS RAISED, HEEL SLID DOWN PLANK INTO DEEP HOLE. WHEN POLE VERTICAL, HOLE FILLED WITH ROCKS, SOIL.

POLE RESTED ON LOG CRUTCH BETWEEN STAGES OF RAISING.

EXPERIENCED MAN DIRECTED POLE RAISING.

N.B. POLE RAISED IN FRONT OF HOUSE DID NOT REQUIRE SCAFFOLD. ROPES WERE TAKEN OVER BEAM OR ROOF

CELEBRATION CEREMONIES INCLUDED CARVER DANCING WITH TOOLS TIED AROUND HIS WAIST.

Islands, the frontal board of a carved mortuary pole has fallen away, leaving the remains of the burial box visible. Now thickly moss covered, the rocks still hold down the covering boards, as they have for perhaps a hundred years, against the force of winter gales.

A *double-post mortuary* consisted of two poles a short distance apart, with a boxlike construction of planks connecting the two. Inside, the structure had space for two or three burial boxes for members of the same family. Occasionally, mortuary poles were not carved and had a frontal board carrying only the crest.

House posts formed an integral part of the house structure. Depending on the style of the house, one large single post at the rear wall and a pair of posts at the front (or two pairs, one at the front and one at the rear) supported the main beams upon which the roof beams rested. These interior posts carried bold carvings, also representing family lineages and histories. In the Kwakiutl dance house at Alert Bay, two large thunderbirds incorporated into the rear wall posts spread their great wings, dwarfing the people who stand beneath them.

A Kwakiutl village that gave large potlatches might install *blanket posts* on the beach. These were two slender, uncarved posts, about forty paces apart, topped by a single crest carving. Great quantities of blankets to be given away at a potlatch or given in payment of a copper were piled in high mounds between the two posts — a means both of measuring out the quantity and impressing guests with the host's wealth.

Carving a Pole Carving a pole was a major project undertaken only by a specialist. He began by going to the forest to carefully select a cedar tree, which had to be the right size and have few knots. After the chosen tree was felled and towed back to the village, it was raised on blocks of wood to allow the bark to be removed from all sides. Next came the removal of the sapwood with a D adze; if the pole was not to be round, wood was removed to flatten one side.

The one who commissioned the pole discussed with the artist what crests the pole was to depict or what legend it should illustrate. The artist, free to create his own design within the given requirements, drew the figures freehand on the pole with a stick of charcoal. In the late nineteenth century the Rev. W.H. Collison, minister of the church at Masset, stood watching a skilled carver and was surprised at the apparently reckless manner in which the artist cut away the wood in the initial stages of the work. The Reverend inquired: "Where is your plan? Are you not afraid to spoil your tree?" According to Collison, the carver replied: "No; the whiteman, when about to make anything, first traces it on paper, but the Indian has all his plans here," and pointed significantly to his forehead.

The carver generally worked behind a brush screen in order to keep the design concealed until it was time for the raising and public viewing, and he often worked with an apprentice. Working from the base of the pole up, the carver roughed in the figures with an adze, a curved knife and sometimes a chisel. Starting at the base again, he refined the design and roughed in the details, working with clean, sure strokes of the knife. To prevent the log from cracking through drying out, he kept it damp by pouring water over the areas being carved, both before he started work and when he finished for the day. Next, he took care of the fine details — the feathers, claws, cross-hatching on a beaver's tail and so on — and added any projections such as beaks, fins, outstretched arms or wings. For these he carefully carved a mortice and tenon joint with a perfect fit and held the projection in place by driving in two or more wooden pegs as required. Most carvers adzed the carved surface all over to give it a textured look; they considered the work unfinished if the wood remained smooth.

In early times paint was applied sparingly, if at all, mainly to accent eyebrows, mouth, nostrils and other features, though different cultural groups had differing preferences. In general, red, black, white and blue-green were the colours used. When commercial paints were introduced, carvers often turned to them with gusto, until some poles were totally covered in paint. In later years, such garish nontraditional colours were used for repainting old poles that the well-known anthropologist Wilson Duff worked with the British American Paint Company (BAPCO) to develop a nonglossy "totem pole red," "totem pole blue-green" and other colours in order to retain the traditional look of the old poles and to paint new ones.

The artist who carved the pole received considerable payment for his labours, particularly if he was famous for his work. Those who felled the tree, transported it and helped to raise the pole also received payment. In postcontact times, payment consisted of guns, blankets and items that could be traded for other goods. A pole carved in about 1867 in Skidegate, Queen Charlotte Islands, as a memorial to Chief Skedans, has the value of the pole recorded on the back. The 23 parallel lines marked on the wood each represent 10 blankets, the large copper represents a value of 40 blankets, and the small copper 20 blankets. (A "copper" is a shield-shaped piece of copper that represents wealth.) The total of 290 blankets had a value of $2.00 each, so the cost of this memorial pole was $580, a considerable sum at the time. The pole is now in Stanley Park, Vancouver, British Columbia.

Once completed, the carved cedar log had to be taken to the site of its raising. A hundred or more people were needed to shoulder a large pole, or to carry it on crosspieces. In this modern, mechanical world of heavy-duty equipment, the pole is still carried the traditional way, and while the physical burden of so heavy a log is great, the feeling of elation that follows is greater.

The raising of a pole had to be accompanied by a potlatch, with feasting, speeches, gift giving, dancing, drumming, singing and other festivities. Wearing his carving tools about his waist, the carver danced around the newly finished pole in celebration. The sculptured work of art came under critical judgement from onlookers, who appraised and discussed its size, design and quality of work. After a long hiatus, poles are again being raised in villages and even cities — along the coast and elsewhere. Witnessing this event brings a special kind of excitement, especially if the pole is a large one, which makes its raising all the more precarious. I well remember the collective roar that rose from the great crowd in Skidegate as Bill Reid's splendid pole, 17.4 m (57') tall, reached the vertical position, high and triumphant against a clouded sky. The joyful feeling of satisfaction that filled those who had hauled on the ropes was shared by the rest of the crowd. It was a stirring, memorable moment.

Traditionally, when a pole stood upright in the hole dug for it, its base was packed around with rocks as large as a man could handle, with smaller stones and earth added to fill in. The heavy rocks protected the pole from being uprooted by the fierce winds that often pounded the coast, especially in winter, and also allowed for drainage to help prevent the wood from rotting. Many poles along the coast have been leaning at a steep angle for decades without falling, held in place by rocks. At Nin-

IMAGE REPRESENTING
RIVAL CHIEF. KW 35

GRAVE FIGURE DEPICTING MAN
HOLDING MASK OVER FACE
1.32m [52"] CS 20

SLAVE CARRYING A CHIEF.
NOTE ARISTOCRATIC FACE OF
CHIEF COMPARED WITH THAT
OF SLAVE. 1.30 m [51½"] KW 3

SPEAKER'S POST.
MAN STOOD BEHIND,
MADE ANNOUNCEMENTS
THROUGH OPEN MOUTH
2.33 m. [7'8"] KW 3

CARVED FIGURES IN
WHALER'S SHRINE.
ABOUT LIFE SIZE. WC 75/12

GRAVE FIGURE REPRESENTING
MYTHICAL SEA BEAR, WITH TWO
WHALE DORSAL FINS. ABOUT 1.2 m
[4'] TS 75/2

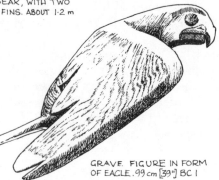

GRAVE FIGURE IN FORM
OF EAGLE. 99 cm [39"] BC 1

CATAFALQUE, REPRESENTING FROG
CREST, SUPPORTED CHIEF'S COFFIN UNTIL
IT WAS PLACED IN TOP OF MORTUARY POLE,
ABOUT A YEAR AFTER DEATH. HA 75/6

CATAFALQUE IN FORM OF
BEAVER. HA. 75/67

82

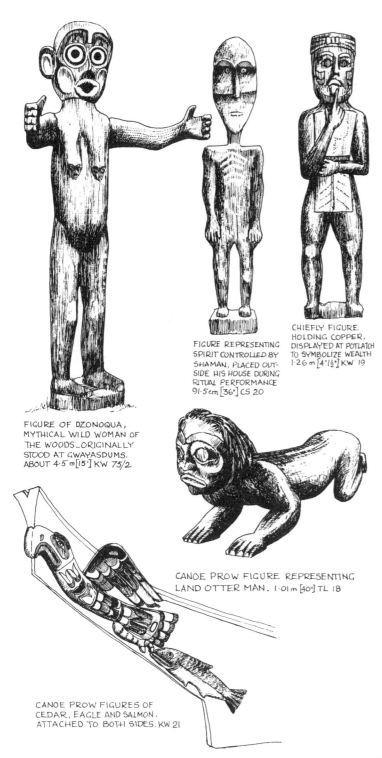

FIGURE OF DZONOQUA,
MYTHICAL WILD WOMAN OF
THE WOODS—ORIGINALLY
STOOD AT GWAYASDUMS.
ABOUT 4·5 m [15'] KW 75/2

FIGURE REPRESENTING
SPIRIT CONTROLLED BY
SHAMAN, PLACED OUT-
SIDE HIS HOUSE DURING
RITUAL PERFORMANCE
91·5 cm [36"] CS 20

CHIEFLY FIGURE
HOLDING COPPER,
DISPLAYED AT POTLATCH
TO SYMBOLIZE WEALTH
1·26 m [4'1½"] KW 19

CANOE PROW FIGURE REPRESENTING
LAND OTTER MAN. 1·01 m [40"] TL 18

CANOE PROW FIGURES OF
CEDAR, EAGLE AND SALMON,
ATTACHED TO BOTH SIDES. KW 21

stints, circles of rocks protrude from the soil in cavities where poles once stood.

These carved cedar monuments, like other important and prestigious possessions, had names that generally referred to the design or the legend they depicted. People took great pride in having the tallest pole or the finest carved by the best artist, and there was much rivalry between villages regarding status and power. The quantity and quality of food at the accompanying feast, as well as of the gifts given to everyone, especially important and high-ranking people, were remembered and talked about long after the event. And it is much the same today.

Carved Figures　The carver's creativity in large-scale art went beyond totemic poles and posts to cover a wide range of human and animal figures, either smaller or larger than life. Generally commissioned by the head of a household, these figures played a specific part in the coast peoples' ceremonial and spiritual life.

As a welcoming gesture to important guests arriving by canoe for a feast or potlatch, a large carved figure of a human was placed at the edge of the beach, facing out to sea. It might have arms outstretched in welcome, or a hand shading its eyes in a scouting manner, watching for the visitors' arrival. The host family, dressed in their finest ceremonial garments and headdresses, gathered at the beach front, singing and dancing to receive the high-ranking guests with appropriate pomp and ceremony. In all likelihood, a carved and painted figurehead at the prow or one on each side of the bow decorated the arriving canoe. Another part of the greeting ceremonies was the speaker's post, a carved ancestral figure with an open, perforated mouth; the officially appointed speaker stood behind it to announce the names of guests as though the ancestor himself was receiving the visitors.

During Kwakiutl dance ceremonies, elaborate, theatrical enactments took place, and spirit figures sometimes seemed to rise up out of the floor (from a box secretly buried in the earth) or to fly across the room. These puppetlike figures, often carved of lightweight cedar and manipulated by strings invisible in the firelight, gave credence to the belief in the presence of the spirits and the power of the performers.

A particularly great potlatch or other grand occasion called for the carving of a commemorative figure of the host chief. Such sculptures were raised aloft for special

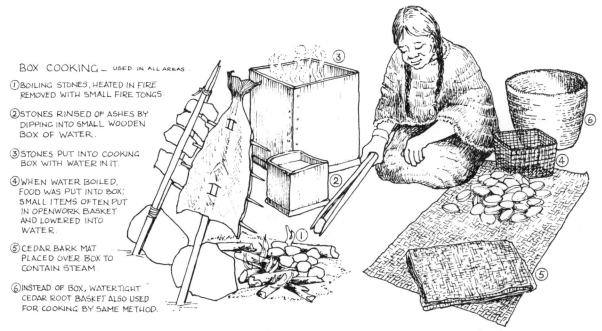

BOX COOKING — USED IN ALL AREAS.

① BOILING STONES, HEATED IN FIRE REMOVED WITH SMALL FIRE TONGS.

② STONES RINSED OF ASHES BY DIPPING INTO SMALL WOODEN BOX OF WATER.

③ STONES PUT INTO COOKING BOX WITH WATER IN IT.

④ WHEN WATER BOILED, FOOD WAS PUT INTO BOX; SMALL ITEMS OFTEN PUT IN OPENWORK BASKET AND LOWERED INTO WATER.

⑤ CEDAR BARK MAT PLACED OVER BOX TO CONTAIN STEAM.

⑥ INSTEAD OF BOX, WATERTIGHT CEDAR ROOT BASKET ALSO USED FOR COOKING BY SAME METHOD.

occasions, either on a pole in front of the house or high on the gable as a proud statement of self worth. In another way of declaring his superiority, a chief might erect a ridicule pole or figure that showed a rival chief in some belittling attitude. A shame pole would be displayed to show contempt for a rival's misdeeds or an unfulfilled social obligation: the carving represented some aspect of the event, and if it did not shame the person into paying the debt, fulfilling the promise or otherwise making good his shortcomings, it stood as a reminder of his disgrace for all to see.

Some carved figures held great spiritual significance. A Coast Salish shaman who took part in the spirit canoe ceremony had a carved representation of his spirit assistant planted in the ground beside him, and a Tlingit shaman's guard figure watched over him while he slept. Very small carved figures were part of many a shaman's medicine bundle, a powerful means of helping to cure the sick. Guard figures watched over a shaman's grave and that of others, too: the Coast Salish often placed one or more standing figures at a grave, and northerners frequently placed a carved crest animal at the site.

On the west coast of Vancouver Island, certain shamans of villages that did not have access to migrating whales built special shrines of cedar planks and posts. Set apart from the village, these shrines housed human skulls and simply carved human effigies that were used in association with the whaling cult that sought to call whales ashore.

STEAMBENT WOOD   One of the most outstanding items manufactured by Northwest Coast woodworkers must surely be the bentwood (or bent-corner) container. No other people in the world devised a large wooden container by kerfing and steambending a single plank to form four sides. The Inuit did make containers using a bentwood technique but seldom used kerfs and lacked a supply of suitable wood for making large storage boxes.

Boxes and Chests   Bentwood containers with a height greater than the width are termed boxes, while those with a length greater than their height are referred to as chests. Boxes varied in size from small to quite large. Some were undecorated; others were either carved or painted, sometimes both. The undecorated cooking box, made in varied sizes, sat beside the fire, partly filled with water. A woman dropped heated stones into the box to bring the water to a boil for cooking food. If food required longer boiling, she replaced the cooled stones with freshly heated ones.

TELESCOPING CHEST
LID FIT COMPLETELY
OVER THE SIDES.

TELESCOPING CHEST, CARVED WITH FIGURES OF THREE BEARS, GENEROUSLY INLAID WITH OPERCULA OF RED TURBAN SNAIL. 50·1 cm [19¾"] HIGH . TL 20

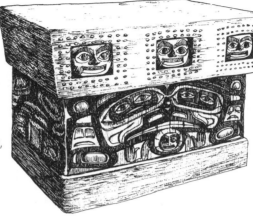

STORAGE CHEST, WITH LID UNUSUAL FOR ITS PROPORTIONS AND CARVING – INLAID WITH 182 OPERCULA EACH SIDE. 66 cm [26"] TL 28

STORAGE BOX WITH PAINTED DESIGN CENTRED ON ONE CORNER. ENTIRE BOX OF CEDAR WOOD, OPERCULA INLAID ON LID. 55·8 cm [22"] TL 21

SUPERB CARVED AND PAINTED CHEST – VALUABLE PROPERTY OF WEALTHY PERSON, USED FOR STORING CEREMONIAL REGALIA AND WEALTH ITEMS.   99 cm [39"] TL 12

BENTWOOD BOX OF CEDAR BEARING CLASSIC BLACK AND RED DESIGNS ON FRONT AND SIDES. 39·3 cm [15½"] TS 20

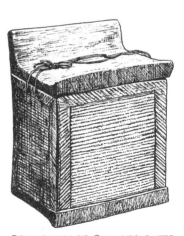

FOOD STORAGE BOX, DECORATED WITH ROWS OF FINELY CHISELLED GROOVES – CORD TIED LID ON. 27·3 cm [10¾"] WC 21

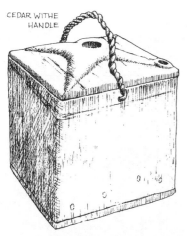

WATER BUCKET _ USED ON CANOE JOURNEYS.
LARGE OPENING FOR FILLING; SMALL HOLE
FOR DRINKING, USING A HOLLOW TUBE _
PLUGS IN BOTH PREVENTED WATER
SPILLING. 22·8 cm [9"] HIGH. MK 12

SHAMAN'S BOX WITH CARVED FRONT
52 cm [20½"] TS 2

Very large cooking boxes used for preparing large quantities of food for a number of guests at a big feast were also brought into service to render oil from eulachon by boiling the pre-rotted fish. The oil floated to the top and was scooped up and poured into smaller bentwood boxes. Eulachon oil was regarded as a valuable trade item, as well as a symbol of wealth by those who lavished it upon the food of their guests. Boxes containing foods or oil for trade were made in standard sizes to simplify trading calculations. The large boxes containing oil were particularly strong and could hold 45.3 kg (100 lbs.).

Domestic boxes, plain or fluted, provided storage for foodstuffs such as dried fish, fish eggs, dried berry cakes, fresh crabapples in water, rhizomes, nuts and dried seaweeds, as well as the oil of seal, whale or eulachon. A plain bentwood box with a handle across the top became a bucket to carry and store water in the house. Plain boxes were also used to store general items such as the tools, implements and supplies of craftspeople. Often, however, a creative carver added a design to his own work box. A shaman housed the mystical paraphernalia of his profession in a small box that he took to a ritual curing or other ceremony. The fisherman or sea mammal hunter took his gear along in a small box shaped to fit neatly into the narrow bow of his canoe. The weaver used urine as a mordant in dying wool; thus, a urinal box was both a household convenience and collector of urine (which had several uses). Because ghosts and malicious spirits had a revulsion for this bodily waste, the placement of the box by the door served another useful purpose by protecting the inhabitants. A small box stood at the left side of a woman while she spun twine from nettle fibre or cedar bark. The prepared strands, or roving, lay coiled in the box and were covered with sand to prevent them from tangling. As the spinner needed more fibre, she simply pulled it from the box. A basket weaver kept a small box of water at hand to keep the basketry material damp and flexible while working.

When a family made a long journey, perhaps to the fish camp or summer village, they loaded their canoe with boxes full of possessions, as well as empty ones in which to bring back winter food supplies; people used these boxes as seats while travelling. Those who went on trading journeys carried their trade goods in boxes and chests. All canoe travellers took along a food box and a water box. The latter had a tightly fitting lid with two holes in it, each stoppered with a wooden plug. The box was filled through the larger hole; a person who wanted a drink unplugged the smaller hole, inserted a hollow tube of wood and used it like a drinking straw. This prevented any spillage of the precious water, especially during a rough passage.

Bentwood boxes were another valuable trade item, and often the ones made for trade had elaborate and complex designs, either painted or carved, sometimes both, on all four sides; red and black were the most commonly used colours. Similar designs also embellished the large and handsome chests, sometimes made of yellow cedar; these often incorporated a third colour, blue-green, in the backgound areas. Some designs had inlays of sea otter teeth, opercula or occasionally pieces of abalone shell; the front often depicted the head and trunk of a creature, while the back represented its hindquarters. Generally these designs were stylized almost to the point of abstraction, with body parts minimized or rearranged, but a few of the more elaborate ones had a face or head carved in three dimensions.

The spirit of the crest figure that embellished a box or chest dwelt within and guarded the contents for the owner. These masterpieces of the woodcarver's art became highly prized family heirlooms and were passed down from generation to generation. Many of the chest designs are among the most remarkable of any on the Northwest Coast; their elegant, balanced and complex compositions represented a high point of the creativity of the northern peoples.

The value of a chest was high, and a wealthy chief might trade for one, or commission an artist-carver to make one. In it he stored his valuable ceremonial possessions, and on important occasions he seated himself on it. A high-ranking family might own several chests, some filled with their dance robes and blankets, furs, masks, rattles, head and neck rings, talking sticks, coppers and other paraphernalia used for ceremonial and state occasions. Other chests and boxes held the finely carved dishes, bowls, ladles and horn spoons used for special feasts. At a potlatch and on certain occasions, the magnificent chests and their contents were set out in a display of opulence to validate the wealth and status of the household. During the singing and dancing of feasts and celebrations, people drummed on the various boxes about the house.

A particularly interesting style of chest had an extending or telescoping lid, built either for strength or to increase the capacity. David Samwell, a surgeon on Vancouver's expedition, recorded: "They appear so much like our chests at first view that we took them for the work of Europeans, being made with lids, one half of the Box is made to enclose the other."

Bentwood boxes served the peoples of the Northwest Coast in death as well as in daily life; when a person died, the body (in a flexed position) was placed in a bentwood box, with the head at the corner where the steambent plank was joined, to allow the soul to escape through the crack. This burial box was often placed in some type of gravehouse, on top of a platform of planks

SMALL BOX, WITH PERFORATIONS FOR THONG TIES. 14.6cm [5¾"] NWC 4

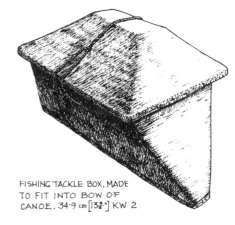

FISHING TACKLE BOX, MADE TO FIT INTO BOW OF CANOE. 34.9cm [13¾"] KW 2

or in the top of a mortuary pole, but not all peoples did so. The southern Kwakiutl took the burial box some distance from the village and placed it in a tall tree, tying it to the branches with cedar bark rope. They preferred a tree that leaned over the water of a chasm and removed the lower branches to render the burial box inaccessible. High-ranking families of the Westcoast people placed the burial box in a cave (above high tide) owned by the bereaved family; many boxes accumulated in these caves over the years.

Bentwood Bowls No feast of a high-ranking northerner was complete without the use of exquisitely shaped and carved bentwood bowls, made from a single plank of yellow cedar (or other wood).

The woodworker carved the four sides of the bowl to give them bulging contours and cut the undulating rim to

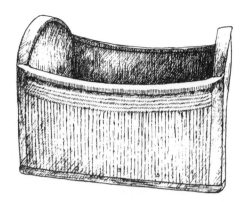

BENTWOOD BOWL WITH FLUTED SIDES
33·6 cm [13¼"] KW 2

CARVED BENTWOOD BOWL, WITH OPERCULA
INLAID AROUND RIM — BASE OF CEDAR
WOOD. 25·4 cm [10"] HA 3

BOWL FOR OIL, CARVED AND PAINTED TO
REPRESENT A BEAVER, RIM INLAID WITH
OPERCULA — BASE OF CEDAR WOOD.
25·3 cm [10"] WIDE. TL 27

shape — all before steaming and bending the plank. Like the bentwood box, he joined the corner by pegging or sewing, and pegged on the base. The bowl did not have a lid, but occasionally had a woven cedar bark covering shaped to fit over the top and sides. The wide rim of the bowl carried a decoration, often of opercula, sometimes of sea otter teeth. The elegant grace of the bowl's contoured sides and the undulating rim gave the container a fluid form. Often a sculptured animal head emerged from the low relief carving at the ends, imparting a vitality that reflected the richness and strength of the culture.

Large bentwood bowls held quantities of food or oil at a feast; smaller ones were used for lesser amounts of food or for individual use. As with other valuable items, a noteworthy bowl had a name, which the person carrying in the filled bowl announced to the assembled guests.

Box Drums The deep, resonant drumming that rolled through the dance house during a Kwakiutl ceremony came from the box drum, a large instrument made in much the same way as a bentwood box, but painted differently. Slender in width and open at one end, the drum was sometimes suspended by ropes from a house beam, and the drummer, his fists wrapped in shredded cedar bark, pounded out the beat for the dancers. In another method, he kneeled on the floor, leaned the drum against his left thigh and beat time with his fists. The awesome sound of the box drum added much to the excitement of the dramatic enactments of the Winter Ceremonials.

Making a The skill of the Northwest Coast wood-
Bentwood Box worker revealed itself in the best of the bentwood boxes and chests. Meticulous measuring ensured that the wooden container would have even sides, vertical corners, a flat base and a lid that fit with exactness. Without ruler, set square or compass, the box-maker used his own system of geometry for measuring and calculating. By studying the many boxes and chests in museums and other collections, it is clear that artisans devised a variety of ways for joining a box corner. So, too, they undoubtedly followed various procedures for boxmaking; the following gives a general outline of box construction by a Kwakiutl.

After splitting a plank from a felled red cedar tree, the boxmaker painstakingly prepared it for evenness of

BOX DRUM _ MYTHICAL SEA-BEAR DESIGN.
97·5 cm [38½"] TL 15

BOX DRUM _ BEAR DESIGN.
91·2 cm. [36"] TL 16

BOX DRUM RESTED AGAINST DRUMMER'S
THIGH — OR SUSPENDED FROM ROOF BEAM —
BEATEN WITH FISTS WRAPPED IN CEDAR
BARK. KW 75/2

length, width and thickness, using measuring sticks that each represented a given measurement of the box. He made sure that all corners and edges of the plank were perfectly true, and that the plank had a smooth, finished surface. Using measuring sticks and a straight-edge, he calculated where the corners of the box should be and scored vertical lines on the wood. Half a finger-width to the right of each line, he scored another line; between each pair of lines, he cut a kerf. The kerfs had to be precise and without slivers. In addition, he sometimes grooved the wood on the reverse side of the kerf to facilitate bending.

The next step was to steam the plank. In the earthen floor of his house, close to the fire, the woodworker dug three narrow pits to correspond in length and spacing to the kerfs on the board. With wooden tongs, he lifted out small, heated stones from the fire and placed them in the pits. He covered the stones with dulse and dead eelgrass, filling the pits to overflowing, then poured water into each pit. As clouds of steam rose, he placed the board down, ensuring that each kerf was over a pit. Over each groove on the reverse side of the kerfs, he placed seaweed, a row of hot stones and more seaweed, before adding water. As the steam permeated the wood, the thinned areas of the board eventually softened.

When the boxmaker thought the board was ready, he removed all the seaweed and rocks. Working quickly, he moved the board to a flat area of the floor and slipped the "board protector" over one end of the plank. Near the edge of the first kerf he placed a length of cedar wood across the plank's width, so that part of it extended over each side. Standing over the board, with one foot on each end of the crosspiece, he then took the ends of the board protector in his hands and carefully drew it upwards, bending the plank at the kerf. This was the crucial part: the wood could crack, break or not bend sufficiently if the kerfing and steaming had not been properly done. He attended to trouble spots in the kerfs with a sharp knife, making sure the grooves were cleanly cut to allow perfect bending.

After he had bent the wood to a ninety-degree angle, and the kerf folded over onto itself (or closed up, depending on the type of kerf), the boxmaker removed the board protector and slid it over the other end of the plank. He bent the middle kerf and then the third kerf in

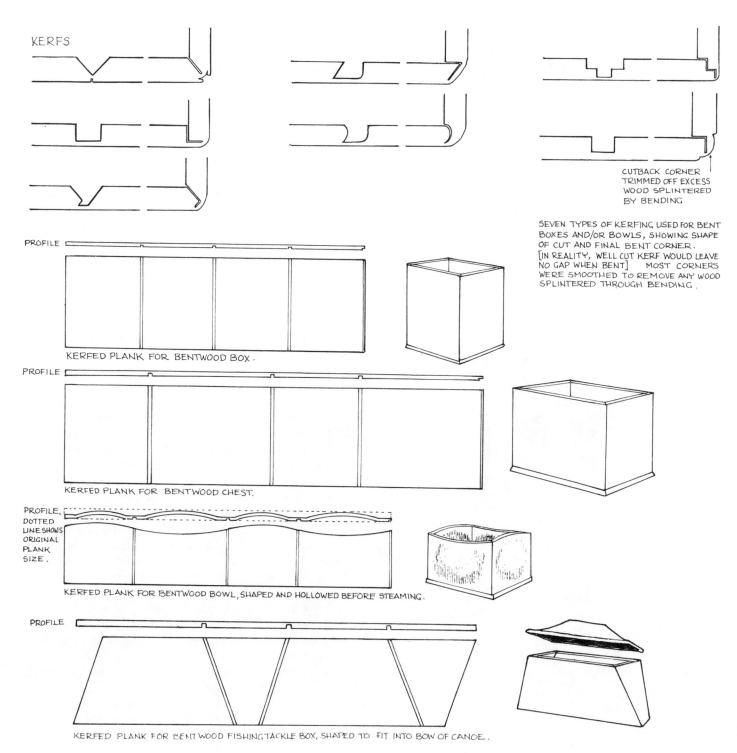

KERFS

CUTBACK CORNER
TRIMMED OFF EXCESS
WOOD SPLINTERED
BY BENDING

SEVEN TYPES OF KERFING USED FOR BENT
BOXES AND/OR BOWLS, SHOWING SHAPE
OF CUT AND FINAL BENT CORNER.
[IN REALITY, WELL CUT KERF WOULD LEAVE
NO GAP WHEN BENT]   MOST CORNERS
WERE SMOOTHED TO REMOVE ANY WOOD
SPLINTERED THROUGH BENDING.

PROFILE

KERFED PLANK FOR BENTWOOD BOX.

PROFILE

KERFED PLANK FOR BENTWOOD CHEST.

PROFILE.
DOTTED
LINE SHOWS
ORIGINAL
PLANK
SIZE.

KERFED PLANK FOR BENTWOOD BOWL, SHAPED AND HOLLOWED BEFORE STEAMING.

PROFILE

KERFED PLANK FOR BENTWOOD FISHING TACKLE BOX, SHAPED TO FIT INTO BOW OF CANOE.

STEPS IN FORMING A BENTWOOD BOX. KW *34

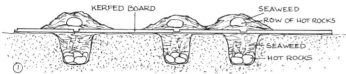

KERFED BOARD

SEAWEED
ROW OF HOT ROCKS

SEAWEED
HOT ROCKS

① STEAM PITS FOR SOFTENING KERFS CUT INTO BOARD_ WATER WAS POURED ONTO ROCKS IN PITS AND ABOVE KERFS.

② BENDING BOARD AT FIRST KERF, USING BOARD PROTECTOR. PRESSURE OF MAN'S WEIGHT ON CROSSPIECE ALONG EDGE OF KERF PREVENTED IT FROM BREAKING.

BOARD PROTECTOR

③ STEAMBENDING NEARLY COMPLETED.

④ TWO STICKS ACROSS CORNERS ENSURED BOX HAD 90° ANGLES_ ROPE HELD SIDES IN POSITION UNTIL WOOD COOLED.

⑤ CORNER DRILLED AND SEWN WITH CEDAR WITHE OR PEGGED.
⑥ BASE FITTED AND SECURED BY DIAGONAL PEGGING.

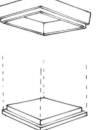

DIAGRAM SHOWING FORM OF BASE AND LID.

METHODS OF JOINING BENTBOX CORNERS

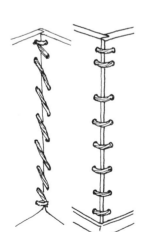

HORIZONTAL SEWING
LEFT: INSIDE OF BOX.
RIGHT: OUTSIDE OF BOX.

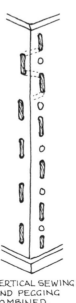

VERTICAL SEWING AND PEGGING COMBINED.

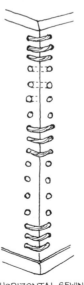

HORIZONTAL SEWING AND PEGGING ALTERNATED.

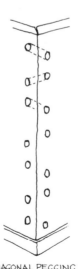

DIAGONAL PEGGING

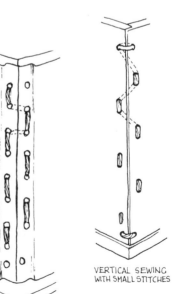

VERTICAL SEWING, WITH PEGS DRIVEN IN TO TIGHTEN STITCHES.

VERTICAL SEWING WITH SMALL STITCHES

the same way, leaving only a single fitted corner to be joined. Taking a length of cedar bark rope previously soaked in water, he wrapped it several times around the bent plank to prevent it from springing open or warping. With the rope in place, he drilled a hole diagonally through the open corner. Taking a slender, pointed peg of yellow cedar (or some other wood harder than the red cedar of the box), he moistened it with saliva and drove it into the drillhole. At intervals of three finger-widths, he drilled other holes, alternating diagonal directions, and drove in pegs. As an alternative to pegging, the box-maker could use cedar withes to sew the corner together, drilling holes two finger-widths apart.

After careful measuring, he fitted a bottom to the box, pegging it on with diagonally drilled holes. Finally, he fitted and shaped the lid so that its inside lip sat comfortably within the box rim. If he was also a good artist, he painted a design on the four sides using, as a rule, red and black paints. To add to the value of the box, he might carve the design in low relief, setting off the painted areas to advantage, as well as decorate the outer rim of the lid with inlaid opercula or sea otter teeth.

Contemporary native artists have revived the skills of making bentwood boxes and these are, as previously, valuable and highly prized by their owners.

PLANKS AND BOARDS Cedar planks — straight, broad and lightweight — provided Northwest Coast inhabitants with a near-perfect building material for their housing needs. They also used planks and boards in a number of other ways. For dance performances, initiation ceremonies, a girl's puberty ceremony and other special occasions, large boards were joined together to form a huge screen, which had an elaborate family crest painted on it. This screen formed a backdrop to the event and also gave the dancers a place to change masks and costumes out of the audience's sight. The dance house had a separate room at the rear for this, constructed of planks, which was strictly out of bounds for the uninitiated.

On certain ceremonial occasions, a northern chief sat with grandeur in an extravagantly carved and/or painted seat. Constructed from wide boards, this legless seat, sometimes called a settee, was placed on the platform at the rear of the house — the most honoured place.

Inside Westcoast houses, partitions made of boards

WOMAN STRETCHED SEA OTTER SKIN OVER CEDAR BOARD, PEGGING OR TYING IT DOWN FOR SCRAPING. WC ✱ 43

FISH-DRYING RACK OVER FAMILY HEARTH — SPLIT CEDAR PLANKS PLACED OVER FRAMEWORK. WC ✱ 43

often formed sleeping compartments against which people could lean, facing into the house, during the day. Wide boards placed across poles or logs formed beds for those who did not sleep directly on the plank platforms. To store fish and other dried foods, householders suspended boards, above head height, with rope from the beams and rafters. This not only kept provisions safe from dogs and insects but prevented them from becoming mouldy because the rising warmth of the fire kept the food dry.

To help keep the house warm, a wide cedar board was placed over the open doorway. If a weaver lived in the house, she might have a pattern board for a Chilkat

A well-known Tsimshian dance screen, with a dragonfly design, originally made of four long planks joined horizontally. Courtesy National Museums of Canada, 62244

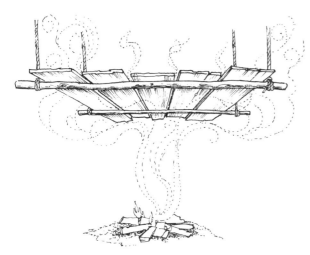

PLANKS SUSPENDED OVER FIRE IN SMOKEHOUSE HELPED
SPREAD SMOKE AND HEAT MORE EVENLY, PLANKS APPROX.
1·2 m [4'] LONG. WC ✳43

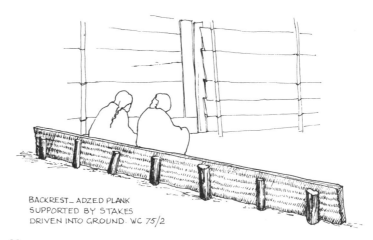

BACKREST_ADZED PLANK
SUPPORTED BY STAKES
DRIVEN INTO GROUND. WC 75/2

PLANK SHELF FOR FOOD STORAGE
HUNG FROM ROOF BEAMS WITH CEDAR BARK ROPE. CS *53

CHIEF'S SETTEE, SET ON HOUSE PLATFORM,
OCCUPIED BY CHIEF ON CERTAIN CEREMONIAL
OCCASIONS. CARVED AND PAINTED DESIGN
ATTRIBUTED TO CHARLES EDENSHAW. 1·36 m [4'5½"]
HA 2

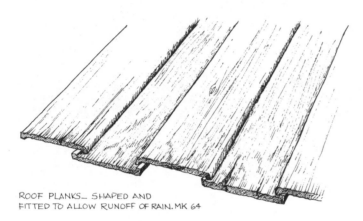

ROOF PLANKS—SHAPED AND
FITTED TO ALLOW RUNOFF OF RAIN. MK 64

PATTERN BOARD COMPOSED OF THREE PLANKS, HAVING
LITTLE MORE THAN HALF THE PATTERN FOR CHILKAT
BLANKET. WEAVER COPIED DESIGN, REVERSING IT FOR
OPPOSITE HALF. THIS BOARD USED FOR BLANKET ON
PAGE 151, BUT NOTE OCCASIONAL DEVIATIONS. 95 cm [37⅜"]
TL 31 COURTESY BILL AND MARTY HOLM.

PLANK DRUM. SEVERAL PEOPLE WITH WOOD
BATONS BEAT OUT A RHYTHM IN UNISON KW *52

PLANK DRUM WITH UNUSUAL
DESIGN. 3·05 m [10'] CS 12

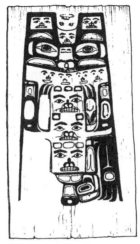

PATTERN BOARD FOR CHILKAT
TUNIC, WITH BEAR DESIGN.
1.22 m [48"] TL 16

ONE LONG PLANK ACROSS THREE CANOES FORMED STAGE FOR
LARGE GROUP OF DANCERS. KW 75/12

HOUSE PLANKS LASHED BETWEEN TWO CANOES TO MAKE
EXTRA SPACE FOR FREIGHT. WC 54

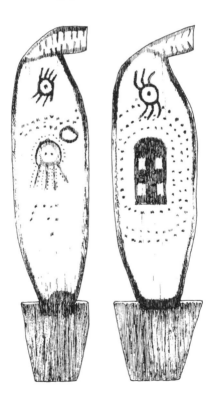

SPIRIT BOARDS, CUT FROM CEDAR
PLANKS AND PAINTED – USED IN SPIRIT
CANOE CEREMONY, AN ELABORATE
RITUAL FOR CURING THE SICK.
APPROX. 1.7 m [5'8"] CS 12

HINGED POWER BOARDS
USED IN DRAMATIZED
CEREMONIALS.
2.66 m [8'9"] KW 52

PLANK PLACED ACROSS
CANOE GUNWALES TO
FORM PLATFORM FOR
CEREMONIAL DANCER
ON ARRIVAL AT VILLAGE.
[WASP DANCE] KW 75/2

95

blanket. Although women skilled in this type of weaving prepared the materials and wove the complex blankets, tradition held that the men should create the designs. On a large, smooth cedar plank the artist painted half of the symmetrical pattern for the weaver to copy; she reversed the design to complete the other half of the blanket or garment.

The Kwakiutl used power boards as part of special performances in the winter ceremonial dances. Tall and slender, carrying painted and perforated designs, the boards were joined together with hinges so that they could give the appearance of growing taller and taller, eventually diminishing with an undulating movement. They represented a supernatural creature, most likely Sisiutl, a being of great power and potential danger for anyone who looked upon it.

A Coast Salish shaman used a different kind of board in a major curing ceremony that enacted a spirit journey undertaken to retrieve a patient's lost soul. Painted to represent mythical beings, spirit boards were set up to form a canoe, while the shaman and his spirit assistants (who were represented by carved figures) stood within and symbolically paddled to the Land of the Dead. When eventually the lost soul was recovered, the shaman turned the lead plank of the spirit canoe from north to south and paddled homeward to restore the patient's soul to him. Should it be necessary to move a sick or injured person, a strong plank was used as a stretcher.

Boards and planks played a versatile and practical part in canoeing. People fitted boards to the bottom of the inside of a canoe (leaving a space open for bailing) to keep their possessions or freight dry. They also lashed strong planks across the gunwales of two canoes to provide extra carrying capacity, such as might be required by families returning from the salmon fishing grounds, and to provide additional stability for the loaded canoes. The Kwakiutl placed planks across the gunwales of a single, large canoe to form a platform for the offshore ceremonial dances and speechmaking they performed when arriving at a village for a special occasion. Some canoe owners rigged their craft with sails, an idea borrowed from early sailing ships. Although some peoples used matting for sails, others, such as the Quinault Coast Salish, stepped a short mast lashed to a thwart and used thin horizontal boards sewn together for a wooden sail, set at right angles to the canoe. At journey's end, when a canoe was taken ashore, planks instead of mats might be used to cover the craft to protect it from the sun or to prevent it from filling with rain.

Although most peoples had elaborate burials for those of high rank, they had simple customs for commoners. The Haida built a platform of planks on top of a single or double pole and deposited the body on this, covering it with moss or stones, while the Westcoast people wrapped the body of a commoner in a mat, placed it on a plank and lashed it to the branches of a tree.

To facilitate the raising of a pole or post, a plank was placed upright at the back of the hole into which the pole was to go. As the pole was raised, its heel, positioned over the hole, slid down the board, ensuring that the base of the pole went to the bottom of the hole without difficulty. This simple but effective technique is still used for raising new poles.

OTHER EVERYDAY USES Cedar wood provided material not only for housing, canoes, poles, boxes and chests but also for a host of additional items that met the needs of daily life.

Canoeists had slender cedar poles for pushing their dugouts upriver or pushing off from a beach, and also had paddles that were often carved from yellow cedar. Some Haida carvers used yellow cedar for the handles of their adzes. Along the coast, women had digging sticks, also of yellow cedar, with which to dig up clams, roots and bulbs or to pry shellfish from rocks.

Fishermen made simple wooden floats for their fish nets or carved elaborate floats in the form of birds and animals to support their halibut fishing lines. They also used cedar slats to make lattice fences for fish weirs and large basketlike structures for trapping large quantities of fish. Both fishermen and hunters had long shafts of lightweight cedar for their spears and harpoons. Salish hunters used pliable yellow cedar saplings to make bows, which they often traded to inland peoples who did not have ready access to that wood. They made straight, lightweight shafts of red cedar for their arrows, which they kept in quivers made from blocks of hollowed-out cedar.

Cedar sticks made good kindling and, while cedar wood burned too fast for general cooking fires, it did

CANOE BAILER . 24 cm [9½"] WC 2

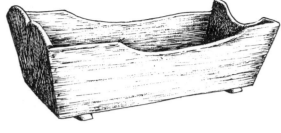

CHILD'S CRADLE – DESIGN AND MANUFACTURE INFLUENCED
BY EUROPEAN CONTACT . 95.2 cm [37½"] KW 9

CEDAR CANOE BAILER . 25.2cm [10"] WC 9

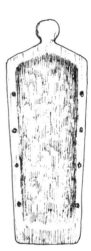

CRADLE FOR SMALL
BABY. DRILLED HOLES
HELD THONGING FOR
SECURING INFANT.
CS 60

GROUND SLATE KNIFE , WITH
CEDAR WOOD HAFT – WOMAN'S
KNIFE USED MOSTLY FOR FISH.
12.8 cm [5"] CS 31

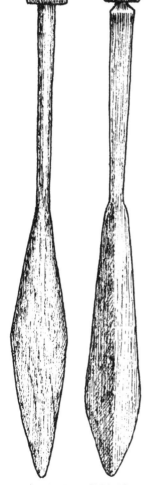

PORCUPINE HAIRS SET INTO SPLIT
WOOD LASHED WITH SINEW OR
CEDAR BARK TWINE –

PAINT BRUSHES WITH CEDAR HANDLES – 26 cm [10¼"] HA 3

YELLOW CEDAR PADDLES.
LEFT. 1.52 m [5'] NWC 9
RIGHT. 1.52 m [5'] TS 31

DIGGING STICK – OCCASIONALLY OF CEDAR,
THOUGH GENERALLY OF A HARDER WOOD –
USED BY WOMEN FOR DIGGING BULBS, ROOTS.
NWC

TORCH USED WHEN DIGGING CLAMS ON LOW TIDE
AT NIGHT, MADE OF CEDAR STICK SPLIT AT ONE END
TO HOLD CEDAR BARK AND SPRUCE PITCH. WC ✕ 66

prove suitable for curing and smoking hides, as it contained little pitch. Women used wooden skewers to cook pieces of meat, fish or clams; they pierced the food through with one end of the skewer and pushed the other end into the ground so that it leaned towards the fire. To barbecue salmon over a fire, they set the fish into a split cedar stake and spread out the succulent flesh with slender cedar sticks.

Slats of split cedar were lashed together to make drying racks of different kinds for fish, herring roe and berries. The posts and crossbars of the southern two-bar loom, used in weaving wool blankets, were also cedar.

The peoples of the Northwest Coast were fond of games, and cedar often supplied the material with which to create them. Women played a game using cedar sticks a little thinner than a pencil; while blindfolded, they had to drop as many sticks as they could through a small ring

CEDAR SAPLING POLES FOR POLING CANOE UP RIVER. TS 75/12

NORTHERN TYPE HALIBUT HOOK,
SET WITH LINE, SINKER AND FLOAT.
CARVED ARM OF YEW WOOD,
BARBED SHANK OF YELLOW CEDAR.
28 cm [11"] TL 31 COURTESY JOHN
HAUBERG.

TACKLE BOX, CARVED FROM SINGLE
BLOCK OF CEDAR. 25·3 cm [10"] WC 4

CANOE BOX CARVED FROM CEDAR, WITH SLOPING ENDS TO
FIT BOW OR STERN OF CANOE. 33 cm [13"] WC 2

COD LURE – PUSHED
DOWN INTO DEEP
WATER, RISING LURE
WAS FOLLOWED TO
SURFACE BY CURIOUS
COD, WHICH WAS THEN
SPEARED. 34·5 cm [13½"]
KW 12

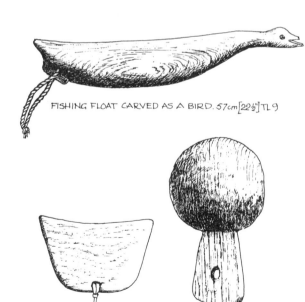

FISHING FLOAT CARVED AS A BIRD. 57 cm [22½"] TL 9

FISHING FLOATS
OF CEDAR

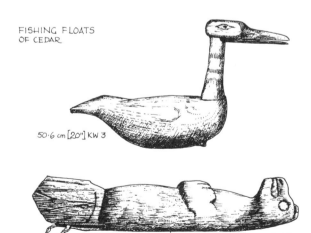

50·6 cm [20"] KW 3

FLOAT CARVED TO REPRESENT SEA OTTER. 47 cm [18½"]
KW 3

20·3 cm [8"] NWC 13

34·2 cm [13½"] NWC 1

25·3 cm [10"] WC 9

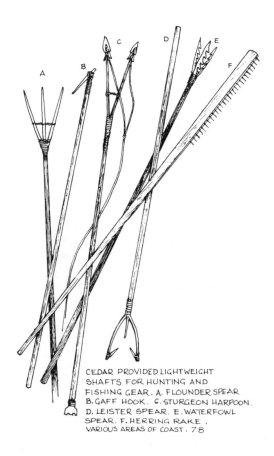

CEDAR PROVIDED LIGHTWEIGHT
SHAFTS FOR HUNTING AND
FISHING GEAR. A. FLOUNDER SPEAR
B. GAFF HOOK. C. STURGEON HARPOON.
D. LEISTER SPEAR. E. WATERFOWL
SPEAR. F. HERRING RAKE.
VARIOUS AREAS OF COAST. 78

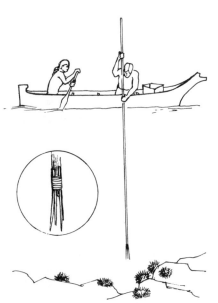

SPEAR FOR TAKING LARGE RED SEA
URCHINS – CEDAR SHAFT 3·6 m [12'] LONG
OR MORE, WITH FOUR POINTED YEW
WOOD PRONGS LASHED AT END. WC ✳ 66

LATTICE FENCING FOR SALMON
WEIR – SPLIT CEDAR STICKS
LASHED WITH CEDAR WITHES.
APPROX. 1·2 m [4'] CS 56

FUR SEAL HARPOON HEAD WITH
PROTECTIVE CASE. 20·3 cm [8"] HA 2

FISH CLUB OF
CEDAR. 45·6 cm
[18"] WC 9

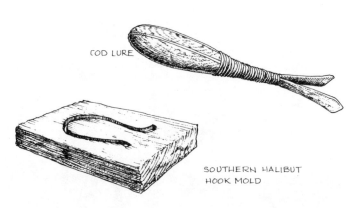

COD LURE

SOUTHERN HALIBUT
HOOK MOLD

ALONG ALL AREAS OF COAST, MANY ITEMS OF FISHING GEAR
WERE MADE OF CEDAR. 78

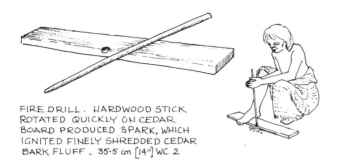

FIRE DRILL. HARDWOOD STICK
ROTATED QUICKLY ON CEDAR
BOARD PRODUCED SPARK, WHICH
IGNITED FINELY SHREDDED CEDAR
BARK FLUFF. 35·5 cm [14"] WC 2

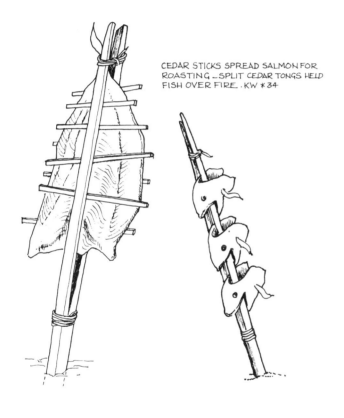

CEDAR STICKS SPREAD SALMON FOR
ROASTING — SPLIT CEDAR TONGS HELD
FISH OVER FIRE. KW *34

ARROWS WITH SHAFTS OF CEDAR — LONGEST 86 cm [34"] NWC 4

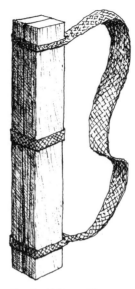

QUIVER — MADE FROM
BLOCK OF CEDAR, SPLIT
AND HOLLOWED OUT —
BOUND WITH BRAIDED
CEDAR BARK. 1·2 m [4'] WC 43

QUIVER OF SPLIT
CEDAR WOOD. 92 cm
[36"] TL 21

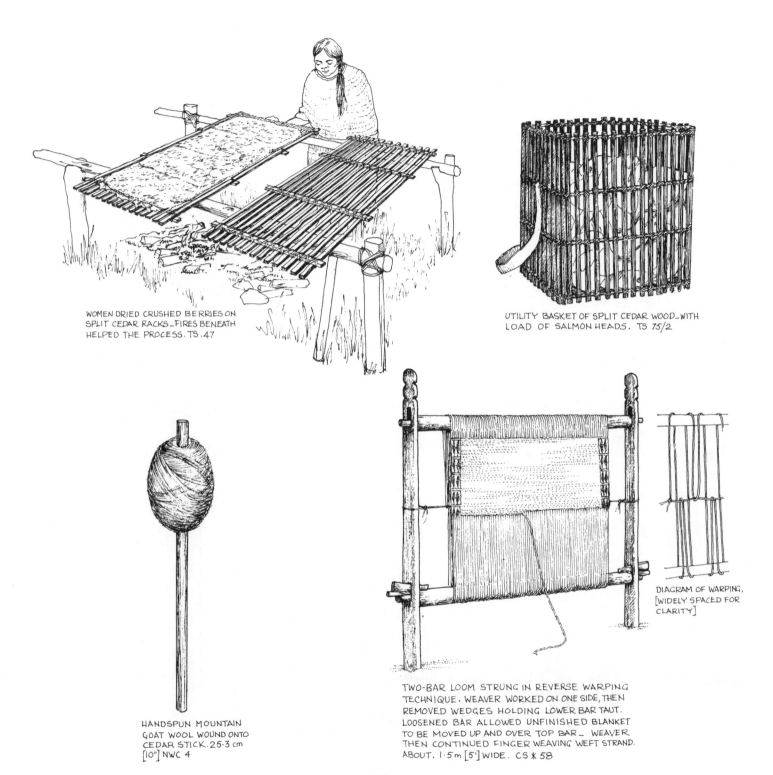

WOMEN DRIED CRUSHED BERRIES ON
SPLIT CEDAR RACKS — FIRES BENEATH
HELPED THE PROCESS. TS .47

UTILITY BASKET OF SPLIT CEDAR WOOD — WITH
LOAD OF SALMON HEADS. TS 75/2

HANDSPUN MOUNTAIN
GOAT WOOL WOUND ONTO
CEDAR STICK. 25.3 cm
[10"] NWC 4

TWO-BAR LOOM STRUNG IN REVERSE WARPING
TECHNIQUE. WEAVER WORKED ON ONE SIDE, THEN
REMOVED WEDGES HOLDING LOWER BAR TAUT.
LOOSENED BAR ALLOWED UNFINISHED BLANKET
TO BE MOVED UP AND OVER TOP BAR — WEAVER
THEN CONTINUED FINGER WEAVING WEFT STRAND.
ABOUT. 1.5m [5'] WIDE. CS * 58

DIAGRAM OF WARPING,
[WIDELY SPACED FOR
CLARITY]

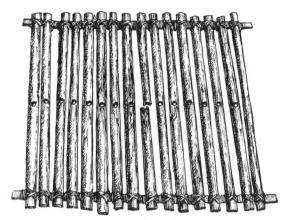

LOOM FOR WEAVING TUMPLINES. CEDAR WOOD
SLATS LASHED WITH CEDAR ROOT. 30·5cm [12"] KW 2.

BASKET FRAME – GAVE CEDAR BARK AND GRASS BASKETS
STRAIGHT, EVEN SIDES, AND HELPED WEAVER WHILE
MAKING INTRICATE DESIGNS 45cm [17¾"] WC 2

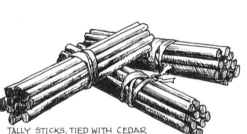

TALLY STICKS, TIED WITH CEDAR
BARK IN BUNDLES OF TEN, TO
KEEP SCORE IN GAMBLING GAMES.
STICKS 11·4 cm [4½"] KW 12

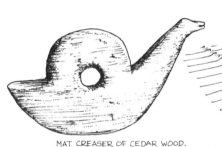

MAT CREASER OF CEDAR WOOD.
17cm [6¾"] CS 9

USED FOR CRIMPING CATTAILS AND TULE
REEDS IN MAKING MAT. GROOVE ON
UNDERSIDE OF CREASER FITTED OVER
TRIANGULAR MAT NEEDLE. CS 53

GAME GENERALLY PLAYED
BY WOMEN – BLINDFOLDED
PLAYER TRIED TO DROP
CEDAR STICKS INTO TARGET
RING. KW * 36

CEDAR BARK AND SWAMP GRASS
BASKET WOVEN OVER WOODEN
FRAME OF DIFFERENT TYPE. WC * 76

attached to a stick driven into the ground. Another game, played by a girl or a woman, used a small bat made from a thin piece of cedar board; the player batted a shuttlecock of feathers attached to a piece of thimbleberry stem to see how long she could keep it going. Tally sticks used in gambling games were also cedar.

This short review of some of these additional everyday uses for cedar wood is by no means complete, but it should give the reader some idea of the wide variety of roles it played in the daily life of those who depended so much upon it.

OTHER CEREMONIAL USES   Throughout spring, summer and fall, many coast peoples were at their summer villages and camps, fishing, hunting, gathering and preserving food. With the onset of shorter days and longer nights, they returned to the security of their winter villages in sheltered waters. It was the sacred time of the Winter Ceremonials, when supernatural spirits drew close and made their presence known. The sacred winter dances took different forms among the many nations and tribes of the coast, but the Kwakiutl developed their ceremonials to the most elaborate and complex degree. Staged with all manner of masks, costumes, and theatrical props and tricks to enhance the telling of the legends, the dances and dramatics impressed spectators with the power of the supernatural spirits and the mysticism of their world. Lengthy ceremonies also initiated new members into special dance societies.

Among all the villages of the coast, family histories and legends were re-enacted through the use of masks depicting birds, animals, supernatural beings and family ancestors. Because the masks of some of the mythical creatures were of enormous size, lightweight cedar provided the ideal material for their construction. Some masks had lengthy beaks that the dancer opened and snapped shut; some appeared to magically transform from bird to human form in a split second, a feat accomplished by the two halves of an outer mask swinging open — like cupboard doors — to reveal a second mask inside. Some masks had several segments that opened up when the dancer manipulated a complex system of connected strings. Others, also very large, were carried on the wearer's head, rather than his face, and supported by his bent back.

HELMET REPRESENTING WOLF, POSSIBLY OF YELLOW CEDAR, LIKELY USED ONLY AS CREST HAT. 42 cm [16¼"] LONG. HA 12

HEAD MASK OF WOLF — USED IN CEREMONIAL WOLF DANCE 51·3 cm [20¼"] WC 15

HEAD MASK — KILLER WHALE WITH EAGLE. JAWS, FINS AND TAIL ARE MOVABLE AND WERE MANIPULATED WITH STRINGS BY THE DANCER. 1·20 m [47¼"] KW 23

LARGE STURGEON HEAD MASK RESTED ON DANCER'S SHOULDERS AND BACK. HINGED TAIL AND FINS MOVED WHEN DANCER PULLED STRINGS. 1·88 m [6'2"] KW 4

SPECTACULAR CROOKED BEAK MASK USED IN WINTER CEREMONIAL DANCES, CARVED BY WILLIE SEAWEED. LIGHT WEIGHT OF CEDAR MADE SUCH LARGE MASKS MANAGEABLE. 94 cm [37"] KW 2

HUMAN FACE MASK, WITH GEOMETRIC DESIGNS TYPICAL OF WESTCOAST LATE 19 th. CENTURY MASKS. 39·5 [15¼"] WC 2

MASK OF "WEALTHY ONE", CHIEF OF THE UNDERSEA WORLD. 40 cm [15¾"] KW 15

MASK OF MYTHICAL CREATURE HOKHOKW. DANCER OPENED AND CLOSED HINGED LOWER BEAK. CEDAR BARK FRINGE COVERED WEARER'S TORSO. 2·13 m [7'] KW 3

DOUBLE MASK REPRESENTING MYTHICAL RAVEN AND CROOKED BEAK, TRIMMED WITH SHREDDED CEDAR BARK. 1·88 m [6'2"] WC 2

MINIATURE MASK
ATTACHED TO SHAMAN'S
HEADDRESS, WORN
WHILE EXORCISING EVIL
SPIRITS FROM THE SICK.
YELLOW CEDAR, HUMAN HAIR.
10.1 cm [4"] TL 21

SMALL FIGURE USED BY
SHAMAN TO HELP EFFECT
CURES. YELLOW CEDAR AND
HUMAN HAIR. 37cm [14½"] TL 31
COURTESY JOHN HAUBERG

FIGURES REPRESENTING SHAMAN'S HELPER
STOOD UPRIGHT IN GROUND – USED IN SPIRIT
CANOE CEREMONY TO CURE THE SICK.
LEFT. 72.4 cm [28½"] RIGHT. 1.22 m [4'] CS 12

SHAMAN'S SPIRIT FIGURE.
23.5 cm [9¼"] TL 9

SOUL CATCHER – USED BY SHAMAN TO CURE PATIENT SUFFERING FROM ILLNESS CAUSED
BY SOUL LOSS. THOUGH USUALLY OF BONE, THIS ONE CARVED FROM CEDAR. 29cm [11¾"] NWC 4

YELLOW CEDAR RATTLE IN
FORM OF BEAR'S FOOT, WITH
HUMAN FACE ON UNDERSIDE
29·2 cm [11½"] TL 21

RATTLE USED IN
CHILD'S NAMING
CEREMONY.
67·3 cm [26½"] KW 9

RATTLE CARVED FROM BLOCK OF CEDAR, SPLIT AND
HOLLOWED OUT TO RECIEVE SMALL PEBBLES. 43·2 cm
[17"] WC 16

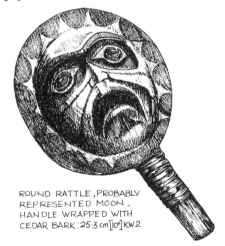

ROUND RATTLE, PROBABLY
REPRESENTED MOON.
HANDLE WRAPPED WITH
CEDAR BARK. 25·3 cm [10"] KW 2

Full appreciation of a mask's mystic power can only come through experiencing the carved image in its proper context — by firelight, on a costumed dancer circling the central hearth of a plank house. To witness the dramatic and characteristic movements of the bird or animal portrayed and to hear the pounding of drums and the chant-like songs is to sense the power of the mask and feel the heartbeat of a great culture.

Most portrait and other small, northern masks were carved from alder, maple and birch, but a very few were of cedar. Carvers among the Westcoast people often split a round of red or yellow cedar to a wedge, and allowed the grain of this triangular shape to influence the design of the mask.

A prestigious type of ceremonial headdress was the wooden hat of the northern peoples, carved in the shape of a crest animal, beautifully painted and often inlaid with abalone shell, sometimes with ermine skins falling from the top of the crown. Wearing a crested button blanket with such a hat, a high-ranking person presented an image of great dignity and wealth. Although generally carved from hardwoods, these were occasionally made of yellow cedar.

Similarly, a "frontlet," the often exquisitely carved plaque at the front of a northern chief's dance headdress, was occasionally made of yellow cedar. Generally inlaid with bright blue-green abalone shell, the frontlet was attached to a headband surmounted by walrus whiskers, sometimes with red-shafted flicker feathers adding to the colour. In addition, ermine pelts cascaded down the sides of the headdress, and occasionally, for a chief of great wealth and high rank, all the way down his back. He wore this on special occasions, such as when dancing to welcome important guests to his house or a feast.

Festive and initiation ceremonies, in addition to those performed by a shaman for curing the sick, calling the salmon to return upstream and on many other occasions, usually included the use of rattles. Created from a wide assortment of materials — pecten shells, puffin beaks, deer hooves, hollowed wood and pebbles — rattles were of many different types. Simple bird-form rattles used by Westcoast people were often made of yellow cedar.

During the War Spirit Dance of the Kwakiutl Winter Ceremonials, a clapper was used in place of the rattle. This generally consisted of a slab of cedar carved to shape and split down the centre; one of the halves was hollowed out at one end. With the two halves lashed together, one half hinged to give flexibility, the instrument was worked by the dancer to produce a resonant, clapping sound.

A variety of single-note whistles, and others with two and three notes, were used to create the sounds of supernatural and spirit creatures. A dancer often concealed a whistle in his costume and even hid a very small one in his mouth, blowing it as he danced. The presence of the spirits about the village, in the weeks prior to the start of the Winter Ceremonials, was manifested by whistling sounds emanating from the nearby forest. Another instrument that produced an eerie, fluttering sound was the bullroarer, a slat of wood attached by a thong to a stick and whirled around the head.

The dancer's staff or wand had a necessary function during the dances. With this long, decorated, paddlelike piece of cedar wood, a man had the task of guiding the masked dancers (who often had difficulty in seeing where they were going) away from the fire and the audience.

Another ceremonial item held in the hand and sometimes carved from yellow cedar was the Speaker's staff. The man appointed as the Speaker carried this staff as his badge of office as he proclaimed the arrival of guests, the gifts given out at a potlatch, the dances to be performed and various other announcements at the behest of the host.

Food played a major part in any important occasion, and enormous feast dishes, carved from a large block of wood into the form of an animal, held great quantities of prepared foods for huge numbers of guests. Women used very large ladles to transfer the food into medium-sized serving dishes, then carried these around to the guests, using smaller ladles to serve out portions into the guests' individual bowls.

In an altogether different ceremonial use of the cedar, the Makah burned the wood and used the ash in ritual face painting — a gesture that may have been a symbolic incorporation of the powerful spirit of the cedar.

CLAPPER 25.3 cm [10"] NWC 9

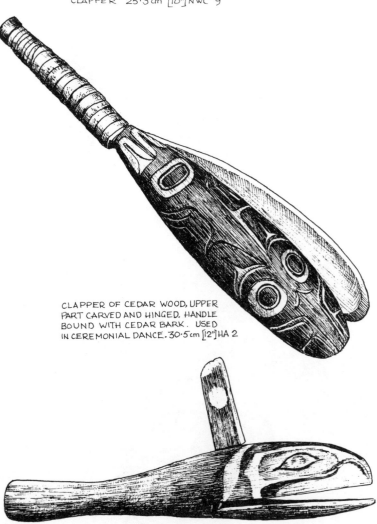

CLAPPER OF CEDAR WOOD, UPPER PART CARVED AND HINGED. HANDLE BOUND WITH CEDAR BARK. USED IN CEREMONIAL DANCE. 30.5 cm [12"] HA 2

CLAPPER IN FORM OF KILLER WHALE. LOWER JAW HINGED 28.5 cm [11¼"] KW 3

FISH-SHAPED WHISTLE. 36·8 cm [14½"] KW 9

SMALL WHISTLE WITH
FOUR DIFFERENT NOTES.
16 cm [6¼"] KW 9

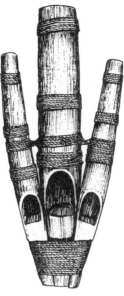

THREE-TONE WHISTLE,
CEDAR SPLIT, HOLLOWED
AND LASHED TOGETHER
WITH STRING. 33 cm [13"]
KW 3

BULLROARER, SWUNG RAPIDLY
THROUGH THE AIR, PRODUCED
WHIRRING SOUND OF SPIRITS.
STICK 47 cm [18½"] MK 12

HORN WITH INCISED
DESIGN. 44·4 cm [17½"] KW 3

WHISTLE WITH TWO CHAMBERS,
AN OPENING ON EACH SIDE.
62 cm [24½"] KW 21

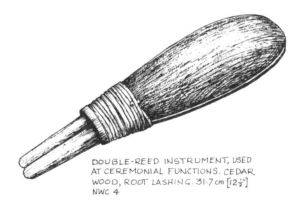

DOUBLE-REED INSTRUMENT, USED
AT CEREMONIAL FUNCTIONS. CEDAR
WOOD, ROOT LASHING. 31·7 cm [12⅓"]
NWC 4

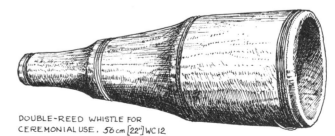

DOUBLE-REED WHISTLE FOR
CEREMONIAL USE. 56 cm [22"] WC 12

CEREMONIAL STAFF.
CARVED AND PAINTED,
INLAID WITH ABALONE.
YELLOW CEDAR, HUMAN
HAIR FRINGE. 1·35cm
[53"] TL. 31. COURTESY
BILL AND MARTY HOLM

SPEAKER'S STAFF.
TWO HOLLOW PIECES
OF CEDAR WITH
PEBBLES INSIDE.
1·43m [56½"] KW? 29

SPEAKER'S STAFF.
INLAID WITH ABALONE,
HELD BY PERSON
MAKING A SPEECH
DURING CEREMONY.
1·19 m [47"] KW 9

FEAST DISH IN FORM OF RECLINING HUMAN. 1·95 m [6'4"] KW 21

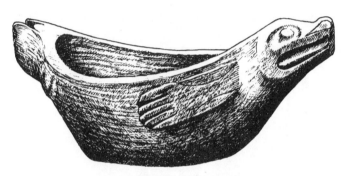

FEAST BOWL CARVED IN FORM OF SEAL 86cm [33⅞"] NWC 4

LARGE AND IMPRESSIVE FEAST DISH, CARVED TO REPRESENT
A WOLF. 3 12m [10'3"] LONG. KW 3

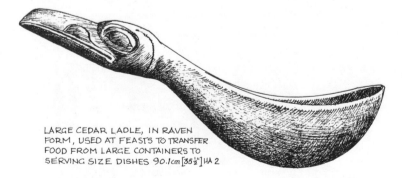

LARGE CEDAR LADLE, IN RAVEN
FORM, USED AT FEASTS TO TRANSFER
FOOD FROM LARGE CONTAINERS TO
SERVING SIZE DISHES 90.1cm [35½"] HA 2

LARGE FEAST DISH IN FORM OF SEAL. 2·18 m [7'2"] KW 3

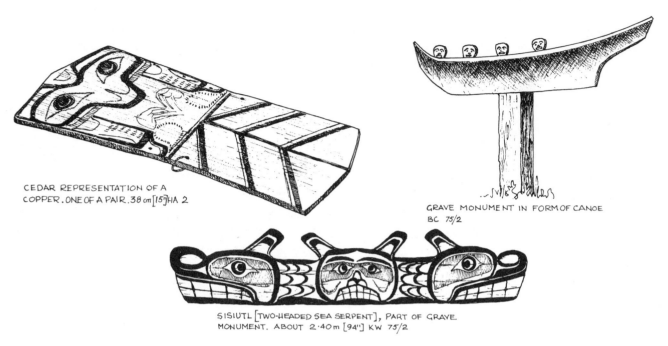

CEDAR REPRESENTATION OF A
COPPER. ONE OF A PAIR. 38 cm [15"] HA 2

GRAVE MONUMENT IN FORM OF CANOE
BC 75/2

SISIUTL [TWO-HEADED SEA SERPENT], PART OF GRAVE
MONUMENT. ABOUT 2·40 m [94"] KW 75/2

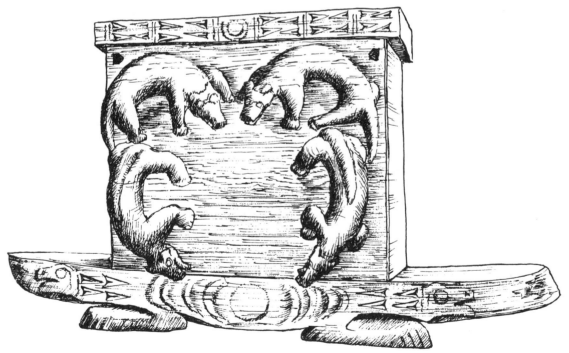

FAMILY TOMB HELD THREE MEMBERS OF ONE FAMILY — FRONT PANEL CARVED WITH FOUR ANIMALS REPRESENTING
FISHERS. PEDESTAL CARVED WITH TWO-HEADED SNAKE. 1·96 m [6'5"] CS 3

PART 4

CEDAR: THE BARK

Working with cedar wood, traditionally recognized as the jurisdiction of men, had its counterpart in the working of inner cedar bark — a task almost entirely carried out by women. Both uses required a knowledge of the tree, technologies and skills that came with experience; both contributed to the essentials of daily living and added richness to ceremonial life, and both provided a means of self-expression and creativity.

GATHERING Different cultural groups gathered the bark of red and yellow cedar at varying times, depending on their geographic location, but it was only during the spring and summer months when the sap was running that pulling off the bark was possible. In the south, the Quinault Coast Salish took the bark of red cedar as early as April. The Hesquiat, on the west coast of Vancouver Island, took it from very slender trees at that time, but waited until May or June to pull from bigger trees. Coast Salish people up the Fraser Valley said the second week in May was best; the Kwakiutl took it in

Photograph by Hilary Stewart
Florence Davidson finishing a hat woven from cedar bark.
Photograph by Ulli Steltzer, courtesy of the photographer

June, and the Haida in July. These times depended on whether spring was early or late, but once the sap was running the bark could be pulled off easily.

Groups of women went together to an area in the forest where there were stands of young red cedars; several men went along to help, since pulling bark was often hard work requiring extra strength. The thickness and quality of the bark depended on the size and growth of the tree, with young ones about two handspans wide, and twenty to thirty-five years old, being considered best for most purposes.

A woman would look for a tall, straight tree, with bark that did not spiral around the trunk and with few branches. She also needed space to back away while pulling bark from the tree, and if this was uphill, so much the better. After selecting a tree, she addressed the spirit of the cedar in a prayer of respect, thanking it for being such a good provider and asking it for its "dress" (the bark), explaining why she needed it. As with all natural resources, whether plant, animal, bird or fish, people expressed gratitude, with the understanding that the resources gave of themselves: to show respect was to ensure a good supply in future years.

113

On the tree's "belly" (the side with fewest branches), the woman used an adze to make a small horizontal cut two finger-widths wide above the flare of the tree's base, then a cut a short way up from each side of this. She pried the bark away with a wooden wedge or a bone tool until she had freed enough for a good grip. Holding the free end of the bark, she walked backwards away from the tree, pulling off a ribbon of bark. Mabel Taylor, a longtime Hesquiat basketmaker now in her eighties and living in Port Alberni, told me that this was the way to check the quality of the bark for length and straightness of fibres — essential qualities for baskets and matting. If the narrow strip did not run "straight up for twenty feet at least" (that is, if it narrowed to a point too soon), then she tried another tree. When a tree proved to be good, she pulled off a second narrow strip a distance from the first. She then pulled the bark between the two strips and was assured of a good long ribbon of even width. Haida weaver Florence Davidson said that she pulled one narrow strip to "make a roadway", then gave a half turn to the bark as she pulled it away. Haida women once sang a lively song as they pulled, chanting:

We want a long strip,
Go up high, go up high,
We want a long strip,
Go up high, go up high.

The higher up the tree that the strip ran, the more difficult it became to pull away from the trunk because of the steep angle. Mabel Taylor solved this problem by tying a rope onto the end of the bark to enable her to back farther away from the tree and increase the angle. Here, too, was where the strength of a man helped a great deal, especially when the upper end was reluctant to come to a point and break away.

Another Westcoast basketmaker, Alice Paul, warned me that it was necessary to move quickly when the great length of bark finally fell to the ground. She also showed me some lengths of bark about 15 cm (6") wide, and said that "In the old days they used to pull maybe a foot wide — but they were experts!"

To pull wide strips of bark from slender trees, the Kwakiutl tied a cedar withe tightly around the trunk at about chest height, then cut the bark horizontally at

GATHERING BARK KW ✗ 34

① WOMAN CHOSE A STRAIGHT YOUNG TREE WITH FEW BRANCHES, SAID A PRAYER TO TREE'S SPIRIT, ASKING FOR ITS BARK.

② ON THE SIDE WITH FEWEST BRANCHES, WOMAN CUT THROUGH BARK TO THE SAPWOOD.

③ AFTER MAKING SIDE CUTS, SHE PRIED BARK LOOSE WITH FLAT-ENDED BONE TOOL.

BARK STRIPPER, TO LIFT BARK AWAY FROM TREE TRUNK, MADE OF BONE – 40·5 cm [16"] BC 2

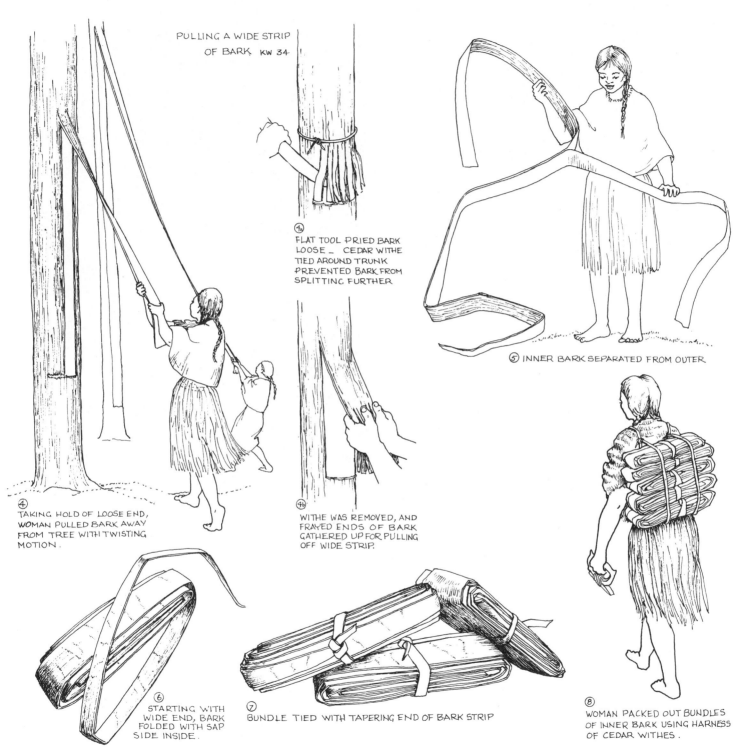

PULLING A WIDE STRIP
OF BARK KW 34

④ₐ FLAT TOOL PRIED BARK
LOOSE — CEDAR WITHE
TIED AROUND TRUNK
PREVENTED BARK FROM
SPLITTING FURTHER

⑤ INNER BARK SEPARATED FROM OUTER

④ TAKING HOLD OF LOOSE END,
WOMAN PULLED BARK AWAY
FROM TREE WITH TWISTING
MOTION.

④ᵦ WITHE WAS REMOVED, AND
FRAYED ENDS OF BARK
GATHERED UP FOR PULLING
OFF WIDE STRIP.

⑥ STARTING WITH
WIDE END, BARK
FOLDED WITH SAP
SIDE INSIDE.

⑦ BUNDLE TIED WITH TAPERING END OF BARK STRIP

⑧ WOMAN PACKED OUT BUNDLES
OF INNER BARK USING HARNESS
OF CEDAR WITHES.

115

ABOVE
NATURAL SCAR ON CEDAR RUNS
FROM BOTTOM OF TREE, TAPERS UP
SHARPLY BETWEEN FLUTES
ON TRUNK OF OLD TREES.

RIGHT
SCAR ON CEDAR, RESULTING
FROM BARK GATHERED
MANY YEARS AGO SHOWS
NEW BARK GROWING IN UNDER
OLD BARK — SCAR PARTIALLY
COVERED.
ARROW SHOWS WHERE
BARK CUT, BUT NOT REMOVED,
HAS HEALED.

FAR RIGHT
BARK HEALING OVER SCAR WITHOUT NEW GROWTH.
BASE OF SCAR MAY ALSO CARRY EVIDENCE OF ADZING.

This cedar on Monas Island, near Tofino, shows evidence of healing on the scar made by bark stripping. 73

about waist height. Using a sharp tool, a man pried the bark loose in several places between the cut and the withe, on the side with the fewest branches; this created a fringe of bark that could not go beyond the withe. He then removed the withe, gathered up the fringed strands in his hands and pulled a wider strip than otherwise would have been possible from a tree of small diameter. Young bark, being strong and tough, was particularly desirable for mat making.

A single ribbon of cedar bark, generally one hand-span wide, could run 12.2 m (40′) and more up the trunk of a good cedar, but pulling it was hard work, especially if the ground underfoot was rough or littered with blow-downs and salal. Once the bark strip came tumbling down, it left a honey-coloured scar, glistening with sap.

Rectangular cuts were made for slabs of bark for canoe bailers and roof planks; these were peeled off from the side, not from the base, by running the hands between the bark and the sapwood.

The question of how much bark to pull off seemed to differ with the cultures. If it was a good tree, Westcoast basketmakers pulled it all; the Coast Salish took about two-thirds, and the Kwakiutl left a strip of four finger-widths on the tree. The Haida said that if you removed all the bark and killed the tree, other cedars nearby would curse you. Generally, one side of the tree had more branches than the other, making it less desirable for pulling bark. This left sufficient bark for the sap to carry nutrients to the roots, allowing for the tree's continued

116

A large old cedar tree with the scars of two bark lengths removed long ago; note how the bark has grown over the sapwood. Windy Bay, Queen Charlotte Islands. 73

between the two, then pulled them apart. Another method was to bend and break the outer bark every four hand-spans, then peel it away from the inner bark. Mabel Taylor said that when she separated bark, she put her foot on one end of the strand to give tension; in earlier times a Westcoast woman squatted at the task. Bits of the outer bark generally adhered to the inner when they were separated. Some women cleaned these off with a knife, but others peeled them off later when preparing the bark for basketry. Vic Mowatt, a Gitksan dancer from 'Ksan who pulls bark for the masks he makes and wears, said the outer bark peeled away cleanly only if it was thick bark from an old tree. Either way, the separation was begun from the top end of the strip; the outer bark used to be taken home for fuel, but nowadays is left in the forest.

Starting with the bottom end, the bark gatherer then folded the strip of inner bark into a hank, sapside inside, and tied up the bundle with the tapered top end. When everyone had a quantity of these, they baled them together with cedar withes, packed them out on their backs to the canoe, and returned home.

Drying   The next step entailed drying out the bark that was so flexible and wet with sap. Some cultural groups hung it up in garlands over a line, while others laid it flat and straight on the ground, turning it frequently. When the bark had dried in the sun and wind for a day or more, it was refolded the same way as before, using the same creases, then stored in boxes or baskets for later use. If it had curled up at the edges, folding was left until evening when the bark became moist again.

A woman found great satisfaction in having a store of neatly bundled cedar bark, smooth and yellow-gold — enough to supply her household needs for the following year. Since bark was best worked when it had thoroughly dried out for a year, she always worked with bark taken the previous season.

UNPROCESSED BARK USES   Lengths of smooth, strong, inner cedar bark filled many everyday needs of a thriving, busy village. Even with its rough outer covering, just as it came from the tree, the bark served many purposes with little or no modification.

As I walked through the moss-floored forest at Windy

growth. A large cedar I saw at Jewitt Lake, near Yuquot, had only a narrow strip of bark remaining. Enquiries revealed that the bark had been taken eight years previously, and the tree was still living.

Many young trees on the coast carry the scars of bark removed long ago. The bark on the edges of pulled strips has grown in considerably, narrowing the width, but on large, old trees, scars made by the removal of slabs, such as for planks, have not.

Separating   To separate the outer bark from the inner bark, the bark gatherer ran a bone knife or similar tool

117

Bay, on the Queen Charlotte Islands, where cedar and spruce reign in splendid majesty, I saw a cedar tree from which a strip of bark about 1.5 m by 0.3 m (5' by 1') had been taken, leaving the sapwood showing. Adze marks in the bark, at the top and bottom of the scar, were still clearly evident, and the growth of bark at the sides hinted at the many years gone by since someone had needed that length of bark. Not far away, another huge, venerable tree bore a similar scar, and further searching revealed three more such trees. One massive cedar bore two scars of bark removal, side by side, both the same deliberate size. Although the base of one strip was slightly higher up the trunk than the other, the top edge was correspondingly higher, indicating that the lengths of bark had been cut to a specific length. The Haida once made boards by taking wide sections of bark and threading salmonberry sticks at intervals through the fibre. Thus flattened, the bark planks were piled up and weighted down with stones until they dried. In trading these to the Nass River people, the Haida received one blanket for two boards.

In many areas of the coast, people built temporary shelters, either a lean-to or a small hut, using bark boards for the sides and the roof, the latter held down with rocks on top of crosspieces. The Salish also used bark to construct sweat houses.

Many types of containers were made of unprocessed bark, including boxes. In one use, a cedar bark plank was kerfed and folded to make a box, with a base and a lid added. Such boxes, used for packing and storage, are rare among museum collections, perhaps because they did not appeal to early collectors or because they had a much shorter life than the wooden boxes. The Quileute, in Washington, regularly made simple bark boxes for storing raw and cooked berries by placing two bark strips at right angles, folding up the sides on scored lines, and sewing the corners with cedar root, but of these also, few remain.

Another type of cedar bark container, used as a makeshift mixing bowl and cooking pot, was made on the spot from bark freshly peeled off a tree. This is described by one R. H. Pidcock in an 1862 publication documenting his adventures on a journey from Bella Coola to Fort Alexandria, on the Fraser River: "they took a strip of cedar bark about 2 feet wide and about 3 feet long which peels off

Florence Davidson, Haida, on a bark-gathering trip near Masset Queen Charlotte Islands. Note the bundled bark in the foreground. Photograph by Ulli Steltzer, courtesy of the photographer.

the tree very easily in spring. About 8 inches from each end they cut it half way through with a knife and take the outside bark carefully off, which leaves the inner bark, which is very pliable. These ends are turned up and tied with a piece of the same bark and a sort of dish is formed, perfectly watertight and rather elegant in appearance. In this they mix flour for bread, and boil water for other purposes by putting red hot stones into it which makes it boil in a very short time."

The Coast Salish made an excellent canoe bailer, using a technique similar to the makeshift pot, by folding up and pleating the ends of a piece of bark. To this they added a handle lashed to the uprights with cedar bark or the bark of western bitter cherry (*Prunus emarginata*). When I made one of these bailers with the outer bark on

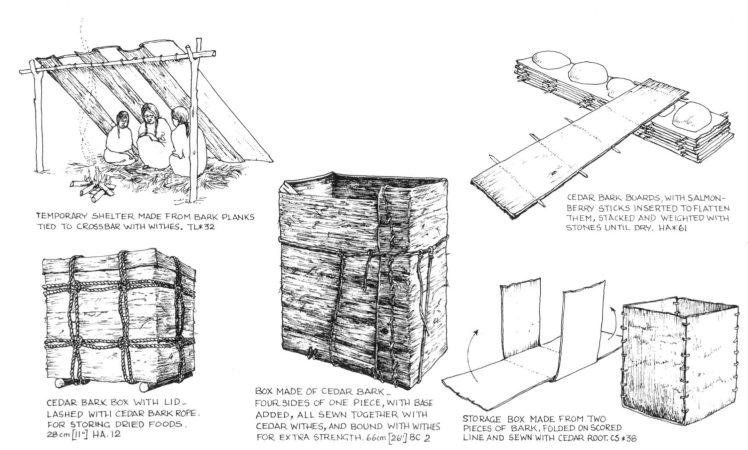

TEMPORARY SHELTER MADE FROM BARK PLANKS TIED TO CROSSBAR WITH WITHES. TL*32

CEDAR BARK BOARDS, WITH SALMON-BERRY STICKS INSERTED TO FLATTEN THEM, STACKED AND WEIGHTED WITH STONES UNTIL DRY. HA*61

CEDAR BARK BOX WITH LID-LASHED WITH CEDAR BARK ROPE. FOR STORING DRIED FOODS. 28 cm [11"] HA.12

BOX MADE OF CEDAR BARK-FOUR SIDES OF ONE PIECE, WITH BASE ADDED, ALL SEWN TOGETHER WITH CEDAR WITHES, AND BOUND WITH WITHES FOR EXTRA STRENGTH. 66 cm [26"] BC 2

STORAGE BOX MADE FROM TWO PIECES OF BARK, FOLDED ON SCORED LINE AND SEWN WITH CEDAR ROOT. CS *38

the outside, I found that as it dried, the edges curled inward, making it less efficient for dipping up water from the rounded floor of a canoe. Further checking on the original bailer which I had copied showed that inserting small slats of yellow cedar wood into the bark along the edges would prevent that from happening, so I soaked my bailer and added the stiffeners. However, when Ed Leon, an elder from Mission, in the Lower Fraser Valley, examined it, he scoffed at the need for stiffeners: "If you make it with the rough bark on the *inside*, then it's gonna try and curl the other way. Won't need any bits of wood in there." I did, and he was right.

An emergency use for a large piece of cedar bark combined survival tactics with an element of adventure. In order to ferry himself across a stream or to fish on a lake, a man could quickly improvise a small craft from a half-cylindrical length of cedar bark peeled from a tree. He could either clamp the two ends tightly between two vertical sticks and lash them in place with root or withe, or

fold up and pleat the ends, as with the canoe bailer. For both types of canoe, he used crossbraces to spread the sides. Legend has it that many a runaway slave made good his escape in such a craft, but the documentation is minimal.

John Jewitt's description of a Westcoast bark cradle does not clarify how this was made, though I picture it as an elongated bailer, without the handle. He wrote: "when they have occasion to go some distance from their houses, the infants are usually suspended across their mother's shoulders, in a kind of cradle or hammock, formed of bark, of about six inches in depth, and the length of the child, by means of a leather band inserted through loops on its edges; this they also keep them in when at home."

Some Salish people used strips of inner cedar bark to securely bind a child in its cradle, arms at its sides. Two other uses of such bark strips were connected with birthing: a length was tied above a woman's abdomen as she

119

MAKING A CANOE BAILER OF BARK

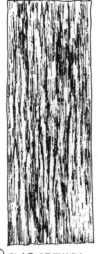
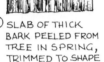

① SLAB OF THICK BARK PEELED FROM TREE IN SPRING, TRIMMED TO SHAPE

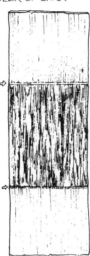

② SLAB SCORED IN TWO PLACES, AND OUTER BARK ON ENDS REMOVED

SLOTS CUT IN HANDLE ALLOW BARK TO BE RECESSED

③ ENDS PLEATED AND FOLDED UP. HANDLE SET INTO A SPLIT IN PLEATED BARK AND LASHED IN PLACE WITH WITHES.

CANOE BAILER OF FOLDED BARK WITH WOODEN PEGS INSERTED INTO EDGES TO PREVENT THEM FROM CURLING INWARD. HANDLE 19 cm [7½"] CS 4

pulled on a rope attached to a tree during labour, and a strip was tied around her waist after delivery to prevent her from swelling up again. At puberty, a young girl in ritual seclusion wore a cedar bark belt to help her achieve a slender waist.

A Westcoast whaler made a protector for his harpoon head from a folded length of inner cedar bark. One of these, unearthed at the Ozette archaeological site, still contained the head of the whaling harpoon. Often the whaler tightly wrapped his three-ply harpoon line with long strips of cedar bark to protect it from abrasion and give it extra strength. A hunter frequently lashed feathers to his arrow shafts with narrow strips of bark, and his wife used strips of bark to hang up rows of smelt and eulachon to dry and smoke. She threaded dozens of fish on one string, passing the end through the gill and mouth, so that they all hung vertically from the strip, taking up a minimum of space. She dried and smoked clams the same way, leaving them on their string for storage. The Tsimshian rendered eulachon oil by boiling the rotted fish in water; as the oil rose to the surface, they used a U-shaped strip of cedar bark to gather and scoop it up.

The complete list of uses for unprocessed bark would be lengthy, but let me conclude with an interesting

CANOE BAILER 30·4 cm [12"] CS 31

assortment. One means of transporting fire was to enclose smouldering bracket fungus or punk wood in a clamshell or sometimes in folded cedar bark. A woman's labret, usually made of stone or wood, was occasionally of bark. The Kwakiutl made a ball, used in a batting game, by tightly rolling skunk cabbage leaves into a small sphere and wrapping it with a strip of cedar bark. Artists used templates made from hide or more often from inner cedar bark, cut and folded in half to be sure both sides were alike. Each represented some main element of the design; by drawing around the template on one side of the design, then using it for the other side, exactness and symmetry were assured.

MAKESHIFT COOKING POT OF FOLDED BARK_
HOT STONES DROPPED IN MADE WATER BOIL. BC✱37

TWO TYPES OF MAKESHIFT OR EMERGENCY CANOES MADE
FROM LARGE PIECE OF CEDAR BARK PEELED RIGHT OFF
THE TREE. NWC✱44

INNER CEDAR BARK USED IN SKIMMING OFF
EULACHON OIL DURING RENDERING. TL✱42

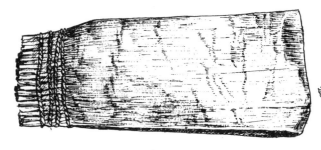

FOLDED INNER BARK PROTECTED HEAD OF WHALE
HARPOON DURING STORAGE. 22.8cm [9"] WC 9

INNER CEDAR BARK PROTECTOR ON
WHALING HARPOON HEAD, WITH
WHALING LINE. 22.8cm [9"] WC 2

REEL OF CEDAR BARK STRIP,
WOUND AROUND CEDAR STICKS,
READY FOR USE AS LASHING. KW 79

CRUSHED AND DRIED BERRIES FOLDED INTO CAKE, TIED WITH STRIPS OF INNER BARK, STORED FOR WINTER USE. 33cm [13"] NWC 4

INNER BARK, WRAPPED AROUND GRIP OF BOW, CONCEALED HUNTER'S CHARM FOR GOOD AIM. WC 2

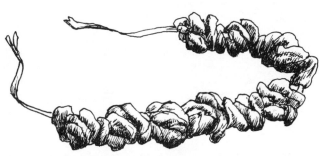

CLAMS, DRIED AND STORED STRUNG ON STRIP OF INNER BARK. CS 1

TOSS BALL USED IN GAME. CEDAR BARK STRIP WRAPPED AROUND CORE OF ROLLED UP SKUNK CABBAGE LEAVES. ABOUT 9cm [3½"] KW ⚹ 36

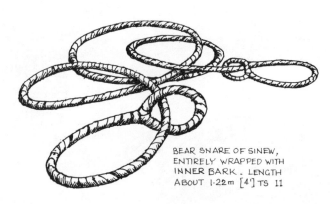

BEAR SNARE OF SINEW, ENTIRELY WRAPPED WITH INNER BARK. LENGTH ABOUT 1.22m [4'] TS 11

GROUSE HEAD RATTLE, HANDLE BOUND IN CEDAR BARK. 22.5 cm [8⅞"] KW 9

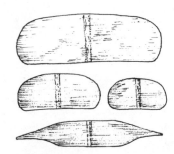

INNER BARK TEMPLATES, USED BY ARTISTS TO ENSURE SYMMETRY IN DESIGNS SUCH AS THOSE ON BENTWOOD BOXES. THESE BELONGED TO FAMED ARTIST/CARVER CHARLES EDENSHAW. TOP ONE, 22.8cm [9"] HA 12

PAD TO CURE CARBUNCLE, MADE FROM FOUR PIECES OF INNER CEDAR BARK, WITH FIR PITCH BETWEEN EACH, THEN TRIMMED TO SHAPE.

FINISHED PAD 7cm [2¾"] KW ⚹ 36

The author demonstrating how to beat cedar bark by the stone-on-stone method. 73

With the modern world so full of artificial materials, there is a real pleasure to be had from running one's fingers along a piece of inner cedar bark, especially on the sap side, and feeling the silken smoothness of the fine grooves and ridges, as well as sniffing its pungent scent.

PROCESSING   The versatility of the inner bark of the cedar lay in a woman's knowledge of how to process the hard, dried bark into a soft, flexible material. She prepared it in different ways to suit various needs: to obtain long, flexible, separate strands, she split the thickness and width of the inner bark; and to obtain shredded or soft-shredded bark, she beat it with a special implement. Processing methods for the inner bark of yellow cedar were similar, but entailed periods of soaking to enable it to be worked satisfactorily.

Shredding   There were several uses for the inner bark in its natural state, but generally it needed some modification. Shredding was one of the most common, and though the tools and methods for this differed along

the coast, the end result was the same.

First the bark had to be thin (that is, from a young tree), free of pitch (pulled at the right time of year) and completely dry. Some women even passed the bark over the fire just before working it, to ensure its crisp dryness. Bark that was too thick simply separated out into many layers, and pitchy or damp bark would not shred well.

A woman of the Westcoast used a handled bark shredder, with a V-shaped edge, generally made of heavy yew wood. She used her left hand to pass the flat, stiff bark across a block of wood, hitting it at the block's edge with the bark shredder. Slowly, she moved the bark forward and repeated the striking to separate and soften the many layers of bark.

Wally Henry, a Coast Salish of the Fraser Valley, has done a lot of research on working with cedar bark. He shreds the bark over a rounded edge to lessen the chance of its breaking. He said that the harder the pounding, the more layers that separated out. As an example, he showed me a very thick piece of bark about 4 mm (3/16″) thick, which had separated into about twenty layers. Because of the thickness, however, it need further processing to reach the fibrous stage.

To shred inner cedar bark, a Kwakiutl woman used an old paddle with the blade supported diagonally from the ground. She squatted over the handle end, passed a heated strip of bark over the edge of the paddle, and beat it with a wide, bladelike bark shredder, made of wood or the nasal bone of a whale. A Quinault Coast Salish woman used a similar method, but lashed the paddle or a sharp-edged board between two uprights at waist level and stood to work the bark.

Vic Mowatt, from 'Ksan, beat the bark as he moved it back and forth over a gutter-shaped groove in a plank. Early bark shredders of northern people were often stone, and these, too, were used to beat bark placed over a groove, generally cut into the house platform.

Soft-shredding   With the bark shredded, there were diverse ways of working it further, depending on the product to be made and who was making it. For a roughly woven cape, skirt or blanket for everyday use in many areas, a woman took the shredded bark in her hands and ruffled it by rolling it back and forth, working it into lengths of rolled strands. She put oil or bear grease

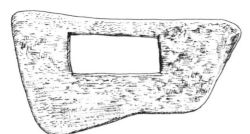

BARK SHREDDER OF WHALEBONE — EDGE WORN DOWN THROUGH MANY YEARS OF USE. 22·8 cm [9"] WC 9

NORTHERN TYPE BARK SHREDDER. OF STONE. 16·5 cm [6½"] TS 2

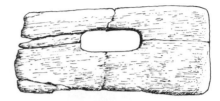

BARK SHREDDER OF WHALEBONE FROM AN ARCHAEOLOGICAL EXCAVATION, DATED BETWEEN 1000 BC AND AD 800. 28 cm [11"] WC 1

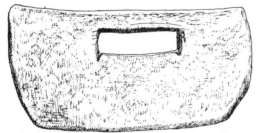

BARK SHREDDER OF WHALEBONE. 28·5 cm [11¼"] WC 9

BARK SHREDDER OF YEW WOOD. 58·3 cm [23"] KW 26

BARK SHREDDER OF WOOD WITH CARVED FIGURE EACH END OF HAND GRIP. 30·7 cm [12⅛"] WC 26

BARK SHREDDER, MADE OF WHALEBONE, WITH PAINTED DESIGN OF SISIUTL, MYTHICAL TWO-HEADED SEA SERPENT. 50 cm [20½"] KW 2

on her hands to further soften the shredded bark and help it shed rain.

For diapers, towelling and certain medicinal uses, the shredded inner red cedar bark was further softened by ruffling between the two hands; the fine particles that fell away were gathered up and used as tinder for the fire drill.

To achieve softness, Wally Henry soaked the inner bark for several days, adding seal or fish oil to the water (he had tried vegetable oil but found it inferior). Then he laid the partially dried bark on a flat stone and beat it with a small flat-based stone. When the bark dried, he worked the beaten fibres between his thumbs, like scrubbing laundry. Alice Paul said she soaked the bark in fresh water for three weeks, pounded it, dried it, then worked the loose strands between her fists, in a tight rotating movement. Oil on her hands helped to soften the fibres — dogfish or ratfish oil in the old days.

I tried the stone-on-stone method on bark previously shredded into layers, and found that fairly gentle beating was necessary to avoid breaking the wet bark fibres. In fact it took a few hours of practice until I consistently did it correctly. It was tedious work, but when the bark dried and I ruffled it, I achieved excellent results. It seems likely that this method may have been preferred for bark too thick to successfully shred when dry.

Quinault Coast Salish and Tlingit women twisted the fibrous strands to soften them further, and there were likely other ways of working the bark in the hands for that final soft-shredded material.

Processing Yellow Cedar Bark   The inner bark of the yellow cedar is tougher than that of red cedar and was valued more highly. It was cut and pulled by the same method as for red cedar bark as soon as the sap began to run. In the south, the Westcoast people gath-

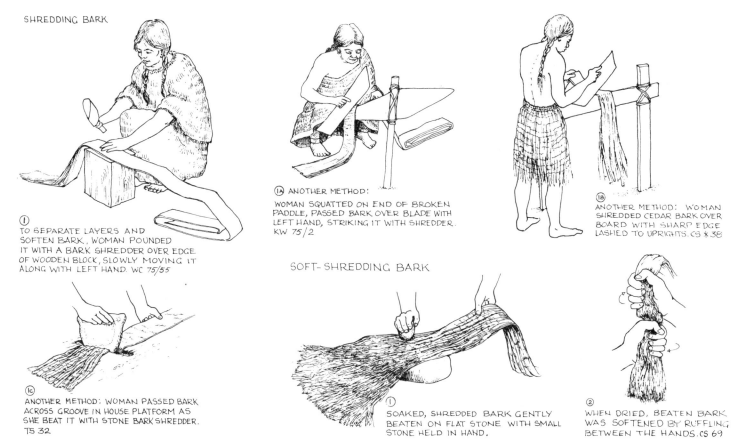

SHREDDING BARK

① TO SEPARATE LAYERS AND SOFTEN BARK, WOMAN POUNDED IT WITH A BARK SHREDDER OVER EDGE OF WOODEN BLOCK, SLOWLY MOVING IT ALONG WITH LEFT HAND. WC 75/55

①A ANOTHER METHOD: WOMAN SQUATTED ON END OF BROKEN PADDLE, PASSED BARK OVER BLADE WITH LEFT HAND, STRIKING IT WITH SHREDDER. KW 75/2

①B ANOTHER METHOD: WOMAN SHREDDED CEDAR BARK OVER BOARD WITH SHARP EDGE LASHED TO UPRIGHTS. CS ✻38

①C ANOTHER METHOD: WOMAN PASSED BARK ACROSS GROOVE IN HOUSE PLATFORM AS SHE BEAT IT WITH STONE BARK SHREDDER. TS 32

SOFT-SHREDDING BARK

① SOAKED, SHREDDED BARK GENTLY BEATEN ON FLAT STONE WITH SMALL STONE HELD IN HAND.

② WHEN DRIED, BEATEN BARK WAS SOFTENED BY RUFFLING BETWEEN THE HANDS. CS 69

ered it by the end of May, while in the north, the Haida went up into the high country in July to pull it. Florence Davidson said that there was only a two-week period when yellow cedar bark could be taken before the pitch came into it, making it sticky and difficult to work.

After six to eight days of exposure to sun and wind dried out the yellow cedar bark, it was then soaked. Here too, methods differed. A Westcoast woman submerged the bark for fourteen days or longer, using pegs and crosspieces to hold the bark strands under water. A Kwakiutl woman took the bark to a quiet tidal pool, which had relatively warm water, weighed the bark down with stones and left it for twelve days. She returned to the tidal pool with her whalebone bark beater and a flat stone, and processed the bark on the beach. Pulling the narrow end from the water, she laid it on the stone and pounded it. She returned home with the beaten bark and hung it up to dry on a fish drying rack,

covering it with mats at night to keep off the dew. After four days of drying, she folded the bark and stored it in a basket until winter, when she would work on it.

Florence Davidson held the bark of yellow cedar in high regard because it split cleanly and evenly. In her basketry, she used it for rows of twining in between the rows of plaiting in red cedar bark. In my experiments with it I found it quite pitchy, but easy to split without running off, less brittle and very strong. To eliminate the pitch, Tlingit women boiled the bark for at least a day, rinsed it in clean water and softened it by twisting and working the fibres in their hands, as they did for red cedar bark, without the aid of an implement. A Westcoast woman put oil on her hands before working with pitchy bark. Each cultural group then soft-shredded the yellow cedar bark, using methods similar to those used for the red but with differing implements.

John Jewitt, who was quite familiar with cedar bark

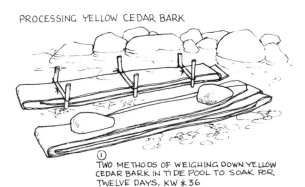

TWO METHODS OF WEIGHING DOWN YELLOW CEDAR BARK IN TIDE POOL TO SOAK FOR TWELVE DAYS. KW * 36

WHALEBONE BARK BEATER FOR USE WITH YELLOW CEDAR BARK. 22.8" [9"] WC 9

② WOMAN POUNDED SOAKED BARK WITH BEATER OF WOOD OR WHALEBONE, GROOVED ON UNDERSIDE. KW * 36
WHEN DRIED, BEATEN BARK SOFTENED BY RUFFLING IN SAME MANNER AS RED SOFT-SHREDDED BARK. WC 68

SPLITTING THICKNESS OF BARK

① END BENT OVER TO SEPARATE LAYERS

② DIVIDED LAYERS SPLIT APART, WITH KNUCKLES TOGETHER TO PROVIDE TENSION WC 72

SPLITTING THE WIDTH

STRAND OF BARK USED AS GAUGE WHEN SPLITTING OTHERS OF SAME WIDTH — SURPLUS TRIMMED OFF WITH THUMBNAIL. WC 68

garments and even wore them for a while, wrote a description of the preparation: "A quantity of this bark is taken and put into fresh water, where it is kept for a fortnight, to give it time to completely soften; . . . it is then taken out and beaten upon a plank, with an instrument made of bone, or some very hard wood, having grooves or hollows on one side of it, care being taken to keep the mass constantly moistened with water."

The instrument described by Jewitt was the whalebone or yew wood bark beater. Because of the amount of oil in fresh whalebone, a beater of this material gave the tool the necessary weight and probably imparted some of the oil to the bark also. When I beat wet bark with an ungrooved piece of wood that was handy, I found the bark kept sticking to the wood and concluded that the grooves on the underside of the beater would prevent this from happening by breaking up the implement's flat surface.

Ensign Alexander Walker left a perceptive and important account of the Westcoast people's preparation of bark for clothing. He referred to the bark as being that of pine, a generic name for conifers in his day: "The Cloth is made from the inner bark of the pine, which after being soaked in water, is beated with an Instrument of bone. . . . One preparation is not sufficient, for it undergoes a second and third soaking, and as many beatings, before it is reduced into threads, or is fit for weaving."

Because of its strength, only yellow cedar bark was used for the core of the warp of Chilkat blankets. Its superior quality also meant that it was made into capes and blankets for high-ranking people along most areas of the coast.

While this account of the preparation of inner bark is far from exhaustive, it does show the diversity of ways in which Northwest Coast women handled this remarkable fibre, the dress of Long Life Maker.

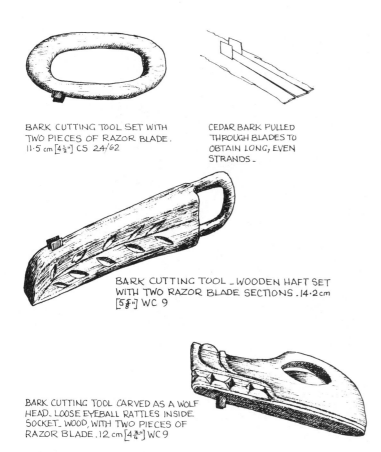

BARK CUTTING TOOL SET WITH
TWO PIECES OF RAZOR BLADE.
11·5 cm [4½"] CS 24/62

CEDAR BARK PULLED
THROUGH BLADES TO
OBTAIN LONG, EVEN
STRANDS.

BARK CUTTING TOOL – WOODEN HAFT SET
WITH TWO RAZOR BLADE SECTIONS. 14·2 cm
[5⅝"] WC 9

BARK CUTTING TOOL CARVED AS A WOLF
HEAD. LOOSE EYEBALL RATTLES INSIDE
SOCKET. WOOD, WITH TWO PIECES OF
RAZOR BLADE. 12 cm [4¾"] WC 9

Splitting the Thickness For basketry, matting, rope, braiding and any item that required long, even strands, a woman split the thickness of the bark into continuous individual layers. Shredding the bark split the thickness, too, but randomly and unevenly. For general purposes, splitting a length into three layers gave her three qualities of bark: rough, from the outer side, suitable for coarse mats and baskets; medium, from the centre, good for fishing lines, ordinary baskets, mats and hats, and fine, from the inner layer, for finely woven and braided items. Kwakiutl women split the bark into three layers while it was still fresh, starting from the wide or bottom end. Most other groups split from the top down, after soaking the dried bark for a few hours. Alice Paul said that splitting could be done wet or dry, but that wet was easier. By working directly from the folded bundle, she always knew which was the top, since the bottom end was folded inside.

Splitting the thickness of the bark was a skill, one still practised today. A woman bent the top edge back and forth, working it with her fingers or her teeth, to cause the several layers to separate. She could then select the required thickness for splitting off. For very fine baskets and matting, the bark required splitting again; the thinner the layers, the more flexible the resulting product. Holding an end in each hand, she split two layers apart, maintaining an even tension. Should one layer begin to thin out, she held it still and continued splitting by pulling away the other. "You feel it in your hands," Alice Paul said, and after considerable practice I knew just what she meant.

Splitting the Width In addition to splitting the thickness of the cedar bark into layers, a basketmaker also split its width into strands — both had to be appropriate for the item to be made. Coarse matting might have strands 2.5 cm (1") wide, and a fine, cross-warped basket 2 mm (1/16") wide. A Westcoast woman split off narrow strands by holding the bark in her right hand and pulling the index finger of her left hand down along the initial split, as far as the required length. Watching Mabel Taylor do this so exactly, I asked her why, when I split bark, it sometimes tapered and ran off. "Must be from a no good tree," she said and laughed, pointing out the importance of using bark pulled in a long, uniform piece. The old way of splitting the bark, she said, the way her mother-in-law did it, was to hold one end in the mouth. To ensure uniformity of width when splitting or to even up a strand of bark, she placed one of the correct width over a wider or uneven one and split off the surplus with her thumbnail.

For speed and precision in splitting bark (and grasses), several groups used a wooden tool, often decoratively carved, set with two parallel pieces of razor blade. Although such tools could originally have been set with microblades of obsidian, it seems probable that they were devised after the introduction of razor blades. Taking this idea one step further, Wally Henry created an implement for splitting three or four strands at a time. It has three sharp Exacto blades set into slots, and a nut-and-bolt device for easy replacement of the blades.

BASKETRY AND OTHER WEAVING Just as men took great pride in the art of woodcarving, enjoying the high status that went with fine design and creativity, so the women of the Northwest Coast enjoyed the prestige and praise that came from their skill in basketry — which was, and still is, exclusively a woman's art.

All women made baskets, but the specialists who excelled in various types of basketry devoted much time to their art and were not required to perform all the usual household tasks. They began learning the craft as children, encouraged over the years by a mother or older female relative. At the time of puberty, when young women were secluded away from the mainstream of family life — for several weeks or months among some groups — they concentrated on practising basketry and other skills.

Regional basketry styles differed considerably in technique and made use of a range of fibrous materials, depending on what was available and abundant in each area. With the spruce tree so prolific in the north, the Haida and Tlingit used a great deal of spruce root in their basketry, while Westcoast women, who had access to several species of sedge grass, produced a distinctly different looking basket. Naturally the inner bark of the cedar (almost always red cedar) had a role in basketry, either as warp, weft or both, and often in combination with cedar roots, withes or some other material. Baskets with both warp and weft of cedar bark were usually neither rigid nor watertight. Weaving the strands in diagonal plaiting gave great flexibility to the work — ideal for large, folding, sacklike bags for storage or travel, and for wallet-type folding pouches. Cedar bark baskets tended to have less decoration than those made of other materials; the overlay patterns were plaid or geometric and used bark strands dyed black or, occasionally, red.

Bark was dyed either shredded or in strands. A Coast Salish woman in Puget Sound dyed bark when it was freshly pulled and still wet with sap. For red, she took the inner bark of red alder (*Alnus rubra*), chewed it to a paste and spat this onto the wet cedar bark, then put it into the sun for fast drying to prevent it from becoming too dark a red. When the dye had taken, she rubbed off the paste. For black, she took dried, year-old cedar bark — because this took the colour better — and buried it in black swampy mud, leaving it for only a few days, other-

A Coast Salish woman holding the start of a cedar bark basket or possibly a hat similar to the one being worn, 1895. Courtesy Vancouver City Archives

wise it would rot. When she washed off the mud, the bark was stained a permanent black.

In all the homes, villages and camps along the Northwest Coast, basketry filled a vital need as a container, both for storage and for transportation of goods. While some baskets had multiple uses, others were made for a specific purpose. Certain customs and uses varied with the cultural areas, but many were similar. Women gathered berries, camas bulbs, clover roots, salmonberry shoots, nuts and other foods in cedar bark baskets and used large baskets to store various dried provisions for winter. In cooking, they used an open-weave cedar bark basket as a strainer and stored sets of flat, spatular-type

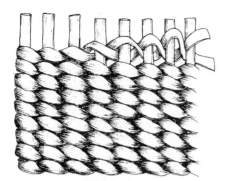

TWO-STRAND TWINING:
WEFT STRANDS CROSS OVER EACH
OTHER BETWEEN EACH WARP.

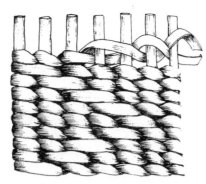

TWILLED TWO-STRAND TWINING:
WEFT STRANDS CROSS OVER TWO OR
MORE WARP STRANDS TO CREATE
A PATTERN.

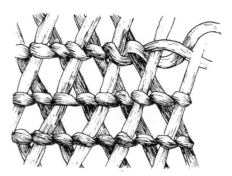

DIAGONAL WARP TWINING:
TWO-STRAND TWINING ON WARP THAT
RUNS DIAGONALLY IN TWO DIRECTIONS.

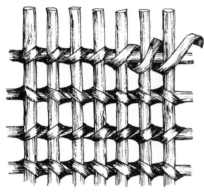

WRAPPED CROSSED WARP:
A SINGLE WEFT STRAND IS WRAPPED AROUND
RIGID WARP AND HORIZONTAL ELEMENT, AT
THEIR INTERSECTION.

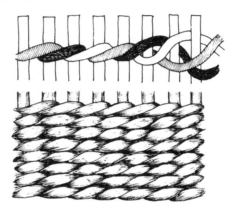

THREE-STRAND TWINING:
ON OUTSIDE OF BASKET, WEFT STRANDS
CROSS TWO WARPS; ON INSIDE, ONE WARP.

YEW WOOD IMPLEMENT USED BY MABEL
TAYLOR TO FLATTEN AND SMOOTH OUT
TWINED STRANDS ON BASKETRY –
[STONE USED IN EARLY TIMES] 17·8 cm [7"] WC 68

IMPLEMENT
BASKETRY   FLATSTONE

FINISHING BASKET RIMS

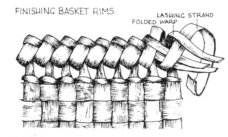

LASHING STRAND
FOLDED WARP

CEDAR BARK BASKET – WARP STRANDS FOLDED
OVER TO FORM BASKET RIM AFTER FIRST
PASSING OVER LASHING STRAND.

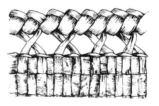

WITH WARP VARIATION

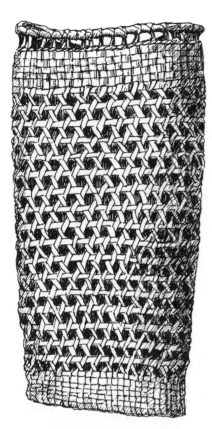

WEDGE BAG, OF CEDAR BARK
WITH DIAGONAL WARP _ TO
HOLD SIX SPLITTING WEDGES.
47cm [18½"] WC 2

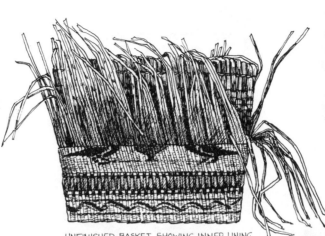

UNFINISHED BASKET SHOWING INNER LINING
OF PLAITED CEDAR BARK, WITH OUTER COVERING
OF SWAMP GRASS TWINED OVER CEDAR BARK
WARP. 40·5cm [16"] WC 10

BASKET OF CATTAIL LEAVES, WITH
OVERLAY OF BEARGRASS [WHITE] AND
CEDAR BARK. RIM. 26·5cm [10½"] DIAM.
PUGET SOUND. CS 24/62

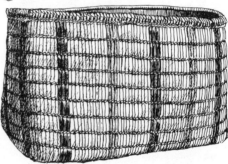

FLEXIBLE BASKET WITH BANDS OF BARK DYED
BLACK AND LIGHT RED. 31·7cm [12½"] KW 9

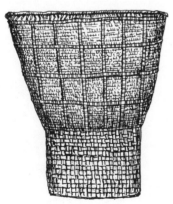

WHALER'S BAG _
78·5cm [31"] MK 12

CEDAR BARK
WARP, WIDE
AND NARROW
BARK WEFT.

WHALER'S BAG _ TO HOLD WHALING
EQUIPMENT. 1·06m [42"] WC 12

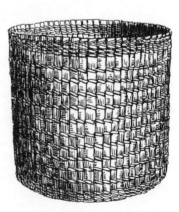

ROUND BASKET _ ROW OF TWO-STRAND
TWINING OF YELLOW CEDAR BARK
BETWEEN EACH PLAITED ROW OF RED
CEDAR BARK .15cm [6"] HA 31

PLAITING – TWILLED WEAVE:
WEFT STRAND CROSSES OVER AND UNDER
TWO OR MORE WARP STRANDS.

PLAITING – CHECKERBOARD WEAVE:
WEFT STRAND CROSSES OVER AND UNDER ONE
WARP STRAND.

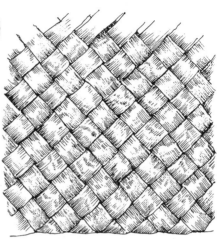

DIAGONAL PLAITING – CHECKERBOARD WEAVE,
CAN ALSO BE TWILLED WEAVE.

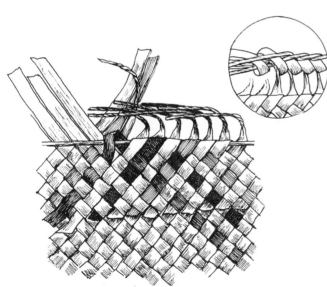

METHOD OF FINISHING RIM OF DIAGONALLY PLAITED BASKET.
INSET SHOWS FINAL STAGE, FORMING RIM.

spoons, used for eating soopolallie berries (*Shepherdia canadensis*), in special, woven bark containers. A mother could fashion a makeshift baby cradle by flattening two bark baskets, slipping one partly inside the other, and adding a rim of cedar withe for strength. In the home, a cedar bark pouch filled with the seed fluff of fireweed (*Epilobium angustifolium*) served as a pillow, and a Coast Salish woman kept her ball of roving in a basket of bark while spinning.

Men, too, used a variety of cedar bark baskets. A whaler had a large, specially shaped basket for carrying his harpoon points and lanyards. Such bags were fine examples of the weaver's art, often with self-designs that no doubt reflected the wealth and status of the whaler. He also kept the great lengths of rope used with the whaling harpoon coiled up in a large, open-mouthed basket, so that when a whale was harpooned, the rope ran out smoothly without tangling.

Many other men, including fishermen and woodworkers, also used basketry containers made specially for carrying or storing the implements, tools or other paraphernalia associated with their occupation or position. A shaman kept his ceremonial rattle in a woven cedar bark container, taking it out to use in curing a patient, calling the salmon upriver or making a change in the weather

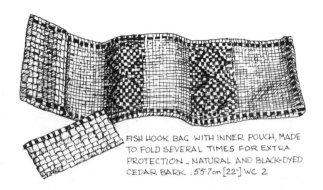

FISH HOOK BAG WITH INNER POUCH, MADE TO FOLD SEVERAL TIMES FOR EXTRA PROTECTION – NATURAL AND BLACK-DYED CEDAR BARK. 55.7cm [22"] WC 2

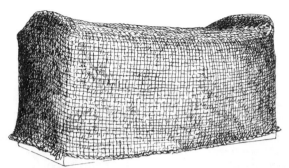

PLAITED COVER FOR BENTWOOD BOWL. 53 cm [21"] NWC 9

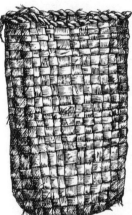

COARSELY PLAITED BAG USED AS POTATO SACK. 68.5cm [27"] BC 2

PLAITED BASKET, SQUARE BASE. 14.5cm [5¾"] HA 31

DIAGONALLY PLAITED BASKET WITH COMPLEX DESIGN IN BARK DYED RED. HEIGHT. 12.7cm [5"] TS 9

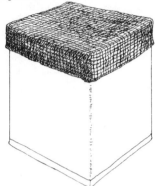

PLAITED CEDAR BARK LID FOR STORAGE BOX. 35.4 cm [14"] TL 21

UTILITY BASKET OF CEDAR BARK WITH DESIGN IN SAME BARK DYED BLACK. 35.5 cm [14"] TL 26

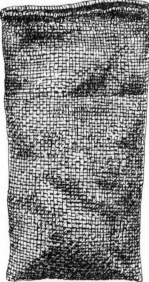

BAG OF PLAITED CEDAR BARK CONTAINING EAGLE DOWN, SYMBOL OF PEACE AND FRIENDSHIP, USED IN CEREMONIES. 30.5 cm [12"] TL 12

MONEY POUCH ONCE OWNED BY CHIEF SHAKES – DIAGONALLY PLAITED CEDAR BARK. 25.3 cm [10"] TL 22

SHAMAN'S RATTLE BAG – FINELY WOVEN OF CEDAR BARK – DIAGONAL PLAITING. 33 cm [13"] TS 12

DIAGONALLY PLAITED CASE FOR STORING CEREMONIAL APRON OF MOUNTAIN GOAT WOOL. 50.6 cm [20"] BC 2

FLEXIBLE BASKET IN DIAGONAL PLAITING
WITH STRANDS OF CEDAR BARK DYED RED
AND BLACK TO CREATE PLAID DESIGN.
THONGING FOR BASE SUPPORT. 25.5 cm [10"]
CS 31 COURTESY SHYAMALI TAN.

PLAITED CEDAR BARK BASKET, HANDLES
OF CEDAR BARK ROPE, DESIGN OF BARK
STRANDS DYED BLACK. 29 cm [11½"] HIGH, PLUS
HANDLES. TS 31

QUICKLY MADE BASKET USING WIDE STRANDS
OF BARK, NATURAL AND DYED BLACK.
BARK OF BRAIDED HANDLE TWISTED INTO ROPE
TO SUPPORT BASE. 16.5 cm [6½"] HIGH. HA 31

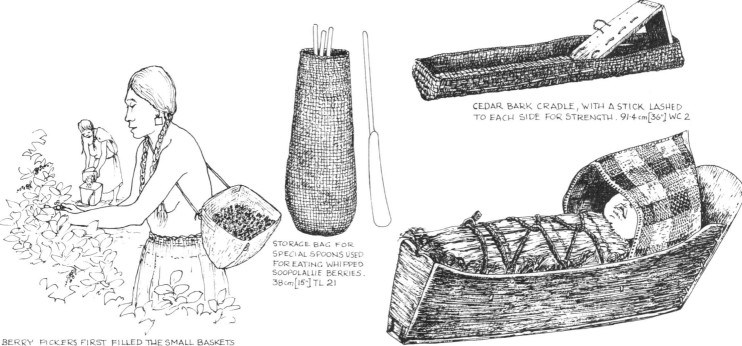

BERRY PICKERS FIRST FILLED THE SMALL BASKETS
THEY CARRIED, THEN EMPTIED THESE INTO A LARGER
BASKET NEARBY. THIS IN TURN WAS EMPTIED INTO
AN EVEN LARGER BASKET IN THE CANOE AND TAKEN
HOME. KW * 36

STORAGE BAG FOR
SPECIAL SPOONS USED
FOR EATING WHIPPED
SOOPOLALLIE BERRIES.
38 cm [15"] TL 21

CEDAR BARK CRADLE, WITH A STICK LASHED
TO EACH SIDE FOR STRENGTH. 91.4 cm [36"] WC 2

BABY WRAPPED IN SOFT-SHREDDED CEDAR BARK, PLACED ON BED
OF SAME MATERIAL IN CEDAR CRADLE. HOOD OF WOVEN CEDAR
BARK PROTECTED INFANT'S FACE FROM ASH AND DUST. KW40

MULTIPLE-STRAND BRAIDING

① FOUR OR MORE CEDAR BARK STRANDS FOLDED OVER HORIZONTAL STRAND OF BARK.

② ALL CROSSING STRANDS INTERWOVEN. FAR RIGHT STRAND [a] FOLDED AND WOVEN THROUGH.

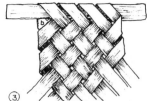

③ FAR LEFT STRAND [b] FOLDED AND WOVEN THROUGH. LEFT AND RIGHT STRANDS WOVEN ALTERNATELY.

SQUARE BRAIDING

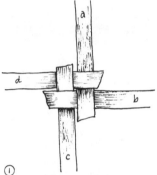

① ENDS OF LONG CEDAR BARK STRANDS POSITIONED AS ABOVE.

② STRAND [a] FOLDED DOWN OVER [d] AND [b]

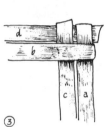

③ STRAND [b] FOLDED LEFT OVER [a] AND [c]

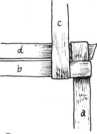

④ STRAND [c] FOLDED UP OVER [b] AND [d]

⑤ STRAND [d] FOLDED RIGHT OVER [c] AND TUCKED UNDER [a]. FOLD-AND-TUCK SEQUENCE CONTINUED.

⑥ FINISHED BRAID

THREE-STRAND BRAID USING DOUBLE STRANDS.

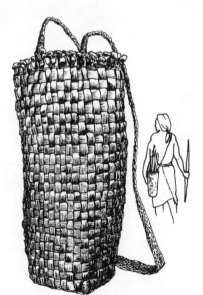

HUNTER'S QUIVER, WITH BRAIDED SHOULDER STRAP. BASKET HEIGHT 30·8 cm [13¾"] WC 4

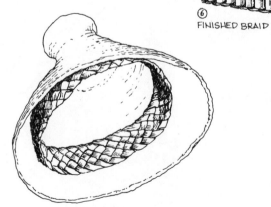

BRAIDED BAND INSIDE HAT GAVE FIRM FIT TO THE HEAD. BRAID 4·7 cm [1⅞"] WIDE WC 31

134

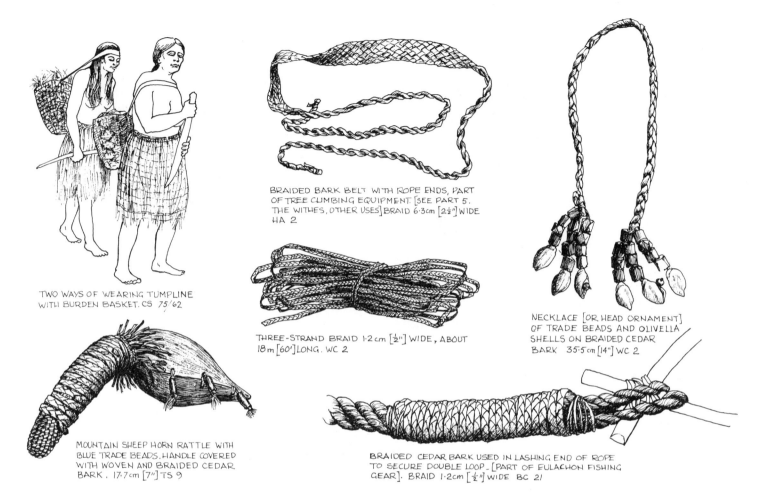

TWO WAYS OF WEARING TUMPLINE
WITH BURDEN BASKET. CS 75/62

BRAIDED BARK BELT WITH ROPE ENDS, PART
OF TREE CLIMBING EQUIPMENT. [SEE PART 5.
THE WITHES, OTHER USES] BRAID 6·3 cm [2½"] WIDE
HA 2

THREE-STRAND BRAID 1·2 cm [½"] WIDE, ABOUT
18 m [60'] LONG. WC 2

NECKLACE [OR HEAD ORNAMENT]
OF TRADE BEADS AND OLIVELLA
SHELLS ON BRAIDED CEDAR
BARK 35·5 cm [14"] WC 2

MOUNTAIN SHEEP HORN RATTLE WITH
BLUE TRADE BEADS, HANDLE COVERED
WITH WOVEN AND BRAIDED CEDAR
BARK. 17·7 cm [7"] TS 9

BRAIDED CEDAR BARK USED IN LASHING END OF ROPE
TO SECURE DOUBLE LOOP. [PART OF EULACHON FISHING
GEAR]. BRAID 1·2 cm [½"] WIDE BC 21

and for other needs. A chief stored eagle down — a symbol of peace and friendship — in a small cedar bag and used it on ceremonial occasions. He would place a handful of down in the open top of his dancing headdress when he danced to greet and welcome his guests to a feast or some other occasion, so that the white down floated gently to the ground before them.

Workers used baskets to carry away soil when excavating a house floor or a pit for implanting a post or pole. People going on long journeys took their possessions or trade goods in the canoe in large cedar baskets as well as boxes. A small, baglike, flexible basket filled with dentalium shells represented a standard measure for trading. Miniature baskets, often later sold to the tourist trade, had their origins as displays of technical skill or as gifts for small children.

Well-made baskets had value as trade items and exceptionally fine ones were presented to high-ranking women as potlatch gifts, a great honour for the basket's maker. After European settlement brought a new kind of commerce, one person, at least, kept his money in a cedar bark container: Tlingit Chief Shakes's money pouch, diagonally woven of cedar bark, a little frayed, is displayed at the Tongass Historical Society Museum in Ketchikan, Alaska.

The art of basketry in cedar bark, as well as spruce root, bear-grass and other materials, has never died out. The past decade has seen a lively renewal of this work as many older women revive their traditional skills. A few younger women, too, are taking the time to learn and practise this very ancient and satisfying art form.

A Haida woman weaving an intricate design into a cedar bark mat. Courtesy Field Museum of Natural History, Chicago, 16319

MATTING   Of all the items made from inner cedar bark, the woven mat must surely have been the most versatile, serving a wide range of uses from birth to death.

Northern mats, woven suspended from a frame, tended to be stiffer and coarser than those of the southern people. In addition to the plain mat, designs ranged from twilled weave, stripes and plaids (using bark dyed black and red) to more complex weaves of patterned squares. In addition, some mats had designs painted on the surface.

The bark strands used for weaving ranged in width from a fine 5 mm (3/16″) to a coarse 20 mm (¾″) or more. Sizes of mats also varied, depending on their purpose, and most families possessed a good assortment of them. Within the house, people often placed mats on the walls to help insulate them and to stop drafts from the cracks between the planks. These wall mats measured about 1.2 m (4′) wide and were twice as long or even longer, usually painted with designs. Large mats were also used as dividers between family units; these had an advantage over plank dividers, since mats could be removed easily to accommodate large gatherings. Captain Cook recorded another household use for mats: "There are holes, or windows, in the sides of the houses to look out at, having bits of mats hung before them, to prevent the rain getting in." People also hung mats from doorways to help keep out the cold and spread mats, held down with planks and rocks, over leaky spots on the roof.

Canoeists made good use of mats on their voyages, which often took them across wide stretches of ocean and

Two well-known Kwakiutl carvers, Charley James and Mungo Martin, beside a cedar bark mat painted with Sisiutl (a supernatural two-headed sea serpent) and a copper; in the background is a thunderbird pole. Courtesy Vancouver City Archives

through rough weather. While they always kneeled to paddle a small canoe, most dugouts required them to sit up on the thwarts; to add a measure of comfort, paddlers used folded cedar bark mats as cushions. Mats also protected both passengers and cargo from being drenched by windblown waves and spray. In later years, after sailing ships from other lands became a familiar sight along the coast, some canoe owners rigged their craft with a mast and a large, coarsely woven cedar bark mat sail or two. And in summer, when canoes were hauled up onto the beach to await their next journey, their owners left some water inside and covered them over with old mats to prevent the wood from drying and cracking in the sun.

The peoples of the coast made good use of mats in their daily life and work. They often used a cedar bark mat for kneeling on while digging clams, for cleaning fish on or for spreading out berries to dry, and they might cover a box of steaming fish or a steam cooking pit with a small mat. To ease the discomfort of a loaded burden basket, both men and women often folded a bark mat to make a protective pad for their back. In some areas a woman birthed her newborn onto a clean cedar bark mat, and mourners wrapped the body of a deceased person in a mat before placing it in a burial box that they might also wrap in a mat.

Several ceremonial and ritual occasions involved the use of cedar bark mats. The Tlingit welcomed a visiting chief of high rank when he arrived at a village by canoe

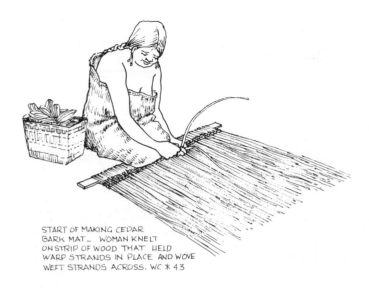

START OF MAKING CEDAR
BARK MAT — WOMAN KNELT
ON STRIP OF WOOD THAT HELD
WARP STRANDS IN PLACE AND WOVE
WEFT STRANDS ACROSS. WC ✱ 43

ONE EDGE HELD
BY TWINING
OVER FOLDED
BARK STRANDS.

OTHER EDGE WITH
BARK STRANDS
FOLDED BACK AND
TUCKED IN.

METHOD OF FINISHING EDGE ON
PLAITED MAT. KW 40

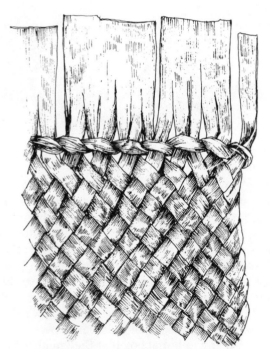

START OF DIAGONALLY PLAITED MAT USING
WIDE STRANDS, DIVIDED INTO NARROWER ONES.
TWINED EDGE HELD NARROW STRANDS IN PAIRS.
KW 40

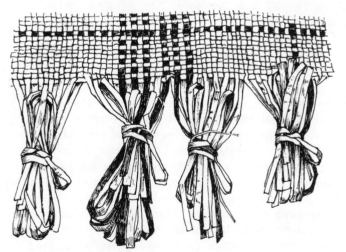

SECTION OF UNFINISHED CEDAR BARK MAT WITH PLAID DESIGN —
STRANDS AVERAGE 4mm [$\frac{3}{16}$"] NWC 4

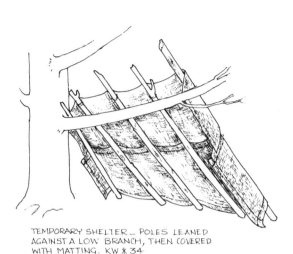

TEMPORARY SHELTER — POLES LEANED
AGAINST A LOW BRANCH, THEN COVERED
WITH MATTING. KW ✱ 34

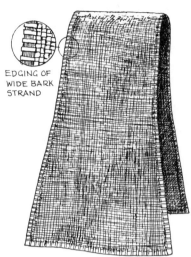
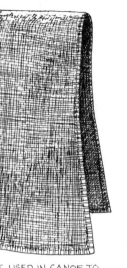
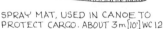

EDGING OF
WIDE BARK
STRAND

SPRAY MAT, USED IN CANOE TO
PROTECT CARGO. ABOUT 3 m [10'] WC 12

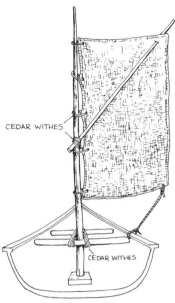

CEDAR WITHES

CEDAR WITHES

LARGE MAT, 1·22 m x 1·83 m [4'x6'],
RIGGED AS SAIL. WHEN NOT IN USE,
MAT ROLLED AROUND MAST. WC ✱ 43

by placing him on a sturdy bark mat and carrying him up the beach to the host chief's house. Similarly, as part of a Tsimshian First Salmon Ceremony to honour the return of this life-giving fish, they placed the first salmon to be caught on a newly made cedar bark mat and sprinkled it with eagle down — a symbol of friendship and welcome. Among some peoples, the First Salmon Ceremony ended by wrapping up all the salmon bones and uneaten parts in a cedar bark mat and putting it into the river. This ensured that the fish would go back to the salmon country at the edge of the sea and relate that they had been respectfully treated; then the other salmon would follow upriver. During a whale hunt, the whaler's wife lay quietly at home, covered with a cedar bark mat, to ensure that the harpooned whale behaved quietly and did not swim far out to sea. As part of a Coast Salish puberty ritual, a young girl remained in the house for four days, secluded in an area screened off with matting. Kwakiutl people hung a large painted mat from the crossbeam of a house to form a screen for their dancers during ceremonies. Behind it they changed masks and costumes and attended to other offstage preparations.

At social functions and other events, the host family unrolled long narrow feast mats 6.1 m to 9.1 m (20' to 30') long to provide clean seating for their guests.

Because strands of bark this length would have been unmanageable for the weaver, the mats were made on the diagonal; new strands were joined in at the edges and folded back diagonally to make the join invisible. There were also smaller food mats, plaited and twilled in design, for two to four people. After a feast guests took home surplus food wrapped in matting. Families and guests used mats to gamble on, to give as potlatch gifts and at day's end to sleep upon.

In a Kwakiutl ceremony pertaining to a chief's purchase of an expensive copper, the chief took the copper from its box lined with shredded cedar bark and laid it on a bark mat before making a speech to the assembled crowd. Along the Nass River, a person stood on a mat during a naming ceremony, and in that area a chief stood on a mat during part of a pole-raising ceremony. This custom has not lapsed with the years. In 1982, a 16.5 m (55') totem pole carved by Nishga artist Norman Tait was raised by the traditional method in front of the Field Museum in Chicago. Among the many Northwest Coast people flown in for the event was the carver's grandfather, Rufus Watts. The elderly chief, resplendent in his button blanket and impressive eagle headdress inlaid with abalone shell, followed tradition by standing on a large ceremonial mat while he related the story of the

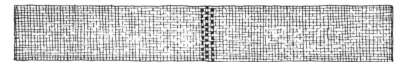

SHAMAN'S MAT ~ TO SPREAD OUT RITUAL EQUIPMENT ON. 1·83m [6'] TL 12

FOOD SERVED ON FOLDED MAT 85cm
x 25cm [34" x 10"] KW * 34

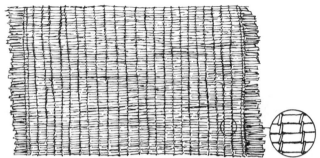

COARSE MAT TO CLEAN FISH ON ~ BARK STRANDS
TWINED WITH BARK ~ 1·27 m [50"] KW 12

REINFORCED EDGE
GAMBLING MAT 35·5cm [14"] WIDE. KW 12

GUEST MAT, TO ENSURE CLEAN
SEATING AT A FEAST. 30cm x 6m [12" x 20'] KW 12

DETAIL OF WEAVE

RAIN PONCHO MADE FROM TIGHTLY
WOVEN MAT, FOLDED. CHECKERBOARD
AND TWILLED PLAITING IN NATURAL AND
DYED BLACK CEDAR BARK CREATES
DESIGN. 88·7cm [35"] HA12

RAVEN DESIGN PAINTED ON PLAITED BARK MAT
1·64 m [64½"] KW OR HA 46

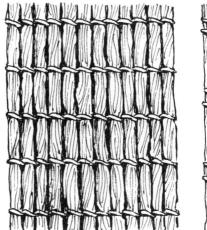
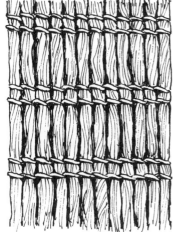

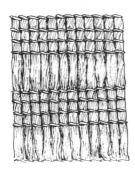

UNUSUAL WARP FOR CEDAR BARK BLANKET. NWC 26

pole to the assembled crowd. Specially woven for the occasion, the mat brought to that bustling Midwest city the soft scent of cedar and a touch of the Northwest Coast, as fully costumed Nishga people danced to the sound of the drum.

CLOTHING   For peoples who lived in a raincoast environment, where heavy downpours, frequent rain, drizzle, chill winds and often fog characterized the weather for much of the year, outer clothing had to be warm, practical and water-repellant. While loose garments of hide were certainly not unknown, they were not suitable as outerwear in the inclement weather. Clothing made from shredded and oiled cedar bark, however, gave protection from both rain and cold. The bark's multiple layers of fibre afforded good insulation and, when wet, dried quickly by the fire.

In good weather, little or no protection was required, and until missionaries imposed their European standards of modesty on the people, men often went about without clothing. Nor was it improper for women to wear only a skirt, though this practice was generally confined to indoors.

On the subject of the native clothing of the Westcoast people, Captain Cook remarked: "Two pieces make a

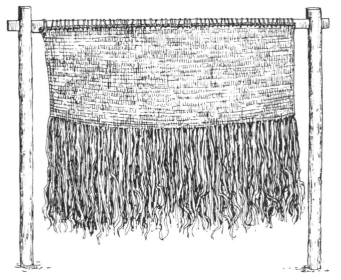

UNFINISHED SHREDDED CEDAR BARK BLANKET. NWC 75/12

141

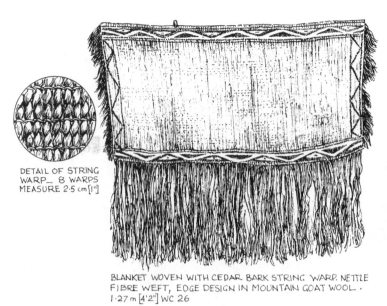

DETAIL OF STRING
WARP_ 8 WARPS
MEASURE 2·5 cm [1"]

BLANKET WOVEN WITH CEDAR BARK STRING WARP. NETTLE
FIBRE WEFT, EDGE DESIGN IN MOUNTAIN GOAT WOOL ·
1·27 m [4'2"] WC 26

FRINGED BLANKET, COLLECTED 1778 BY COOK EXPEDITION. 1·58 m [5'2"] WC 26

VARIOUS WAYS OF WEARING CEDAR BARK BLANKET

KW 75/47

KW 75/12

KW 75/47

BLANKET WRAPPED AROUND WAIST,
HELD IN PLACE WITH CORD OR BRAID.
WC 75/2

142

BLANKET COLLECTED BY COOK C.1780, MADE WITH CEDAR BARK WARP,
MOUNTAIN GOAT WOOL WEFT, RED AND BLACK DESIGN PAINTED
ON REPRESENTS OYSTERCATCHER AND TWO SKATES. 1·52 m [5']
PROBABLY WC 26

WC 75/47

CEDAR BARK BLANKET
FOLDED TWICE SERVED AS
SIMPLE CRADLE _ CEDAR WITHES
HELD INFANT SECURELY. WC #43

WC 75/21

WC 75/2

CS 75/47

WC 75/47

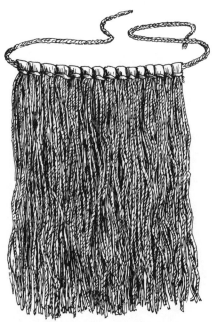

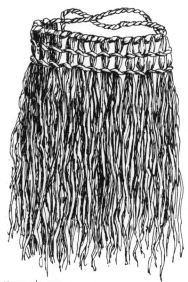

SHAMAN'S SKIRT OF SHREDDED CEDAR BARK, WITH PANELS DYED BROWN, AN ANIMAL PAW, BIRD HEAD AND WHITE FUR. 68·4 cm [27"] TL? 12

WOMAN'S APRON OF SHREDDED CEDAR BARK, SUSPENDED FROM BARK BRAID, PLIED INTO THICK FRINGE OF CORD. 66 cm [26"] LONG. KW 40

FEMALE'S APRON OF SHREDDED BARK OVER BARK ROPE, WITH TWO ROWS OF TWINED BARK FOR WAIST BAND 68·5 [27"] TS 12

complete dress, that is a cloak and a petticoat . . . the one is tied over the shoulders and the other is wrapped around the waist and reaches the middle of the leg." The "petticoat" was likely a woven bark rectangular garment, now generally referred to as a blanket, which could be worn in several ways. A woman wrapped it around her waist and let it hang to the ankle or hoisted it up above her chest so that it hung to the knee. Both men and women used this blanket as a cape and tied it under the chin or folded it over double in front; sometimes they belted it at the waist and tied or pinned it over one shoulder to free their arms for work. Women also wore a skirt of loose lengths of shredded cedar bark attached to a waistband, and a female shaman sometimes wore a ceremonial dance apron of loose bark strands held together by a few rows of twining at the top.

The fabric for quality clothing was comprised of bundles of soft-shredded yellow cedar bark, twined at intervals with cedar bark, nettle or wool string. To make a blanket, the weaver hung long lengths of these bundles over a rope attached to a crossbar between two uprights. Starting at the top, she made several close rows of twining to ensure a firm, strong edge, then followed this by rows of twining spaced about one finger-width apart. She strengthened the bottom edge with more closely twined

rows and cut off the surplus bark to form a fringe or added a fringe. After witnessing this work, John Jewitt wrote: "In order to form the cloth, the women, by whom the whole of this process is performed, take a certain number of these skeins and twist them together, by rolling them with their hands upon their knees into hard rolls, which are afterwards connected by means of a strong thread, made for the purpose." Recent attempts by native people at reviving this art have been successful, though enormously time consuming. Yet Cook remarked that this work, all done by women, was "performed with surprising dispatch," which can only point to the skill and experience of those early garment makers.

Cook also noted that women "have another cloak . . . it is close[d] all around with a hole in the middle just big enough to admit the head through." This was the attractive cedar bark cape of tailored weaving which fitted around the shoulders, flaring as it hung down to the waist or lower. The flare was accomplished by adding extra bundles of shredded cedar bark, bent over double, at strategic places as the work progressed. So expertly was this done that evidence of the addition was visible only on the inside of the cape.

Some blankets and capes had a painted design or, according to Jewitt, were "painted red with ochre the bet-

This detail of a watercolour sketch by John Webber of Cook's expedition, 1778, shows a Westcoast woman weaving a yellow cedar bark blanket; there are various bark and root baskets to her left. From Cook, A Voyage to the Pacific Ocean . . .

ter to keep out the rain." One such cape, loaned by the Royal Ontario Museum, was part of a travelling exhibition of Canadian spinning and weaving entitled "The Comfortable Arts." Probably from the west coast of Vancouver Island, the cape bore a simple design of several seals painted in red and black. When I examined the garment, I noticed that the small horseshoe-shaped ends of the extra, doubled-up bark strands, worked into the cape to make it flare, were on the painted side. This meant that the design had been painted on the *inside* of the cape and that the garment was, in fact, being displayed inside out. In the light of other beliefs and customs of the coast, it seems likely that the hidden depiction of seals was intended to bring success to the seal hunter. Whether worn by the hunter himself or more probably by his wife at home to ensure a successful hunt, the power of the painted seals lay in the secrecy of their presence within the cape.

For most peoples along the coast, protection from the elements consisted largely of these cedar bark garments, with ratfish or some other oil worked in to help repel the rain. Some people wove in other material with the bark: the Makah, for instance, added duck down for extra warmth to make a lightweight robe or "blanket." For this, the widely spaced cedar bark warp was woven with a weft spun from cedar bark that had duck down caught up in it. Feathers could be incorporated in the same way to add additional warmth during cold weather, and in many areas soft hide garments worn under bark clothing also gave extra warmth. Some blankets had a border design woven with mountain goat wool. To the north, the magnificent Chilkat blankets, used for ceremonial occasions by those of wealth and rank, were made with a warp of yellow cedar bark twine wrapped in mountain goat wool, with spun wool for the weft.

In heavy rain, a finely woven mat folded double and wrapped around the shoulders formed a type of rain cape for both men and women. Hats, also woven from cedar bark, provided additional protection in inclement weather and shaded the eyes from glare on the water. People of the northern and central coast favoured the wide-brimmed, flat-topped style, while those of the southern coast wore brimless hats in the shape of a tapered dome. Cook referred to these as "shaped like a flower pot" and said that they were "as good a covering for the head as can possibly be invented." These were often double-walled and quite waterproof. Jewitt noted that the Westcoast people wore a hat "when they go out upon any excursion, particularly whaling or fishing."

The well known "Maquinna hat" (first documented as having been worn by the all-powerful Chief Maquinna) carried a distinctive, traditional design depicting a whale hunt. This hat incorporated spruce root with the cedar bark and was worked in a different weave from the contemporary Maquinna hat, which has a cedar bark warp and weft totally covered by wrapped twining in beargrass and the characteristic knob on the top. Dyed strands create the colourful whale hunt design on the creamy white background.

Well-made yellow cedar bark clothing had a good trade value. Westcoast people traded four blankets of yellow cedar bark for one good stone hammer. Among the Quileute, twenty cedar bark skirts could be traded for two birdskin blankets, one whaling canoe or one slave. A single skirt could be worth one fathom of dentalium shells, which were used for jewellery or sewn in designs on ceremonial garments. A fathom (the length of a person's outstretched arms) required about forty of these tusklike shells, found only in deep water.

Worn-out blankets of cedar bark found a use in the

START OF CAPE AT NECKLINE

CEDAR BARK CORD

FINE BARK STRING

LENGTHS OF SOFT-SHREDDED BARK DOUBLED OVER CORD

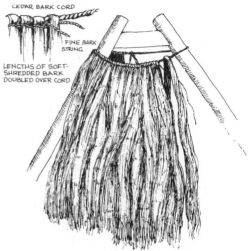

START OF MAKING WOMAN'S CAPE OF SOFT-SHREDDED CEDAR BARK. LENGTH ABOUT 81 cm [32"] CS 63

CONSTRUCTION OF CAPE

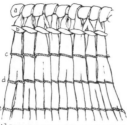

d] WHEN GARMENT FINISHED, TOP EDGE BOUND WITH STRIP OF FUR [NOW BARE] 0·8 cm [5/16"] WIDE.

b] ROW OF TWINING WITH BARK STRAND DIVIDED WARP EVENLY.

c] FIRST ROW TWINED WITH BARK STRING.

d] SECOND ROW OF TWINING DIVIDED MOST WARPS INTO TWO.

e] THIRD ROW OF TWINING DIVIDED REMAINING WARPS, GIVING CAPE ITS INITIAL FLARE. NWC 31

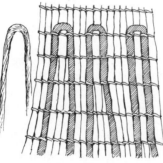

TO GIVE CAPE ITS FLARED SHAPE, DOUBLED STRANDS OF SOFT-SHREDDED BARK WERE ADDED OVER WARP STRANDS. AS WEAVING PROGRESSED, THESE WERE WORKED IN TO FORM EXTRA WARPS AS NEEDED.

WHEN COMPLETED, CAPE WAS TURNED INSIDE OUT TO CONCEAL THIS.

DETAIL OF SINGLE-ROW TWINING

WOMAN TWINED CAPE OVER WOODEN FRAME, LIFTING AND ROTATING GARMENT AS NECESSARY. ROWS OF TWINING CONTINUOUS, ABOUT 2 cm [3/4"] APART. CS 63

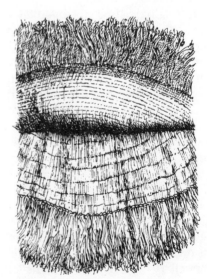

DETAIL OF DOUBLE-LAYERED CAPE. OUTER LAYER SOFT-SHREDDED AND CLOSELY TWINED, INNER LAYER SHREDDED, TWINING WIDELY SPACED. WC 58

WOMAN'S DOUBLE-LAYERED CAPE OF YELLOW CEDAR BARK. 74 cm [29"] LONG. WC 30/58

OUTER LAYER OF CAPE FINISHED OFF WITH SIX ROWS OF TWINING, WITH A CEDAR BARK STRING HELD IN BEHIND EACH WARP STRAND TO CREATE A FRINGE. INNER LAYER FRINGE COMPOSED OF LOOSE, SHREDDED BARK OF WARP STRANDS

CAPE WORN WITH SKIRT. KW 75/47

CHILD-SIZE CAPE. 22·5 cm [10"] LONG. WC 26

SOFT-SHREDDED CEDAR BARK CAPE, TURNED INSIDE OUT, SHOWS RED AND BLACK PAINTED DESIGN, WHICH INCLUDES SEA MAMMALS. 71 cm [24"] LONG. PROBABLY WC 6

RAINPROOF HAT TIGHTLY WOVEN IN THREE-STRAND TWINING. 35·5 cm [14"] DIAM. WC 9

CONTEMPORARY VERSION OF WHALING CHIEF'S HAT, WORN BY HIGH-RANKING WHALERS. CEDAR BARK WARP ENTIRELY COVERED BY WRAPPED TWINING OF SWAMP GRASS BLEACHED AND DYED IN COLOURS, WOVEN IN TRADITIONAL DESIGN DEPICTING WHALE HUNT. 27·9 [11"] WC 31

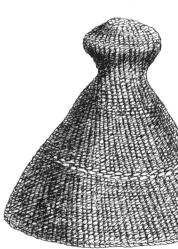

CAPE WORN OVER HEAD TO GIVE BACK PROTECTION. WC 75/12

TWINED CEDAR BARK HAT IN STYLE OF WESTCOAST WHALER'S HAT. 24·8 cm [9¾"] WC 31

COMMON TYPE OF HAT WORN BY MEN AND WOMEN IN MANY AREAS OF COAST. 39·4 cm [15½"] DIAM. HA 31

Four strengths of cedar bark rope ranging in thickness from 0.4 cm (3/16") to 2 cm (¾"). The top two ropes are two-ply, the lower ones, three-ply. The ropes are in the Thomas Burke Memorial Washington State Museum, Seattle. 73

Kwakiutl Hamatsa initiation ceremonial; the blanket was rolled up, tied to the end of a stick and lit from the fire. The smouldering blanket, swung around in a circle, dropped sparks onto the naked initiate. Another use was as a wrapping for the bodies of the dead before placing them in a gravehouse or other receptacle.

By 1875 cedar bark clothing had almost entirely been replaced by European garments, trade cloth and store-bought blankets, and the art of making cedar bark garments fell into decline.

CORDAGE   No one knows how long ago man — or perhaps it was woman — first invented rope, or where and how it was first used, yet early peoples the world over knew the technique for making this essential item. Perhaps lengths of twisted vine in some distant jungle initially inspired someone to ply together two strands of a fibrous plant material, but whatever the source, the basic technology has remained the same ever since.

Cedar bark is naturally strong, with a tensile strength of around 27 MPa (4000 lbs. p.s.i.). Readily available in long lengths and variable thicknesses, it provided Northwest Coast peoples with an excellent material for making all types of cordage: rope, string and fine twine. Although plain strands of inner cedar bark were well suited to certain binding and tying needs, the dried strands were brittle and inflexible, limiting their usefulness. When twisted and plied into a two- or three-strand

MAKING ROPE OF CEDAR BARK

② BOTH STRANDS TWISTED SEPARATELY TO RIGHT.

③ LITTLE FINGER OF RIGHT HAND PICKED UP LEFT STRAND

④ RIGHT HAND TURNED OVER TO LEFT, CROSSING BOTH STRANDS IN THAT DIRECTION

① TWO-PLY ROPE. TWO STRANDS KNOTTED TOGETHER AND HELD BETWEEN TOES.

JOINING ON AN EXTRA STRAND

① NEW STRAND LAID IN BEHIND SHORT END...

② BOTH TWISTED TOGETHER AS ONE.. ROPE MAKING THEN CONTINUED...

③ END CUT OFF WHEN ROPE FINISHED.

MAKING BARK ROPE USING TWO PERFORATED STONES

CEDAR BARK TWINE MADE BY ROLLING TWO STRANDS DOWN THIGH WITH RIGHT HAND; RELEASING LEFT HAND CAUSED TWISTED STRANDS TO PLY TOGETHER. ROLLING STRANDS BACK UP THIGH TIGHTENED PLY. PROCEDURE REPEATED CONTINUOUSLY TL 57

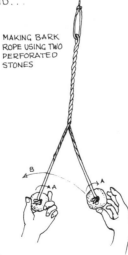
A] STONES AT END OF BARK STRANDS SPUN TO THE RIGHT, TO TWIST UP STRANDS.
B] STONE IN RIGHT HAND PASSED OVER LEFT.. REPEATEDLY.. CREATED 2-PLY ROPE. KW

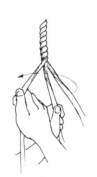
THREE-PLY ROPE. THREE STRANDS USED.. RIGHT HAND CROSSED OVER TO LEFT SIDE FOR EACH PLY

S TWIST AND Z TWIST ROPE. WITH RARE EXCEPTIONS, ALL ROPE AND CORDAGE MADE IN Z TWIST.

The late Hannah Parnell, Haida, making three-ply cedar bark halibut line at Masset, Queen Charlotte Islands. Photograph by Ulli Steltzer, courtesy of the photographer.

A cedar bark rope, 1.3 cm (½") thick, in the Thomas Burke Memorial Washington State Museum, Seattle. 73

filament, however, the bark remained flexible, and by adding in additional strands, any desired length could be achieved.

The ropemaker, often a woman, prepared the dried and split inner bark by cutting it into long, even strands of a width suitable for the size of rope required: a three-ply halibut line, for example, required bark strands about 8 mm (5/16") wide. The start of a two-ply rope began with two strands, moistened for flexibilty, knotted together at one end. Holding the knot between two of her toes and keeping the strands taut in her hands, the ropemaker twisted first one then the other strand to her *right*. When a short length was twisted tightly, she crossed them over each other in the opposite direction, to her *left*. Keeping the tension even, she continued the process of twisting, then crossing (plying), in one smooth, continuous motion. After making two or three spans of rope, she took the knotted end from between her toes, tied it around a post in the ground, and continued working.

When all that remained of one of the bark strands was a short end, the ropemaker took up another length of bark and dipped it into the small box of water close at hand to make it flexible. She placed one end of this strand behind the short end and twisted the two together until they became one. Then she continued twisting and plying as before, until she again needed to add another bark strand. Tight twisting, firm plying and even tension resulted in a neat, strong rope. To avoid fuzzy edges to the rope, she ensured that she always twined the bark in the direction it had been pulled from the tree, from the bottom upwards.

For a stronger rope that was barely thicker, the ropemaker twisted and plied together three strands for three-ply rope. To do this, she always took the right hand strand and simply passed it over to the left, crossing both of the other strands. To make an even stronger but thicker rope, she plied the rope with doubled strands.

I learned to make rope from the late Hannah Parnell,

150

CHILKAT DANCING BLANKET, WORN BY HIGH-RANKING PERSON ON CEREMONIAL OCCASIONS. WARP AND FRINGE CONSISTED OF CEDAR BARK CORD COVERED WITH MOUNTAIN GOAT WOOL, WEFT OF SPUN WOOL. 1·67 m [67½"] TL 54

with a Z twist: that is, the twisted strands lie diagonally from top right to bottom left, as opposed to the S twist, which is the reverse. All rope and string was produced with the Z twist, but cords of both twists were used together for a decorative effect on ceremonial accoutrements.

To make an ordinary cedar bark blanket, with the shredded bark twined in rows about 14 mm (9/16″) apart, a woman required approximately 91.5 m (300′) of fine string. Some blankets made with rows of twining closer together needed over fifty per cent more string. Capes, too, required many metres of twine, and some had an extra fringe of cord. A seamstress used cedar bark twine, a bone awl and a bone needle to sew together a number of pelts to make a long, loose fur cloak; sea otter furs made the finest of these garments, which usually belonged to chiefs and those of high rank and wealth. The exquisitely woven multicoloured Chilkat dancing blanket had a warp of yellow cedar bark cord wrapped with mountain goat wool; the cord gave the blanket substance and weight as well as durability. One blanket used at least 818 m (2685′) of two-ply cedar bark cord, including the long, heavy fringe that swung so beautifully as the wearer danced. Occasionally the top edge of a bird or fish mask had a trim of rope, and the face mask of the Fool dancer in Kwakiutl ceremonies had a rim carved to represent rope.

Rope and string played a vital part in the food quest. Fishermen used rope lines to take halibut and salmon, dipnets of cedar bark string, lashed to their frames with bark cord, to scoop up salmon, smelt, eulachon and herring, as well as cedar bark gill nets, which were held stretched out with anchor lines of rope to catch salmon. Hunters used cedar bark harpoon lines to retrieve sea mammals, and whalers carried cedar bark rope of tremendous strength. Attached to these whaling harpoon ropes were inflated sealskin floats that dragged through the water to slow down and tire the wounded whale as it tried to escape. When the whale was finally killed, a man leaped into the water to cut slits in its jaw and tie its mouth shut with rope to prevent the carcass from filling with water and sinking. The great animal was then buoyed up with floats and towed on strong ropes back to the village. Ropes were also used to tow planks, logs and unfinished canoes back to the village or to tow finished

an elderly woman in Masset, a Haida village in the Queen Charlotte Islands. When I met her she was busy making three-ply halibut line from lengths of cedar bark she kept in a brown paper bag; at her feet was an enamel bowl with water to keep the bark moist for working. Her delicate, gnarled fingers twisted the fibrous material with a speed and exactness that impressed me. Since Hannah did not speak English, and I could not understand Haida, I learned from her in the traditional way — by watching how it was done. Only after practice could I twine two- and three-ply rope evenly and with speed.

To make string and sewing twine in two-ply, there was a different, faster method than twisting and crossing. Holding two strands of bark in her left hand, with their lengths draped over her bare thigh, a woman rolled the strands forward with the palm of her right hand to twist them up and released her left hand to allow the strands to twist themselves up. Then, with a quick, reverse movement, she rolled her hand back along her thigh to tighten the ply. By drawing lengths of unspun cedar over her thigh and repeating the action over and over, she could spin quantities of two-ply twine or thread at quite a speed. Both these techniques produced rope and twine

REEL OF CEDAR BARK TWINE - UNUSUAL FOR ITS
S TWIST. 22·8 cm [9"] NWC 13

RATTLE OF DEER HOOVES STRUNG
TOGETHER WITH CEDAR BARK TWINE
10 cm [4"] CS 9

CRADLE BOARD - SOFT-
SHREDDED CEDAR BARK
BEDDING WITH CEDAR
BARK ROPE FOR LASHING
IN INFANT. CS 53

STRING TIED TO MOTHER'S FOOT
ENABLED HER TO ROCK CRADLE
SUSPENDED BY CEDAR BARK ROPE.
WC ☓43

SPLICED SECTION OF WHALING HARPOON
LASHED WITH CEDAR BARK TWINE, PRIOR TO
WRAPPING WITH CHERRY BARK. WC ☓ 43

METHOD OF LASHING BOX WITH ROPE
FOR TRAVELLING. UNTYING TOP LACING
ALLOWED REMOVAL OF LID FOR ACCESS
TO CONTENTS - KW 40

LARGE DIP NET OF CEDAR BARK
TWINE - FRONT EDGE MEASURES
94 cm [37"] HA 12

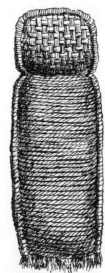

HEAD PRESSER - USED IN HEAD
DEFORMATION OF INFANT,
A SYMBOL OF HIGH BIRTH.
25·3 cm [10"] CS [CHINOOK] 12

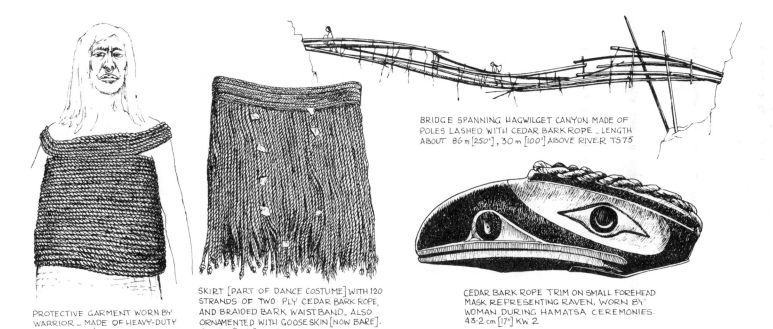

PROTECTIVE GARMENT WORN BY WARRIOR – MADE OF HEAVY-DUTY ROPE. KW 75/12

SKIRT [PART OF DANCE COSTUME] WITH 120 STRANDS OF TWO-PLY CEDAR BARK ROPE, AND BRAIDED BARK WAISTBAND. ALSO ORNAMENTED WITH GOOSE SKIN [NOW BARE]. 89.5 cm [35¼"] KW 9

BRIDGE SPANNING HAGWILGET CANYON MADE OF POLES LASHED WITH CEDAR BARK ROPE – LENGTH ABOUT 86 m [250'], 30 m [100'] ABOVE RIVER TS 75

CEDAR BARK ROPE TRIM ON SMALL FOREHEAD MASK REPRESENTING RAVEN, WORN BY WOMAN DURING HAMATSA CEREMONIES. 43.2 cm [17"] KW 2

canoes to another village for trade. Canoeists used strong rope on their heavy, perforated stone anchors and for lines to control their sails.

House builders relied on cedar bark rope in many ways. They used it to measure out floor plans and to ensure a true rectangle or square by checking distances between specific points. A centre point, for instance, was determined by stretching a rope from corner to corner, then folding the rope in half. They also used rope to raise poles, roof beams and rafters. The smoke hole shutter of a northern house was built so it could be adjusted by pulling a rope from inside the house. Footbridges across narrow canyons relied on long lengths of heavy-duty rope to support their planking.

Indoors, people used rope to stow various items by hanging them from the rafters and to suspend poles over the fire in order to smoke and store dried fish. Some large baskets had rope running beneath the base for reinforcement or around the rim as a drawstring, and baskets often had handles of rope, as did wooden water buckets. The lids of storage boxes were often tied down securely with rope, particularly if they were to be transported. Burial boxes, too, were tied with rope, and some coffins were hauled up to the higher branches of trees by a rope that was then used to tie the box to the tree.

The uses for rope and string among the different peoples along the coast were many, including warfare. To protect his body from injury, a Kwakiutl warrior wore armour comprised of thick rope sewn into a vest-shaped garment. Most warfare was carried out for revenge, to acquire property and to take slaves, who were an important wealth symbol of the rich. One of the warriors was responsible for the rope with which to tie up captured slaves for the victors' return journey. As a defence measure, some Tsimshian villages built a barricaded fort on a hill top, to which the people withdrew when warned of an enemy attack. Outside the barricade they secured large, heavy logs with ropes; when the enemy climbed the hill, they released the ropes, sending the logs rolling downhill with devastating effect.

It should be emphasized that not all cordage was made from cedar bark. Other materials used included stinging nettle fibres, cattail leaves, spruce root, kelp stipes, human hair, bear intestines, animal sinew, hide and, of course, cedar withes.

SHREDDED AND SOFT-SHREDDED BARK USES   In addition to clothing, coast peoples found many uses for soft-shredded cedar bark, whose fluffy fibres had the extra softness and absorbency suitable for towel-

TOWEL OF SOFT-SHREDDED
CEDAR BARK. 32 cm [12½"] CS 21

BABY DIAPERS OF SOFT-SHREDDED
YELLOW CEDAR BARK- EACH ABOUT
FIST SIZE. WC 51/31 COURTESY ULLI
STELTZER

WOODEN GAMING DISCS HIDDEN IN SHREDDED
CEDAR BARK DURING GAMBLING. KW ✕ 36

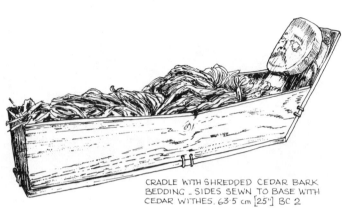

CRADLE WITH SHREDDED CEDAR BARK
BEDDING _ SIDES SEWN TO BASE WITH
CEDAR WITHES. 63·5 cm [25"] BC 2

ling, diapers and other such needs.

Among the Kwakiutl, a woman, aided by a midwife, gave birth straddling a shallow pit that was dug in the house floor, lined with soft-shredded bark to receive the infant. A newborn of the Coast Salish people was wrapped in soft-shredded bark, with a piece of cedar bark blanket around it, before being tied onto its cradle board with wads of soft-shredded bark under its head and at its feet. A child who was to undergo head deformation — a symbol of high rank — had a pad of soft bark (or a pressure board) placed on its forehead; strings laced over this, from each side of the cradle, put a constant, steady pressure on the tiny skull, which ultimately attained the desirable flattened shape.

Most mothers used soft-shredded bark or absorbent moss for diapers and for a mattress in the cradle; some, like the Coast Salish, mixed the shredded bark with bird down for extra softness. Women with access to yellow cedar preferred it to the red cedar bark for their infants' diapers because it was particularly soft when shredded, and for this reason they used it to wash their babies. Women also used the softened bark for menstrual pads. After a feast, where much of the eating was done with

the fingers, guests were given soft-shredded bark on which to wipe their hands. Referring to a feast given by Chief Maquinna at Yuquot, Alexander Walker wrote: "After the eating was finished, a quantity of the bark prepared for making Cloth was presented, and was used as towels for cleaning their hands."

The soft-shredded bark had its place in medicine also, frequently being applied as a dressing to various injuries. These uses are described in the section on healing. In a more drastic measure used by the Kwakiutl, soft-shredded bark was laid on an infected wound and ignited; the slow-burning material cauterized the affected area.

The slow-burning property of bark provided the slow match — a means of transporting fire. Shredded cedar bark was twisted, then wrapped spirally with a plain strip of bark; when lit at one end, it burned slowly for a long time. Fluffy pieces of dry shredded bark made good tinder, and wads of it were used for getting a fire going.

Gambling games, popular along the entire coast, took several different forms, but most of them required a pile of shredded cedar bark as a cover-up for a secret manoeuvre. For instance, a gambler who had to shuffle

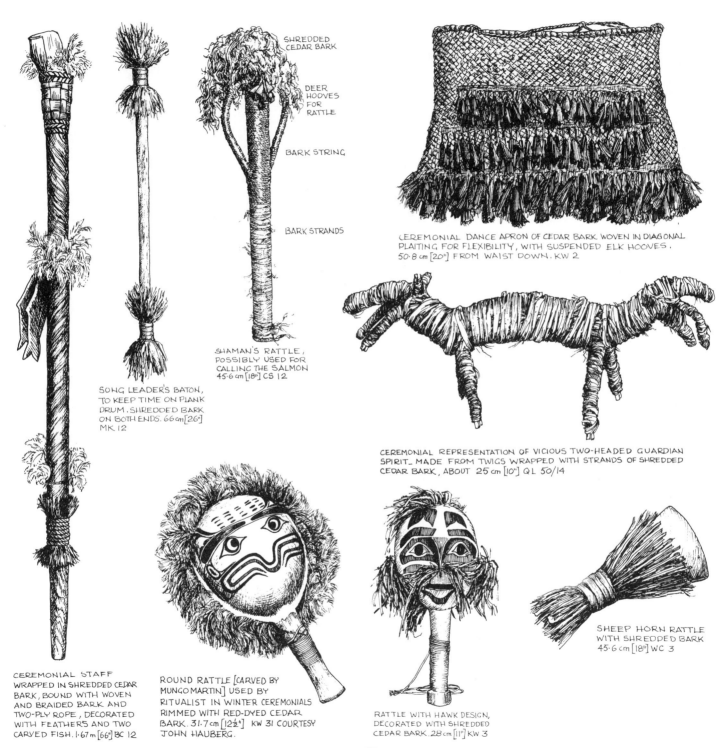

SHREDDED
CEDAR
BARK

DEER
HOOVES
FOR
RATTLE

BARK STRING

BARK STRANDS

SHAMAN'S RATTLE,
POSSIBLY USED FOR
CALLING THE SALMON
45·6 cm [18"] CS 12

SONG LEADER'S BATON,
TO KEEP TIME ON PLANK
DRUM. SHREDDED BARK
ON BOTH ENDS. 66 cm [26"]
MK 12

CEREMONIAL DANCE APRON OF CEDAR BARK WOVEN IN DIAGONAL
PLAITING FOR FLEXIBILITY, WITH SUSPENDED ELK HOOVES.
50·8 cm [20"] FROM WAIST DOWN. KW 2

CEREMONIAL REPRESENTATION OF VICIOUS TWO-HEADED GUARDIAN
SPIRIT MADE FROM TWIGS WRAPPED WITH STRANDS OF SHREDDED
CEDAR BARK, ABOUT 25 cm [10"] QL 50/14

CEREMONIAL STAFF
WRAPPED IN SHREDDED CEDAR
BARK, BOUND WITH WOVEN
AND BRAIDED BARK AND
TWO-PLY ROPE, DECORATED
WITH FEATHERS AND TWO
CARVED FISH. 1·67 m [66"] BC 12

ROUND RATTLE [CARVED BY
MUNGO MARTIN] USED BY
RITUALIST IN WINTER CEREMONIALS
RIMMED WITH RED-DYED CEDAR
BARK. 31·7 cm [12½"] KW 31 COURTESY
JOHN HAUBERG.

RATTLE WITH HAWK DESIGN,
DECORATED WITH SHREDDED
CEDAR BARK. 28 cm [11"] KW 3

SHEEP HORN RATTLE
WITH SHREDDED BARK
45·6 cm [18"] WC 3

PAIR OF BRAIDED KNEE RINGS FOR
CEREMONIAL DANCING. 11·4 cm [4½"]DIAM.
KW 12

PAIR OF WRISTLETS
FOR CEREMONIAL
DANCING. 12·7cm [5"]BC 12

BIRD MASK USED IN HAMATSA CEREMONIES,
STRAPPED TO WEARERS BODY FOR SUPPORT,
LENGTHS OF SHREDDED CEDAR BARK DYED
RED COVERED HIS HUMAN FORM. HINGED
LOWER BEAK MANIPULATED WITH STRINGS.
MASK ABOUT 1·2 m [4'] KW 35

BONE INSTRUMENT PUNCTURED
SKIN TO FACILITATE SEWING
MINIATURE PADDLES TO BODY
OF SECRET SOCIETY INITIATE.
POINT IS BLOOD STAINED.
BONE 14 cm [5½"] KW 12

TOWEL USED BY GIRL AT HER
PUBERTY CEREMONY. 43 cm [17"]
QL 50/14

OCTOPUS PUPPET USED
CEREMONIALLY. MOUTH
AND TENTACLES OF CEDAR
BARK ROPE AND BRAID,
LEATHER BODY. 28 cm [11"]
KW 3

SUPERNATURAL CODFISH MASK
WITH CEDAR BARK FRINGE TO
COVER HUMAN FORM _ MASK
LENGTH 41·9 cm [16½"] KW 3

WOLF DANCER WEARING SHREDDED CEDAR BARK
SKIRT AND WRISTLETS _ SAME MATERIAL ON MASK.
KW 75/12

CEREMONIAL FIGURE
OF WOOD WITH CEDAR
BARK HAIR. 38cm [15"]CS12

GAMING RING _ ONE TEAM ROLLED OR
THREW CEDAR BARK RING TO OPPONENT
WHO HAD TO CATCH OR PIERCE IT WITH
DART. 23 cm [9"] KW 12

and divide a number of gambling sticks (or bones or discs), and hold them in his hands for his opponent to guess which one held a specially marked piece, would do so under a pile of shredded bark. Needless to say, sleight-of-hand also played a part in the skill of the game. Such games were an enjoyable part of the entertainment at feasts and gatherings, and lengthy gambling games are still played along the coast at potlatches and canoe races.

For their ceremonies, the Kwakiutl used many types of costuming and headgear of shredded bark, among them the often elaborate and intricately braided head and neck rings of the Hamatsa initiate and others associated with the ceremonies. Two women attendants wore bird-form headdresses of cedar bark in lieu of wooden masks. The Hamatsa novice wore a different head ring, neck ring, and wristlets for each stage of his initiation on the four nights of dancing. All such ceremonial regalia was dyed red, but one series of dances, the Tsetsika (also termed the Cedar Bark Dances), incorporated both natural and red-dyed bark in its regalia. Dancers in the nonceremonial season wore items of natural bark. The Kwakiutl probably developed the most flamboyant head and neck rings, but other peoples also had their own versions of these ceremonial pieces. For initiation and for curing ceremonies, the Quileute used cedar bark head rings, and a Westcoast father of twins, who was considered to be endowed with supernatural powers, wore a special cedar bark head ring when he ritually called the salmon to return upriver. The Tsimshian, too, used ceremonial headgear of cedar bark.

The process of making paint also involved soft-shredded bark. Red and blue-green were made by grinding certain soft stones to a powder; charcoal was used for black, and the ashes of burned clam shells, for white. All these required a binding agent so that the pigments would adhere to a wood or other surface. To make the binding agent, the Indian artist chewed salmon eggs, while holding in his cheek a wad of soft-shredded cedar bark to filter out the glutinous substance, which he spat onto a paint palette and mixed with the powdered pigment. People used such paints on boxes, masks and other carvings, and occasionally on mats, basketry and clothing.

ELABORATE HAMATSA NECK RING OF SHREDDED CEDAR BARK INCORPORATING FOUR SETS OF CARVED WOODEN HEADS, WITH HANDS AND FEET. 102 cm [40"] KW 12

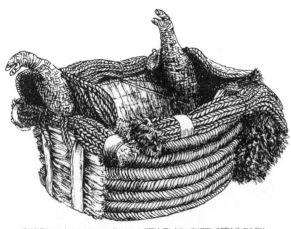

CEREMONIAL HEAD RING WITH ELABORATE CEDAR BARK
BRAIDING THAT INCLUDES TWO BIRDS, PROBABLY EAGLES.
ABOUT 58 cm [23"] CIRCUM. KW 12

SHAMAN'S HEADDRESS - COILED CEDAR BARK ROPE,
CARVED WOODEN HEADS AND HAIR. ABOUT 33 cm [13"] TL45

HAMATSA HEAD RING   19 cm [7½"] KW 3

HEAD RING OF HAMATSA INITIATE.
ABOUT 28 cm [11"] KW 35

HAMATSA HEAD RING   17·6 cm [7"] KW 3

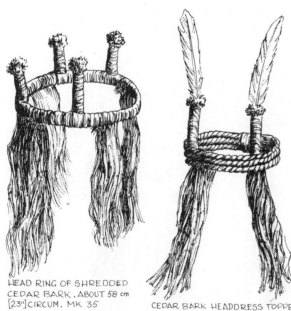

HEAD RING OF SHREDDED
CEDAR BARK. ABOUT 58 cm
[23"] CIRCUM. MK 35

CEDAR BARK HEADDRESS TOPPED
WITH FEATHERS, WORN IN WINTER
CEREMONIALS. ABOUT 58 cm [23"]
CIRCUM. KW 35

HAMATSA HEADPIECE   43 cm [17"] KW 3

HAMATSA HEAD RING 20·3 cm [8"] KW 3

HEAD RING COMPOSED OF FOUR
ROWS OF SQUARE BRAID. 20·3 cm
[8"] DIAM. KW 3

DETAIL: ONE
ROW OF SQUARE
BRAID.

CEREMONIAL HEADDRESS.
ABOUT 56 cm [22"] QL 50

CEREMONIAL HEADBAND OF SOFT-SHREDDED
CEDAR BARK. CS 38

COMPLEX NECK RING OF SHREDDED
AND SOFT-SHREDDED BARK WITH
CARVED HEAD, HANDS AND SKULLS,
ALSO FOOT-SHAPED RATTLES - WORN
IN HAMATSA CEREMONIES. 1.42 cm [4'8"]
KW 7

CEDAR BARK NECK RINGS WORN ON CEREMONIAL OCCASIONS
BY MEMBERS OF GRIZZLY BEAR SOCIETY.
LEFT: 50.6 cm [20"] KW 12   RIGHT: 53 cm [21"] KW 12

TWO TSIMSHIAN CHIEFS IN CEREMONIAL REGALIA,
INCLUDING HEAD RINGS AND NECK RINGS. TS 75/33

UNUSUALLY LARGE NECK RING COMPOSED OF
CEDAR BARK BRAIDING OVER CORE OF
SHREDDED BARK, WITH LONG FRINGES OF
BRAID. 1.37 m [54"] BC 12

PART 5

CEDAR: THE WITHES

GATHERING AND PREPARING Cedar withes are the branchlets that hang down from the main branches of the cedar in long, graceful curves. Some are short, with leaves sprouting part way along, but a few are particularly long, slender and free of any shoots. Occasionally a withe grows directly from the trunk and reaches an extreme length, and these were the most desired by coast peoples for making heavy-duty rope. The best withes were found on cedars standing in swampy areas.

I knew that withes were tough as I had used them for various lashing jobs while camping, but I did not know the real strength of cedar withe until Laurence Brown, professor of metallurgical engineering at the University of British Columbia, conducted a series of breaking load and tensile strength tests for me. He tested a fairly slender, untwisted withe of red cedar (with a cross section of 28 mm² (less than ¼") and found the breaking

load to be 1890 N (425 lbs.). When he tested a two-ply withe rope, it broke at 1690 N (380 lbs.); twisting the fibre gave the withe greater flexibility, but weakened the overall strength. Nevertheless, Dr. Brown was surprised that the tensile strength of the withe, almost 67 MPa (10 000 lbs. p.s.i.), proved to be nearly twice that of a clear specimen of unseasoned cedar wood and about thirty per cent greater than Douglas fir, the strongest softwood commercially available. After examining a section of cedar withe with a scanning electron microscope, he found that though the withe's cell size was about the same as that of cedar wood, the wall thickness was greater, giving the withe a much higher density and hence a greater strength.

Although Northwest Coast peoples did not know the tensile strength of cedar withe, they did have a clear and practical comprehension of its amazing properties and of how to make full use of them. They gathered the slender branches in the spring when the sap was running and the withe was at its most flexible. Being so pliable and fibrous, the withe could not be broken off without excessive twisting and mangling, so it had to be

Photograph by Hilary Stewart

The cells of a red cedar withe, magnified 12 000 times, showing the thick walls that give it particular strength. Photograph by Mary Magor. Courtesy Laurence C. Brown

PREPARING CEDAR WITHES. KW 34

① WITHES CLEANED OF SMALL TWIGS, THEN HEATED OVER FIRE.

② TO REMOVE BARK, HEATED WITHE PULLED THROUGH SPLIT STICK DRIVEN INTO GROUND.

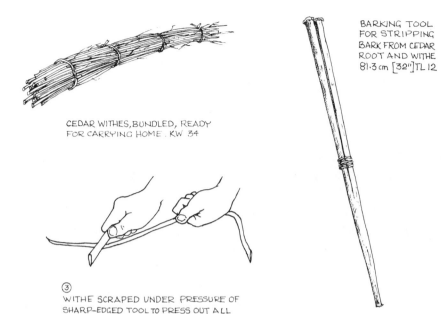

CEDAR WITHES, BUNDLED, READY FOR CARRYING HOME. KW 34

③ WITHE SCRAPED UNDER PRESSURE OF SHARP-EDGED TOOL TO PRESS OUT ALL SAP— AN AID TO FLEXIBILITY.

BARKING TOOL FOR STRIPPING BARK FROM CEDAR ROOT AND WITHE 81·3 cm [32"] TL 12

cut or chopped off. Once the sap had dried out of the withe, it became rigid, but regained some flexibility after being soaked in water a few hours or days, depending on its thickness.

A man who wanted an untwisted withe first chose one of the right thickness, cut it off, coiled it up and heated it over the fire. When the sap had heated through, he placed the thin end of the withe in the split end of a bark stripping tool, which he had driven into the ground. Gripping the top end of the split stick firmly with one hand, he pulled the withe through with the other and stripped off the bark to leave smooth, clean wood.

If a man needed a flexible withe for lashing or tying purposes, he stripped off the bark, then again heated the withe. Holding the thin end in his left hand, he twisted up a short length of it with his right, wrapped that part around his left hand, and continued twisting until he reached the thick end. Twisting the fibrous strands gave the withe permanent flexibility. When I demonstrated this at a lecture some years ago, Ed Leon, a Coast Salish elder, said that when his grandmother twisted withes, she put her foot on the small end and twisted up the withe vertically. For quick or makeshift use, he had another way of softening the withe for flexibility. "Twist it right on the tree," he said, "we used to do that when

we got a deer, to tie up the legs. No need to cut it first and take the bark off." It was further proof to me of the diversity of technologies for accomplishing any one task.

Alice Paul, a Hesquiat basketmaker, told me that withes could be collected later in the year than spring; as the sap subsided, however, the bark adhered to the wood and the withe became less flexible. To remove the bark, it was necessary to bite it off with the teeth, bit by bit.

ROPES   Strong, lengthy two-ply ropes for fishing, sealing and canoe anchor lines were made from withes. The Field Museum in Chicago has an excellent example of this in a coiled rope about 36.6 m (120') long and 9 cm (⅜") thick. Even more impressive is a large coil of heavy-duty three-ply withe rope once used by Makah whalers; it has a uniform thickness of more than 4 cm (1½") and has the precision look of a factory-made product.

Making a long rope required many withes. Alice Paul split the slender branchlets into three and discarded the centre section, which she regarded as not being suitable for making rope. The outer sections she split again into several strands, then softened by soaking them in water. To make two-ply rope, she used several strands together in two bundles, and twisted them in the same manner as for making cedar bark rope, frequently adding in strands

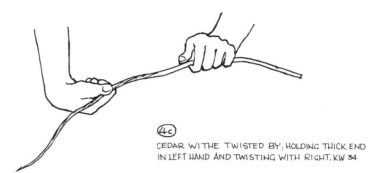

④c
CEDAR WITHE TWISTED BY HOLDING THICK END
IN LEFT HAND AND TWISTING WITH RIGHT. KW 34

④a
CEDAR WITHE TWISTED
VERTICALLY, WITH ONE
END HELD BY THE FOOT.
CS

④b
WITHE TWISTED WITH ONE END HELD IN THE MOUTH. 75/12

WITHE TWISTED WHILE STILL ON THE
BRANCH: FOR MAKESHIFT USE. CS 70

163

DETAIL

WHALING LINE, 3-PLY, TWISTED WITHES OF YOUNG
RED CEDAR. 3.3 cm [1¼"] THICK. MK 12

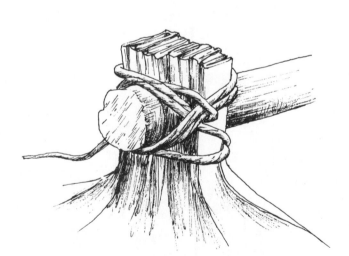

HANDLE OF CEDAR BARK CANOE BAILER
LASHED ON WITH CEDAR WITHE. CS 12

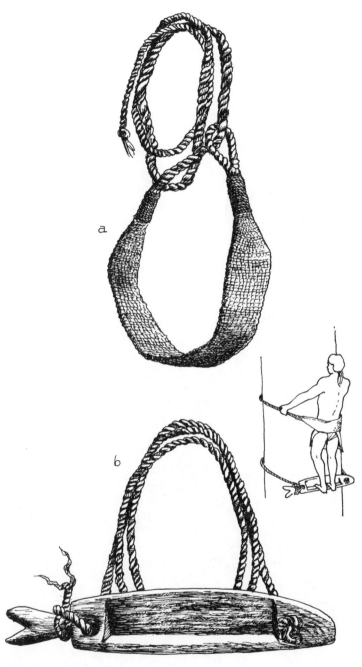

a

b

TWO-PIECE TREE CLIMBING EQUIPMENT.

a] HEAVY BELT WOVEN WITH SPLIT CEDAR WITHES, WITH THREE-PLY
   WITHE ROPE. BELT 12.7 cm [5"] WIDE

b] FISH-SHAPED FOOT LEDGE, WITH WITHE ROPE, HAS CONCAVE BACK
   TO STEADY IT AGAINST TREE TRUNK. 63.5 cm [25"] TL 12

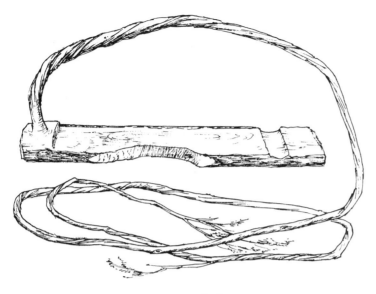

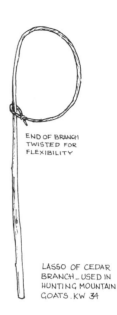

VERY LONG CEDAR BRANCH, ABOUT 4·5m [15'] ATTACHED TO SECTION OF TRUNK, FORMED PART OF TREE CLIMBING EQUIPMENT. HA 2.

END OF BRANCH TWISTED FOR FLEXIBILITY

LASSO OF CEDAR BRANCH—USED IN HUNTING MOUNTAIN GOATS. KW 34

as required to maintain an even thickness and to continue its length.

The Kwakiutl had a different method of making withe rope, and because heavy-duty rope required strong hands, it was generally made by a man. He used only very long slender withes and prepared them in the usual manner — by heating, stripping and twisting. He then laid the withes on a cedar board and pounded them with the butt of a heavy wedge, further breaking up the fibrous strands. Next, he made a steam pit by piling dulse (a seaweed) thickly over red-hot rocks, laid on the withes, and added more dulse before pouring on two buckets of warm, fresh water. Covering the whole thing with cedar bark mats, he let the steam permeate the withes for about ten minutes, pulling them out one at a time as needed to make the rope. When he had twisted about two-thirds of a withe, the ropemaker worked in a new one, always laying the thin end next to a thick, and vice versa, to keep the diameter of the rope even.

To make a short length of two-ply rope, the ropemaker twisted a single withe, then doubled it so that the two halves entwined themselves with a reverse twist.

LASHING AND SEWING   In a culture that did not have nails, screws and bolts, there was a need for withe lashing as a fastening material. Before the Haida used the tongue-and-groove technique for setting wall planks into a baseboard, these were set into the ground, and the edges lashed together with cedar withes. The planks of house partitions and dance screens were also joined together with withes. The Westcoast and Salish tied down their roof planks with withes and hung their wall planks horizontally on slings of withes.

Northern people, who used grooved and perforated mauls, found withes most suitable for lashing these heavy stone heads onto wooden hafts. People also placed a grommet or crown of twisted withe at the top of wooden wedges to prevent repeated blows of the maul from splitting them.

An important part of the art of making boxes was joining the open corner, and for this cedar withes proved ideal. The technique of sewing wood was well developed along the coast and was also used to manufacture and repair wooden items; countersinking the stitch into a groove cut into the wood made an almost invisible join. To prepare withes for sewing, the Kwakiutl, and probably others, first soaked them for four days in urine. This made the strands softer for sewing and prevented them from rotting.

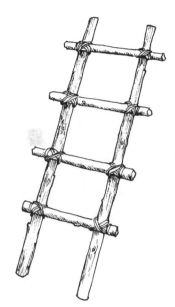

LADDER [POSSIBLY INFLUENCED
BY CONTACT] LASHED WITH
WITHES. WC * 43

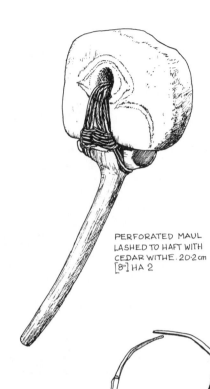

PERFORATED MAUL
LASHED TO HAFT WITH
CEDAR WITHE. 20·2 cm
[8"] HA 2

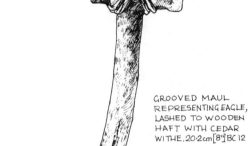

GROOVED MAUL
REPRESENTING EAGLE,
LASHED TO WOODEN
HAFT WITH CEDAR
WITHE. 20·2cm [8"] BC 12

RATTLE - DEER HOOVES STRUNG
ON WITHE HOOP, WITH SECTIONS OF
BIRD QUILLS. 12·6 cm [5"] DIAM. NWC 9

SLENDER WITHES USED
FOR TYING BRAIDS, ALSO
FOR HANGING EAR AND
NOSE ORNAMENTS. WC 43

SET OF WOODEN CLAWS [CATALOGUED AS PANTHER CLAWS]
HELD TOGETHER WITH CEDAR WITHES. 15·2 cm [6"] DIAM. WC 2

BENTWOOD BOX - CORNER SEWN
WITH CEDAR WITHE, AND BASE
ATTACHED TO SIDES WITH SAME
MATERIAL. 40·5 cm [16"] KW 31

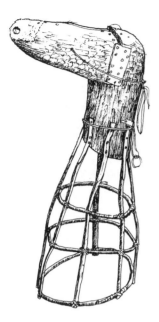

TRANSFORMATION MASK, ONCE
COVERED IN DEERSKIN, OPENED
TO REVEAL HUMAN FACE. FRAME
MADE OF CEDAR WITHES.
61 cm [24"] CS 2

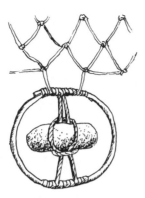

GILL NET SINKER.
STONE HELD WITHIN
CEDAR WITHE HOOP.
HA 32

SINKER STONE
WRAPPED IN STRANDS
OF SPLIT WITHES.
14·6 cm [5¾"] CS 65

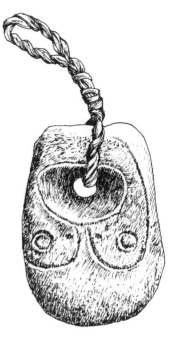

STRONG WITHE LOOP ON
HEAVY STONE SINKER,
FOR ATTACHMENT. 16 cm [6¼"]
NWC 14

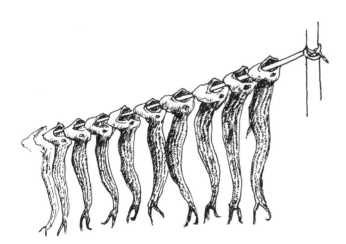

EULACHON, THREADED ON CEDAR WITHE, HUNG UP TO DRY. TS ✳ 32

OTHER USES   Because of their strength, untwisted cedar withes were ideal for making the burden basket — a large openwork container carried on the back with the aid of a tumpline — used for hauling fish, clams, firewood and various household goods. Occasionally the bark was left on before splitting to allow the basketmaker to create a two-colour design, using split withe with and without the brown of the bark.

On canoe journeys, roughly woven withes provided a coarse matting for the bottom of the dugout to help keep the cargo and people's feet dry. Fish nets and duck nets, too, were occasionally made from these tough, fibrous strands, as was the frame for a sea urchin scoop or a crabnet.

The Quinault Coast Salish used untwisted withes for the frame of a makeshift container for meat. They bent two short lengths of withe into hoops, each lashed across with cedar bark. They piled up pieces of meat on one hoop, laid the other hoop on top of the meat, and tied the whole bundle together using cedar bark, with a wide strip of bark for a carrying handle. Another interesting Quinault use of untwisted withe was the makeshift stretcher. They lashed poles together with withes to form a rectangular frame and tied more withes across to support the injured person.

Fishermen used loops or ties of twisted withe to attach sinker stones to the bottom edge of gill and other nets or to carry a fish hook to the sea bottom. Women found withes ideal for stringing up and drying eulachon, herring, smelt and clams; they also tied up bundles of dried salmon with withes before storing them. Westcoast people prepared sea cucumbers for boiling by stringing a dozen on a cedar withe, tying the two ends to form a circle, and dragging the soft invertebrates over barnacled rocks to remove the outer slime.

The Reverend Collison described a good use of cedar branches among the Haida in the late 1880s: "To strengthen an old or weakened canoe . . . they procured a number of cedar branches. These they planed off on two sides [they were probably split], and nailed them about twenty inches apart the whole length of the canoe, which so strengthened it that it was unlikely she would split in a rough sea."

Boughs of cedar, with leaves attached, also served several uses. Fishermen sank these, using sinker stones, in a quiet bay where herring spawned in early spring, returning later to haul out the boughs covered with the edible and much favoured herring roe. When harvesting and drying edible seaweeds, the Kwakiutl interspersed each layer with cedar boughs to provide aeration. Some piled up cedar boughs for bedding, covered them with a deer hide, and no doubt enjoyed the pungent aroma of the tree. Many canoe owners used cedar boughs to protect their beached craft from drying and cracking in the sun.

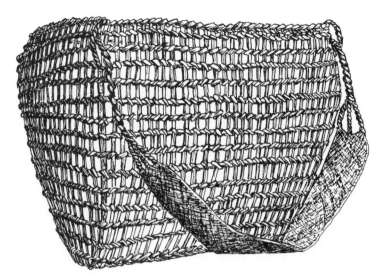

BURDEN BASKET OF SPLIT CEDAR WITHES _ WRAPPED CROSSED WARP OF CEDAR ROOT_TUMPLINE OF WOVEN CEDAR BARK. 50·8cm [20"] WIDE. KW 12

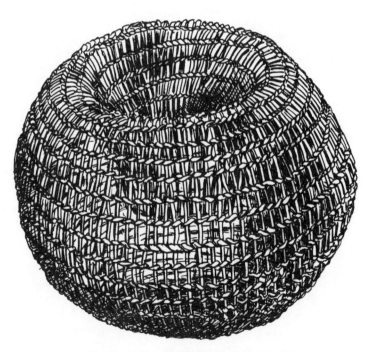

GLOBULAR TRAP FOR CATCHING SMALL ROCK COD USED MAINLY FOR BAIT_ MADE OF SPLIT CEDAR WITHES. 56cm [22"] KW 78

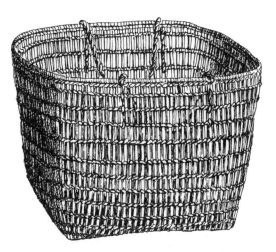

CLAM BASKET OF SPLIT CEDAR WITHES.
WRAPPED CROSSED WARP OF SPLIT CEDAR
ROOT, CEDAR BARK ROPE HANDLE. 26 cm
[10¼"] KW 3

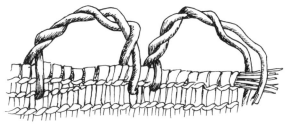

DOUBLE HANDLE ON BASKET MADE WITH SINGLE WITHE. WC 65

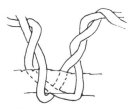

DIAGRAM SHOWS HOW THIS
WAS DONE. AFTER CROES

CRADLE OF WOVEN SPLIT CEDAR WITHES, WITH WHOLE
WITHE ATTACHED TO EACH SIDE FOR STRENGTH..
SHREDDED CEDAR BARK BEDDING. 73·6cm [29"] WC

GENERAL CARRYING BASKET OF
PLAITED SPLIT WITHES. 54·5cm [21½"] TL 12

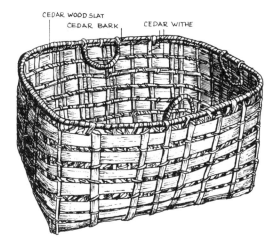

CEDAR WOOD SLAT
CEDAR BARK   CEDAR WITHE

STORAGE BASKET OF CEDAR WOOD SLATS,
WITHES AND BARK. 35·5cm [14"] KW 9

PART 6

CEDAR: THE ROOTS

Generations of Northwest Coast peoples had an intimate knowledge of the cedar tree and they learned how to exploit every part of it. Early inhabitants of the Northwest Coast even dug into the earth to take and use the long, slender roots of this Tree of Life, this Long Life Maker.

GATHERING AND PREPARING In the spring, when the sap coursed through the cedar, men and women went into the forests to collect the cedar's roots as well as its bark. Choosing a spot about 4.5 m (15') away from a large, old tree, a woman used her hardened digging stick of yew or some other hardwood to dig down 61 cm (2') or more. Since the roots should be straight and even, the woman hoped for soil without the rocks and pebbles that made roots grow crooked. Roots growing on old rotten logs were ideal. If she had access to a sandy river bank, the task of digging would be much easier and the quality of roots superior. The Fraser River was once a favourite area for root digging because of its soft, muddy banks.

For the split-root coil basketry so typical of the Coast Salish people, cedar roots about 2.5 cm (1") in diameter were favoured. Some years ago I talked with Mary Jackson, a longtime basket-maker of Sechelt, up the coast from Vancouver, whose skills in the art of coil basketry were superb. Her greatest difficulty was in obtaining sufficient high quality roots; extensive logging in the area had depleted the old, accessible cedars, and she found the roots of second growth cedar to be inferior for splitting, calling them "spindly." In addition, her advancing years made it impossible to trek into the forest, and she was obliged to buy roots from those willing to dig them for her.

Mary Jackson described the work as arduous and tiring, needing much strength and stamina. Having dug roots myself, and not very deeply, I had an understanding of the work involved. It heightened my admiration for those women, with talented and experienced hands, who wrenched raw cedar roots from the moist earth, then

Photograph by Hilary Stewart
Mary Jackson of Sechelt using the author's bone awl to make a cedar root basket. 73

171

COLLECTING AND PREPARING
CEDAR ROOTS. KW 34

① CEDAR ROOTS DUG OUT WITH DIGGING STICK
THEN PULLED UP BY HAND.

② ROOTS CLEANED OF ROOTLETS AND
DIRT, THEN BUNDLED.

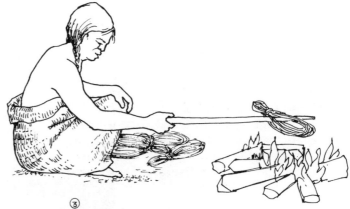

③ BUNDLED ROOTS HEATED OVER FIRE...

④ ...THEN PULLED THROUGH SPLIT STICK TO
STRIP OFF OUTER BARK

⑤ ROOTS SPLIT INTO TWO OR MORE STRANDS,
ONE END HELD IN THE MOUTH. WC 68

172

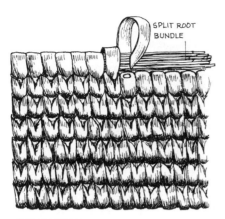

COIL BASKETRY:
BUNDLE OF SPLIT CEDAR ROOT COILED AROUND TO FORM SIDES OF BASKET. UPPER ROW SEWN TO THE ONE BELOW IT WITH SPLIT CEDAR ROOT. CS

BUNDLE OF SPLIT ROOTS COILED TO FORM WEFT OF BASKET.

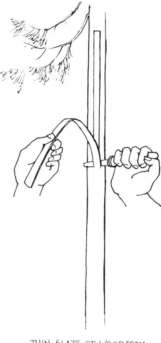

THIN SLATS OF WOOD FROM CEDAR SAPLINGS _ USED IN COIL BASKETRY. CS 70

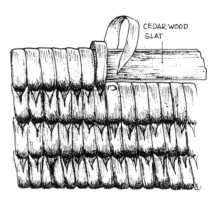

COIL BASKETRY:
THIN SLAT OF CEDAR WOOD COILED AROUND TO FORM SIDES OF BASKET. ROWS SEWN TOGETHER WITH SPLIT CEDAR ROOT. CS

WEAVER PERFORATED CEDAR SLAT [OR SPLIT ROOT BUNDLE] WITH AWL TO ALLOW ROOT STRAND TO PASS THROUGH.

transformed this material into flawlessly crafted works of great beauty and usefulness. There are still several Coast Salish women (Interior Salish, too) who continue to make split cedar root baskets and cradles, but their numbers are slowly diminishing over the passing years.

Once she had some bundles of freshly dug cedar roots, flexible and moist with sap, the basketmaker's next task was to strip off the outer covering. She would do this either by running the root through her hand or by pulling it through a split stick driven into the ground (in the same manner as for cedar withes). Using a sharp knife, she made a diagonal cut on the end that grew closest to the tree, then began splitting the root in half by inserting either a knife or her thumbnail across the centre of the end. She took care to ensure that the initial split followed the natural cleavage line on the root. This was a slight identation, running the length of the root, from which

the rootlets had branched. Small brown knots marked where these had been and acted as a guide to the direction of the split.

When I watched Mary splitting roots, it seemed as though she had only to pull at the two halves for the root to divide down the middle. But when I tried it, I discovered that pulling with uneven tension caused one side to thin out and split right off. Like riding a bicycle, the straight path down the centre relied on the equal balance of bilateral pull.

After splitting the root in half, the basketmaker split off a thin strip, about 1.5 mm (1/16″) thick, from one of the halves. She started it cautiously, then ran it swiftly to the end. Several strips were split off the same root, depending on its thickness. A young woman from Mission, up the Fraser Valley, told me that her mother used to split the root into four quarters and then split each quarter

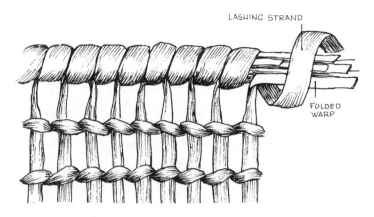

SPLIT-ROOT BASKET. WARPS FOLDED AT RIGHT
ANGLE TO FORM BASKET RIM AND LASHED WITH
SINGLE STRAND OF SPLIT ROOT.

LASHING STRAND

FOLDED
WARP

BASKET OF SPLIT CEDAR ROOT_ OUTSIDE
ENTIRELY COVERED WITH BEAR-GRASS AND
HORSETAIL ROOT IMBRICATION. 25·2 cm [10"]
CS 62/24

into several strips. The freshly split roots were hung to dry before being bundled for storage. The basketmaker kept the fine roots for making berrying and storage baskets, and the coarse ones for burden baskets and general-use containers. She moistened the roots before working with them, keeping a container of water nearby for this purpose.

BASKETRY The Coast Salish used cedar root more than any other coast peoples and made almost all their basketry by the coil method. The combination of the firm, tough root and the coil technique created a rigid basket that was very strong, often watertight and occasionally quite large, qualities different from bark or grass baskets. Newly made cedar root baskets were a light honey colour, but with use, exposure to the air and many years of smoke from fires, the colour mellowed to become a rich warm brown, similar to that of cedar wood.

Many museums have Coast Salish baskets of enormous size, some up to 91.5 cm (36") by 56 cm (22"), many with lids. One of the largest and finest I have seen belonged to a ninety-one-year-old lady; it was a hope chest, made for her when she was a young girl, and is in immaculate condition still.

Characteristic of Coast Salish baskets was the round or rectangular shape, with sides slightly sloping outward towards the top; two- or three-colour geometric patterning was worked over part or all of the basket. Close contact with Europeans was responsible for a number of basketry innovations, obviously made for sale to the newcomers, including such untraditional items as lamp bases, cake stands, suitcases and other assorted household items. Coast Salish women used two materials for the coiled element of their basketry. One was composed of many finely split cedar roots that formed a long, slender bundle, which could be added to as the work progressed; for this the basketmaker used crooked or imperfect roots. The other element was a thin slat of wood split off a cedar sapling, sufficiently pliable to bend into a circle or to take a ninety-degree corner. The basketmaker built up the sides of the basket by coiling the element; the wood slats, however, were generally in discontinuous rows, one upon the other, though they could be in a coil if the basket was a large one. To sew the rows together, she used an awl to make a hole through the top of the lower element, then passed the root strand through the hole to sew it to the upper element. In early times the awl was a bone, sharpened to a point; this was eventually replaced by a metal awl.

The tightness of split-root coil basketry provided the

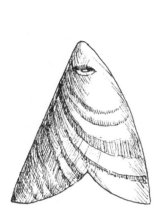

MUSSEL SHELL KNIFE
USED IN BASKET MAKING.
6 cm [2¾"] WC 20

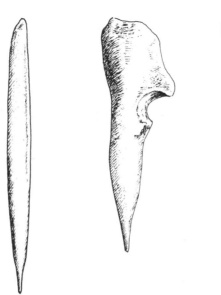

BONE AWLS USED IN BASKETRY.
LEFT: 10·8 cm [4¼"] CS 4
CENTRE: 10 cm [4"] CS 4
RIGHT: 13·3 cm [5¼"] CS 5

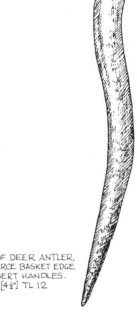

AWL OF DEER ANTLER,
TO PIERCE BASKET EDGE
TO INSERT HANDLES.
11·5 cm [4½"] TL 12

BALL OF SPLIT CEDAR ROOT FOR
COIL BASKETRY. 15·2 cm [6"] DIAM. CS 12

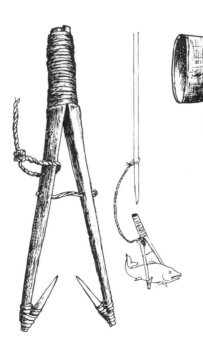

DETACHABLE HEAD OF LEISTER
SPEAR – TWO PRONGS AND
BONE BARBS LASHED WITH
SPLIT CEDAR ROOT. 29 cm [11½"] CS 9

CEREMONIAL WHISTLE LASHED WITH SPLIT CEDAR
ROOT. 56 cm [22"] WC 12

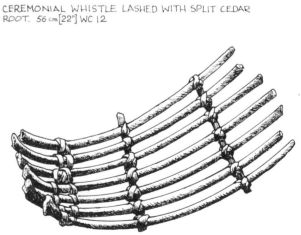

IMPLEMENT FOR LIFTING MEAT FROM COOKING
BOX – SEAL RIB BONES LASHED TO SLATS
WITH SPLIT CEDAR ROOT. 22·8 cm [9"] KW 12

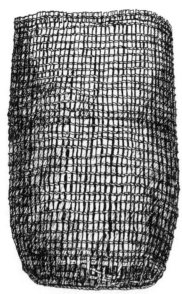

BASKET OF SPLIT CEDAR ROOT,
USED FOR PRESSING EULACHON
RESIDUE DURING RENDERING OF
THE OIL-RICH FISH. 58·3cm [23"] BC 2

HAT WITH PAINTED DESIGN – WOVEN
FROM CEDAR [OR POSSIBLY SPRUCE] ROOT.
31 cm [12¼"] WC 26

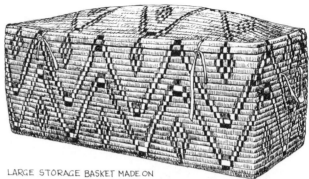

LARGE STORAGE BASKET MADE ON
LINES OF EUROPEAN SEA CHEST – WITH
CHERRY BARK AND REED CANARY GRASS
IMBRICATION. 91·2 cm [36"] CS 31 COURTESY NEIL SMITH

SPLIT CEDAR ROOT BASKET WITH BUNDLE
FOUNDATION – LEATHER HANDLES AND
HINGED LID. 31·7cm [12½"] DIAM. CS 31
COURTESY NEIL SMITH.

LIDDED BASKET OF SPLIT CEDAR ROOT, DECORATED
WITH CHERRY BARK "BEADING" i.e. BARK THAT RUNS
OVER AND UNDER THE ROOT STRANDS. 23 cm [9"] CS 9

HAT OF UNUSUAL SHAPE, PROBABLY OF
SPLIT CEDAR ROOT, TWINED. 21·5cm
[8½"] HIGH. MK 2

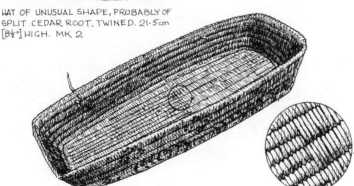

SPLIT CEDAR ROOT CRADLE FOR INFANT
4 TO 6 MONTHS OLD. 80 cm [28"] CS 31

DETAIL SHOWING
REINFORCED BASE.

WATERTIGHT COOKING BASKET – SPLIT CEDAR
ROOT WOVEN IN COIL TECHNIQUE – OVAL SHAPE.
35·5 cm [13¾"] CS 31

Coast Salish with good storage containers as well as watertight vessels for cooking. To use a basket for cooking, a woman lined it with large leaves, partly filled it with water, then added hot rocks. When the water came to a boil, she put in the foods to be cooked; small foods, such as roots, she placed into an openwork basket twined with cedar root, then put the basket into the boiling water.

In her basketry, Mary Jackson worked geometric designs using a characteristic Salish technique called imbrication, which resulted in a design only on the outside of the basket. For this she used strips of the outer bark of western bitter cherry (*Prunus emarginata*) in both its natural mahogany-red colour and dyed black. The traditional way of achieving the black was to bury small bundles of the cherry bark in black swamp mud for a year. That process is now hastened by soaking the bark in mud — or even water — to which rusty iron has been added. The third colour of the design, a light cream, traditionally came from the tall stems of various grasses, particularly that of canary reed-grass (*Phalaris arundinacea*). This grass, which resembles a small bamboo, was particularly prolific in the Fraser Valley in damp, open places; women gathered the stems in late June before the fine grain of the stems grew coarse. Many basketmakers now use dried cornhusks as a readily available substitute; it is quite similar to the grass stems, but lacks their smooth, polished appearance.

Along the coast, women made large burden baskets, in which to gather clams, carry fish or fetch firewood, with a weft of split cedar root in wrapped crossed twining over coarse split cedar withes. They also made tightly woven hats that were waterproof, a distinct advantage on the raincoast.

OTHER USES   Cedar roots, split or whole, provided material for various lashing and sewing requirements such as lashing a bone fish hook barb to its shank, sewing a small split in wood to repair it or to lash together the two halves of a whistle.

Strong, flexible when moistened and abundant, the root of cedar provided coast peoples with yet another versatile material that was a part of everyday life.

PART 7

CEDAR: SPIRITUAL REALMS

The cedar tree touched so many facets of the life of Northwest Coast peoples that it was only natural and right for them to hold the tree in the highest respect and to believe deeply in its healing and spiritual powers.

BELIEFS AND TABOOS Belief in the spirit of the cedar tree had a strong effect on people's lives. When the Kwakiutl pulled bark from a cedar, they took care to leave enough on the tree to ensure its continued growth, for the person who caused a tree to die by taking all the bark would be cursed by the other cedars nearby.

In early times, native people felt that even the stump left after felling a cedar contained life and a spirit. A Tlingit legend tells of Raven, who was roasting some salmon and having an argument with Stump. Eventually, angry Stump deprived Raven of his meal by throwing himself over the fire and the roasting salmon. An old Tlingit pole depicts the orange-shafted flicker (a special family crest) perched on a tree stump —

Photographs by Hilary Stewart

the latter personified as a human with its knees drawn up in front.

The Quileute believed in a supernatural spirit woman who lived in dense brush in the forest and possessed the power to make an expert basketmaker of anyone who caught sight of her. A Westcoast woman who wished to excel in creating basketry designs sought a spirit power to help her; after ritual fasting and bathing, she went into the forest in quest of a vision. Some women acquired supernatural help for their basketry by singing a personal power song as they worked. The Coast Salish of Puget Sound, however, looked to crows for supernatural help in creating superb baskets, since these birds had excelled at this art in the long-ago myth time. The people knew, also, that the great Transformer, who made all creatures in the form they are today, transformed Crow's baskets into clam shells. A close look at the patterns on clam shells, particularly those of the little-neck clam (*Protothaca staminea*), clearly supports this ancient belief. These shells have a texture that looks like weaving, with attractive, geometric patterns not unlike the characteristic designs of Puget Sound baskets imbricated with cherry bark.

Several taboos that concerned working with cedar were related to pregnancy. A man whose wife was pregnant must not twist cedar withe into rope or sew with it, and a pregnant woman must not make baskets, for fear that the umbilical cord would twist around the baby. A pregnant woman also must not shred cedar bark — often sticky with pitch — lest the child also stick and cause a difficult delivery.

RITUALS   Several rituals incorporated the use of the cedar, particularly its bark. Part of the cleansing ritual for a Kwakiutl girl during puberty involved a loose ring of undyed, shredded cedar bark, about 68.5 cm (27") in diameter. A woman companion put this over the girl's head and rubbed her body with it as she moved it down to her feet; the girl then stepped out of the ring, right foot first. The young girl also wiped her face with undyed soft-shredded bark to make her skin a light colour.

Among the Kwakiutl, if a pregnant woman saw anything deformed, ugly or sick (in spite of trying to avoid this), a friend rubbed the offending creature with shredded bark, then touched the woman's back four times with the bark, saying, "This is what would have done it," meaning that it would have affected the unborn child in some way. The bark was then kept in a place where no one would walk over it, such as a corner of the house, until the baby was born. To ensure the child's good health, the afterbirth was kept indoors for four days, then wrapped in four layers of cedar bark. Early in the morning, the bundle was buried in a place where it would be walked over — usually in front of the door, if the child was a boy, or at high-water mark, if it was a girl (to make her excel at clam digging). Some Coast Salish people (the Lummi) ensured a long life for the child by placing the afterbirth in the stump of a large and, therefore, long-lived cedar tree. To make the child grow up brave, they fastened the afterbirth to a cedar's topmost limbs.

HEALING   The ritual and medicinal practices for curing sickness and ailments were numerous. Some illnesses required a ritualistic performance by a shaman to effect a cure, but others responded to simple methods that involved the use of some part of the cedar tree. In some cases the cedar may have provided a convenient material, but in others it was clearly a deliberate choice.

Cedar bark strips found a ready use as a tourniquet to stop bleeding and as bandaging. For instance, the Kwakiutl treated a burn with chewed hemlock needles, covered it with a dressing of soft-shredded bark and then bandaged it with a strip of inner bark. Four pieces of inner bark, half a span long by four fingers wide, formed the basis of a healing pad for a lanced carbuncle. After being spread with perch oil, the pad was heated, covered with eagle down and applied to the sore.

The treatment of both spiritual and bodily illness often incorporated the use of soft-shredded cedar bark. Among the Kwakiutl, people who believed they had been bewitched rubbed their bodies with soft-shredded bark, divided it into four bundles and buried each in front of a house where it would be stepped over. Should one of the houses chosen be that of the witch, the spell would turn against that person. A cure for various diseases required that soft-shredded bark, containing saliva or other bodily waste, be divided into four bundles and placed in four pieces of copper. These were folded over, the edges hammered closed, and then driven into the trunk of a grave tree that contained twins.

Treatment of a person who was spitting blood also made use of soft-shredded bark. For four consecutive days, the blood was collected in a bundle of this material, one each day, and kept until a whale appeared offshore. A friend of the patient then paddled out to the whale and beseeched it in prayer: "I beg you, Supernatural One, to take pity on my friend and restore him to life!" He turned around in his canoe and threw the four bundles of bark into the water, saying, "That is the sickness."

People sometimes used a single cedar withe to aid the recovery of a sick person. Each evening at dusk the patient went to the river to wash; immersing a slender cedar withe in the river, the person listened to the sound of the running water and received a song that would help in healing. Part of an elaborate ritual for curing a chief's sick son called for soft-shredded cedar bark (some of it dyed red) attached to a cedar mat, a quantity of long cedar sticks and eight baskets made of cedar withe.

A deliberate use of yellow cedar, which strengthened the body, is evident in a number of cures for the sick. In one treatment, an old yellow cedar bark blanket was burned and the ashes, mixed with catfish oil, were spread over the afflicted person. To relieve general pains, people chewed leaves of the yellow cedar and rubbed them on the afflicted parts. Painful legs and feet were soothed by a hot footbath of equal parts of fresh and salt water, to which the bark of elder and black twin-berry had been added, as well as the tips of four yellow cedar branches. Among old people, a painful back was sometimes rubbed with cedar branches until blood was drawn; the back was then smeared with a mixture of ground hellebore (*Veratrum viride*) and catfish oil.

Used in conjunction with a sweatbath, yellow cedar aided recovery from an illness that caused localized pain and general weakness. The sweatbath consisted of a long bed of hot stones covered with kelp, another plant and the tips of four branches from four separate yellow cedars. After sea water was poured over this, the afflicted person lay on the steaming bed, covered with a bark blanket, and turned at times to steam all parts of the body. When the stones cooled, the patient was uncovered and rubbed with four bunches of soft-shredded yellow cedar bark, which were later placed under the four cedar trees from which the branch tips had been taken. As the shredded bark dried up, the disease dissipated.

People who suffered from rheumatism found relief in a similar steambath that made use of a small canoe, which was brought to the side of the patient's bed. Into the canoe was put a layer of seaweed, hot rocks and more seaweed; yellow cedar branches were added before water was poured on. The patient lay in the canoe on top of the cedar branches and was covered with old cedar bark mats or blankets. Afterwards, he or she jumped into cold water to frighten away the sickness.

There were, of course, many more ways of healing with cedar among the various coastal cultures, but in general all such remedies recognized the power of the supernatural tree and the peoples' faith in it.

PRAYERS The Northwest Coast peoples had a deep understanding and appreciation of the vital part that the life-giving cedar played in their lives, as well as a pro-

A stand of mature red cedar, Thuja plicata. 73

found spiritual respect for the tree. The supplications they addressed to the spirit of the tree before felling it or taking its bark acknowledged this spiritual bond. A Kwakiutl woman who wanted to pull the bark from a cedar to make a basket for lily roots spoke to its spirit in words such as these:

Look at me friend!
I come to ask for your dress.
You have come to take pity on us,
for there is nothing for which you cannot be used,
because it is your way that there is nothing
for which we cannot use you,
for you are really willing to give us your dress.
I come to beg you for this, Long Life Maker,
for I am going to make a basket for lily roots out of you.
I pray, friend,
to tell your friends about what I ask of you.
Take care friend.
Keep sickness away from me that I may not be killed
in sickness or in war, O friend.

Before felling a cedar in the forest, a Kwakiutl man beseeched the spirit of the tree, with ritual, for the trunk to fall in the right direction. He chiselled into the heartwood and picked up four chips. Throwing the first where he wanted the tree to fall, he said:

O Supernatural One!
Now follow your supernatural power!

He threw down a second chip in the same place and said:

O friend, now you see your leader
who says that you shall turn your head
and fall there also.

He then threw down the third piece in the same place and added:

O Life Giver! Now you have seen which way
your supernatural power went,
now go the same way.

When he threw the fourth chip in the same spot, he ended his plea:

O Friend, now you will go
where your heartwood goes.
You will lie on your face
at the same place.

Answering for the tree with the assurance he sought, the tree faller said:

Yes, I shall fall with my top there.

Before collecting fronds from a young healthy yellow cedar, as part of a cure for his wife suffering with a kidney ailment, a Kwakiutl man sat under the tree and prayed to its spirit:

Look at me, I am to be pitied
on account of my poor wife . . .
sick for a long time
with a swelling of the kidney.
Please have mercy on her
and, please, help each other with your powers,
with our friend, acrid roots of the spruce,
that my wife may really get well.
Please, Supernatural One,
you, Healing Woman,
you, Long Life Maker.

Then he gathered the soft tips of yellow cedar boughs and added spruce roots to make a decoction that his wife drank four times a day. The Coast Salish, who had a similar cure for kidney problems, drank an infusion made by boiling the leaves, bark and twigs of the cedar. They also chewed the cedar's green cones and swallowed the juice to prevent conception.

So strong was the power of Supernatural One, Healing Woman, that a person who stood with his or her back against the trunk received strength from Long Life Maker, the spirit of the mighty — the incomparable — cedar tree.

BIBLIOGRAPHY

Andrews, Ralph Warren. *Indian Primitive*. Seattle: Superior Publishing, 1960.

Arima, Eugene Y. "A Report on a West Coast Whaling Canoe Reconstructed at Port Renfrew." *History and Archaeology*, vol. 5. Ottawa: Department of Indian and Northern Affairs, 1975.

Arima, Eugene Y. *The West Coast (Nootka) People*. Special Publication No. 6. Victoria: British Columbia Provincial Museum, 1983.

Barbeau, Marius. *Totem Poles of the Gitksan, Upper Skeena River, British Columbia*. Reprint. Ottawa: National Museum of Man, 1973.

Barnett, Homer G. *The Coast Salish of British Columbia*. University of Oregon Monograph, Studies in Anthropology No. 4. Eugene: University of Oregon Press, 1955.

Bernick, Kathryn. *A Site Catchment Analysis of the Little Qualicum River Site DiSc 1: a wet site on the east coast of Vancouver Island, B.C.* Ottawa: National Museum of Man, 1983.

Bernick, Kathryn. "Perishable Artifacts from the Pitt River Site DhRq 21." Report to the Heritage Conservation Branch, Victoria, January 1981.

Blackman, Margaret B. *During My Time: Florence Edenshaw Davidson, a Haida Woman*. Vancouver: Douglas & McIntyre, 1982.

Blackman, Margaret B. *Window on the Past: The Photographic Ethnohistory of the Northern and Kaigani Haida*. Canadian Ethnology Service Paper No. 74. Ottawa: National Museum of Man, 1981.

Boas, Franz. "Ethnology of the Kwakiutl." *U.S. Bureau of American Ethnology, Annual Report* 35 (1921).

Boas, Franz. *Kwakiutl Ethnography*. Edited by Helen Codere. Chicago: University of Chicago Press, 1966.

Boas, Franz. *The Kwakiutl of Vancouver Island*. Memoirs of the American Museum of History, The Jesup North Pacific Expedition, vol. V, part II, 1909. Reprint. New York: AMS Press, 1973.

Boas, Franz. *The Religion of the Kwakiutl Indians*. Part 2. Columbia University Contributions to Anthropology No. 10. 1930. Reprint. New York: AMS Press, 1969.

Boas, Franz. *The Social Organisation and Secret Societies of the Kwakiutl Indians*. 1895. Reprint. New York: Johnson Reprint, 1970.

Boxes and Bowls: Decorated Containers by Nineteenth-Century

Haida, Tlingit, Bella Bella, and Tsimshian Indian Artists. Washington: Smithsonian Institute Press, 1974.

British Association for the Advancement of Science. *6th Report on the North-Western Tribes of Canada.* London: British Association for the Advancement of Science, 1890.

British Association for the Advancement of Science. *11th Report on the North-Western Tribes of Canada.* London: British Association for the Advancement of Science, 1896.

Bunyan, Don. "Hewers of Wood." *Heritage West* (Summer 1981).

"Canadian Aboriginal Canoes." *Canadian Field Naturalist* 33 (August 1919).

Carter, Anthony. *From History's Locker.* Vancouver: Anthony Carter, 1968.

Collison, William Henry. *In the Wake of the War Canoe.* Reprint. Victoria: Sono Nis Press, 1981.

Cook, James. *The journals of Captain James Cook on his voyages of discovery.* Edited by J. C. Beaglehole. Vol. 3, parts 1 and 2, The Voyage of the Resolution and Discovery 1776–1780. Cambridge: Published for the Hakluyt Society at the University Press, 1967.

Croes, Dale, ed. *The Excavation of Water-Saturated Archaeological Sites (Wet Sites) on the Northwest Coast of North America.* Ottawa: National Museum of Man, 1976.

De Menil, Adelaide, and Bill Reid. *Out of the Silence.* Toronto: Published for the Amon Carter Museum, Fort Worth, by New Press, 1971.

Dewhirst, John. "Nootka Sound: a 4,000 Year Perspective." Sound Heritage 7:2.

Drucker, Philip. *Indians of the Northwest Coast.* Garden City, N.Y.: Natural History Press, 1963.

Drucker, Philip. "The Northern and Central Nootkan Tribes." *U.S. Bureau of American Ethnology, Bulletin,* 144 (1951).

Duff, Wilson. *Arts of the Raven: Masterworks by the Northwest Coast Indians.* Vancouver: Vancouver Art Gallery, 1974.

Duff, Wilson. *The Upper Stalo Indians of the Fraser Valley, British Columbia.* Anthropology in British Columbia, Memoir No. 1. Victoria: British Columbia Provincial Museum, Department of Education, 1953.

Durham, Bill. *Indian Canoes of the Northwest Coast.* 1960. Reprint. Seattle: Shorey Publications, n.d.

Ellis, David W., and Luke Swan. *Teachings of the Tides.* Nanaimo, B.C.: Theytus Books, 1981.

Ernst, Alice Hensen. *The Wolf Ritual of the Northwest Coast.* Eugene: University of Oregon Press, 1952.

Fine American Indian Art. Public Auction Catalogue. New York: Sotheby Parke Bernet, April 1981.

Fine American Indian Art. Public Auction Catalogue. New York: Sotheby Parke Bernet, October 1981.

Garfield, Viola E., and Linn A. Forrest. *The Wolf and the Raven: Totem Poles of Southeastern Alaska.* Rev. ed. Seattle: University of Washington Press, 1973.

Garfield, Viola E., and Paul S. Wingert. *The Tsimshian Indians and Their Arts.* Seattle: University of Washington Press, 1966.

Goddard, Pliny E. *Indians of the Northwest Coast.* New York: American Museum Press, 1945.

Grim, William C. *Familiar Trees of America.* New York: Harper & Row, 1967.

Gunther, Erna. *Art in the Life of the Northwest Coast Indians.* Portland: Portland Art Museum, 1966.

Gustafson, Paula. *Salish Weaving.* Vancouver: Douglas & McIntyre, 1979.

Hawthorn, Audrey. *Kwakiutl Art.* Vancouver: Douglas & McIntyre, 1979.

Hawthorn, Audrey. *People of the potlatch: native arts and culture of the Pacific northwest coast.* Vancouver Art Gallery with the University of B.C., 1956.

Hebda, Richard. "Pollen Analysis." *Datum* 6:3 (1981).

Holm, Bill. *Box of Daylight.* Seattle: Seattle Art Museum and University of Washington Press, 1983.

Hosie, R. C. *Native Trees of Canada.* Don Mills: Fitzhenry &

Whiteside, 1979.

Inverarity, Robert Bruce. *Art of the Northwest Coast Indians*. Berkeley and Los Angeles: University of California Press, 1950.

Jewitt, John R. *The Adventures and Sufferings of John R. Jewitt, Captive Among the Nootka. 1803–1805. (from the Edinburgh 1824 edition)*. Toronto: McClelland & Stewart, 1974.

King, J. C. H. *Artificial Curiosities from the Northwest Coast of America*. London: British Museum Publications, 1981.

Kirk, Ruth. *Northwest Coast Indian Land and Life*. Seattle: Pacific Science Centre, 1979.

Kirk, Ruth, and Richard D. Daugherty. *Hunters of the Whale: an adventure in northwest coast archaeology*. New York: Morrow, 1974.

Koppert, Vincent A. *Contributions to Clayoquot Ethnology*. Washington: The Catholic University of America, 1930.

Krajina, V. J., K. Klinka, and J. Worrall. "Distribution and Ecological Characteristics of Trees and Shrubs of British Columbia." Faculty of Forestry, University of B.C., 1982.

Krause, Aurel. *The Tlingit Indians: Results of a trip to the Northwest Coast of America and the Bering Straits*. Translated by Erna Gunther. Seattle: University of Washington Press, 1956.

Little, Elbert L. *Audubon Society Field Guide to North American Trees*. New York: Alfred A. Knopf, 1980.

Lobb, Allen. *Indian Baskets of the Northwest Coast*. Portland: Graphic Arts Center Publishing, 1978.

MacDonald, George F. *Haida Monumental Art: Villages of the Queen Charlotte Islands*. Vancouver: University of British Columbia Press, 1983.

Mauger, Jeffrey E. *Shed Roof Houses of the Ozette Archaeological Site: a pre-historic architectural system*. Pullman, WA.: Washington Archaeological Research Centre, Washington State University, 1978.

Moser, Charles. *Reminiscences of the West Coast of Vancouver Island*. Victoria: Printed by Acme Press, 1926.

Moziño, José Mariano. *Noticias De Nutka: An Account of Nootka Sound in 1792*. Translated by Iris H. Wilson. Seattle: University of Washington Press, 1970.

Native Research Project. *Traditional Salish Textiles*. Mission, B.C.: Mission Indian Friendship Centre, 1978.

Niblack, Albert. "The Coast Indians of Southern Alaska and Northern British Columbia." *U.S. National Museum Annual Report, 1888*. Washington: U.S. National Museum, 1890.

Olsen, Ronald L. *Adze, Canoe and House Types of the Northwest Coast*. 1927. Reprint. Seattle and London: University of Washington Press, 1967.

Olsen, Ronald L. *The Quinault Indians*. 1936. Reprint. Seattle: University of Washington Press, 1967.

Phelps, Stephen. *Art and Artifacts of the Pacific, Africa and the Americas: The James Hopper Collection*. London: Hutchinson & Co., 1976.

Pidcock, R. H. *Adventures in Vancouver Island*. 1862.

Powell, Jay, and Vickie Jensen. *Quileute: An Introduction to the Indians of La Push*. Seattle: University of Washington Press, 1976.

Raley, George H. *A Monograph of the Totem Poles in Stanley Park, Vancouver, British Columbia*. Reprint. Vancouver: Raley, 1951.

Ruby, Robert H., and John A. Brown. *Myron Eells and the Puget Sound Indians*. Seattle: Superior Publishing, 1976.

Samuel, Cheryl. *The Chilkat Dancing Blanket*. Seattle: Pacific Search Press, 1982.

Sargent, Charles Sprague. *Manual of the Trees of North America*. Vol. 1. New York: Dover Publications, 1965.

Sendy, John. *The Nootkan Indian*. Port Alberni, B.C.: Alberni Valley Museum, 1977.

Smith, Marian. *The Payallup-Nisqually*. Columbia University Contributions to Anthropology. New York: Columbia University Press, 1940.

Smyly, John, and Carolyn Smyly. *The Totem Poles of Skedans*. Seattle: University of Washington Press, 1976.

Steltzer, Ulli. *Indian Artists at Work*. Vancouver: Douglas & McIntyre, 1976.

Stern, Bernhard J. *The Lummi Indians of Northwest Washington*. 1934. Reprint. New York: AMS Press, 1969.

Stewart, Hilary. *Indian Artifacts of the Northwest Coast*. Seattle: University of Washington Press, 1976.

Stewart, Hilary. *Indian Fishing: Early Methods on the Northwest Coast*. Vancouver: Douglas & McIntyre, 1977.

Swan, J. G. *The Haida Indians of Queen Charlotte's Islands, British Columbia*. 1874. Reprint. Seattle: Shorey Publications, 1972.

Swanton, John R. *Contributions to the Ethnology of the Haida*. 1905. Reprint. New York: AMS Press, 1972.

Thompson, Nile, and Carolyn Marr. *Crow's Shells: Artistic Basketry of Puget Sound*. Seattle: Dushuyay Publications, 1983.

Turner, Nancy. "Native Economic Plants of Totem Park." Davidsonia 2:2 (Summer 1971).

Turner, Nancy. *Plants in British Columbia Technology*. Handbook No. 38. Victoria: British Columbia Provincial Museum, 1978.

Turner, Nancy, and Barbara S. Efrat. *Ethnobotany of the Hesquiat Indians of Vancouver Island*. Cultural Recovery Paper No. 2. Victoria: British Columbia Provincial Museum, 1982.

Walker, Alexander. *An Account of a Voyage to the North West Coast of America in 1785 & 1786*. Edited by Robin Fisher and J. M. Bumstead. Vancouver: Douglas & McIntyre, 1982.

Waterman, T. T. *Notes on the Ethnology of the Indians of Puget Sound*. New York: Museum of the American Indian, 1973.

Yakutat South: Indian Art of the Northwest Coast. Catalogue. Chicago: Art Institute of Chicago, 1964.

INDEX